Books by Bruce Moen

Voyages into the Unknown,
Volume 1:
Exploring the Afterlife Series

Voyage Beyond Doubt
Volume 2:
Exploring the Afterlife Series

EXPLORING THE AFTERLIFE
SERIES

VOL. 3

Voyages into the Afterlife

Charting Unknown Territory

Bruce Moen

HAMPTON ROADS
PUBLISHING COMPANY, INC.

for the evolving human spirit

Cover design by Marjoram Productions
Cover painting by John Edens

For information write:

Hampton Roads Publishing Company, Inc.
134 Burgess Lane
Charlottesville, VA 22902

Or call: 804-296-2772
FAX: 804-296-5096
e-mail: hrpc@hrpub.com
Web site: http://www.hrpub.com

If you are unable to order this book from your local
bookseller, you may order directly from the publisher.
Quantity discounts for organizations are available.
Call 1-800-766-8009, toll-free.

Library of Congress Catalog Card Number: 99-71615

ISBN 1-57174-139-9

10 9 8 7 6 5 4 3 2 1

Printed on acid-free paper in Canada

Dedicated
to
my wife, Pharon
and
the continuing efforts of
ALL
who are working toward fulfillment of

THE EXPLORATION 27 AFFIRMATION

I am much more than my physical body. Because I can perceive that which is greater than physical matter reality, it is my intent through these explorations to contribute to the expansion of human consciousness by experiencing and acquiring knowledge of the realms beyond ordinary consciousness. It is my intent to observe and bring into Conscious Awareness the process of bridging these realities.

In so doing I ask for help to be open, allowing, and serene in perceiving clearly, responding appropriately, and carrying out my intent of service.

I carry out this intent empowered by the group energy of companion travelers and by the acknowledgment of our Oneness in Love. For this help I am truly grateful.

—Reprinted with permission of The Monroe Institute

Contents

Prologue

Scarcely five hundred years ago mariners like Christopher Columbus and Ferdinand Magellan revealed a New World that had always existed beyond the edge of humankind's flat-Earth beliefs. Other explorers, often led by native guides, mapped the wonders and immensities of what had once been a great unknown. Later came ships filled with people whose fear of the edge had been erased by knowledge of the New World's existence. They arrived with the hope of one day living in complete freedom.

In the late 1950s Robert A. Monroe, another Mariner, began having spontaneous out of body experiences that at first led him to fear he might be dying. After overcoming his fear Monroe began exploring the nonphysical world. Bob Monroe was certainly not the first Mariner to explore human existence beyond the physical world, but he's one I knew. Like Columbus and Magellan before him, Monroe made charts and maps of the New World he discovered before he died. I am one of many Explorers who have been using Bob's techniques to push back the edge of another Great Unknown. We've found an inhabited New World, where people have been living beyond death all along. Monroe, now living in the Afterlife, has become a native Guide, who is leading some of us to the Afterlife's wonders and immensities.

The fear of death we carry is erased by Knowledge of what lies beyond our physical world's horizon. I want you to know you don't have to take anyone else's word for what the Afterlife is. You can explore There yourself and learn from your own direct experience. There you might discover not just hope, but also knowledge. The one message I want to be sure to deliver before I die is that when you board your ship for the Afterlife, as we all someday must, there's an opportunity to live in complete freedom.

Voyages into the Afterlife is the third book in my series and is a continuing account of the Afterlife exploration I began in 1992 at The Monroe Institute, when I attended Lifeline, a six-day residential program. Lifeline teaches Afterlife exploration by giving participants practice in retrieval: locating and assisting newly deceased humans who have become lost or stuck due to circumstances of death or beliefs held before departure. The first two books in this series, *Voyages into the Unknown* and *Voyage Beyond Doubt*, tell how I learned the basic techniques. The book you're holding tells how I learned to explore far beyond the basics.

Voyage Beyond Doubt ends with the disappearance of Coach, a nonphysical part of myself some would call a Guide. He is a friend, who helped me learn more about the Afterlife by assisting my explorations. In December 1995 the retrieval of a close friend's father, Joe, led to what I refer to as my *Punky* experience, which finally eliminated all doubt I carried about the reality of our Afterlife existence. Within two days of *Punky*, my friend Coach disappeared. For a brief time I seemed to be in contact with a new Guide, then he too was gone. I felt alone and lost, drifting in and out of depression, grieving the loss for over a month.

But weeks before I'd signed up to attend The Monroe Institute's newest program, Exploration 27, the last program Robert Monroe had a hand in birthing before he died. It was billed as an opportunity to expand exploration of Focus 27, an Afterlife area, beyond what was available through retrievals. There was also talk of exploring Focus 34/35, an area of consciousness called the Gathering in Monroe's second book, *Far Journeys.* Here, contact with intelligences from other parts of our Universe was supposedly possible. Before Coach's disappearance I had been excited by the prospects of voyaging beyond another horizon; afterwards nothing much held my interest. For two months I was unable to make any contact in the nonphysical world. A couple of weeks before the start date of Exploration 27, I began to wonder if perhaps I'd meet a new Guide there. I approached the program hoping that, through it, I might somehow reconnect with the greater part of myself and feel whole again.

As this is the third book in the Exploring the Afterlife series, some of the terms used may be unfamiliar to you. Appendix C contains many of these, and as you bump into them, consider checking the glossary there for explanations and definitions. A fuller understanding will, of course, be gained by reading *Voyages into the Unknown* and *Voyage Beyond Doubt,* the first two books of the series.

chapter 1

Setting Sail

On Saturday, February 17, 1995, I finished my intake interview with Franceen King, a program trainer, and headed outside for a walk on the deck. While slowly pacing the deck's length, looking out over the Virginia countryside, I suddenly felt a presence. It was following beside me as I walked. In a moment I realized the presence encompassed both Dr. Ed Wilson and Bob Monroe, one on my right and one on my left. Bob had died almost a year earlier. Ed had left this world during my third Lifeline program in November 1994. Now each was talking in a whispery voice that I felt more than heard. Focusing my attention, I realized each was telling me a different story. As Ed whispered his story into my right ear, Bob rattled on with his in my left, leaving me mentally jumping back and forth, trying to listen to both stories at once. Very frustrating.

"Hey you guys! Cut that out! I can't understand what either of you is saying if you insist on talking about two different things at the same time," I thought out to them.

They both burst out laughing.

"Ed, I think we finally got his attention," I felt Bob say.

"Yep, he's definitely aware of our presence now," Ed laughed.

"Bruce, that's just a little game we used to play," Bob said, a little apologetically. "Kind of divides your attention, doesn't it!"

"If you're asking if it causes a very distracting, disturbing feeling, like having your mind split in two, I can vouch for that!" I replied, with an inner smile.

"We've been trying to reach you off and on for a while. Then Ed here suggested we try that little game and it worked like a champ."

"Where have you guys been? I've been down in the dumps and haven't heard from you since Coach disappeared."

"We've tried several times to reach you. So have some other friends of yours," Bob said flatly. "Your depression seemed to screen out awareness of our presence."

"Bob, after Coach left I remembered what you wrote in *Ultimate Journey* about how you felt when your INSPEC left. Your words there didn't paint a picture that comes close to describing my experience of loss and gloom! I sure could have used some company."

"Well, that's all behind you now and I'm sure everything's going to turn out fine. Just wait until you see what's in store for you this week!"

"Hope so," I mentally replied.

"Don't you worry about a thing, Bruce," I felt Bob say. "Now go get 'em, Tiger!"

With that, awareness of both Bob and Ed faded away and I felt alone again, standing on the deck at The Nancy Penn Monroe Center, looking out over the Virginia countryside.

I felt somewhat buoyed by Bob and Ed's visit, but over the next few hours a little nervousness started to mix into my excitement. Since Coach's disappearance I had tried to focus my awareness into the nonphysical world many times without success. Maybe I'd lost the ability? Maybe I wouldn't be able to make contact during Exploration 27? Performance anxiety!

Just after dark, my nervousness drove me to step outside into a soft, drizzling rain to smoke a cigarette. Settled down by the familiarity of my habit, I became aware of Bob and Ed again, approaching through the dark night's sky from the west. I opened my awareness to them. They stopped about four feet away, standing side by side and facing me. It was Bob who spoke.

"Bruce, . . . ah . . . Ed and I are really glad you came to participate in this program. We both feel your abilities and energies will be very beneficial to the group. We both just wanted to express our appreciation to you for being a part of this Exploration 27 gathering and tell you we're happy you decided to join in."

"Thanks Bob, I'm looking forward to getting started to see what happens."

"Well . . . ah . . . I'm afraid I've got some bad news for you there," Bob said, his voice a mix of sadness and resignation. "You see, Bruce, nothing much is going to happen for you. What comes for you, won't come until later."

The first anger I felt was just a twinge, then it quickly flared and flew out of me in terse, clenched-teeth thoughts.

"I see, Bob," I felt myself say, as more anger welled up inside me and filled my being. Then, barely containing it, I spit out red flares in his direction, "So what's in it for me?"

"Well, all I can tell you is, what's in it for you comes later," he said with a serious tone. His voice carried the sadness of a doctor bearing bad news that he was powerless to change. Then the two of them slowly turned their backs to me and began moving away in the direction they came from. As they disappeared into the rainy night's darkness I felt my anger still rising. I was extremely upset!

"Yeah, right! Maybe two weeks or a month after I get back home to Denver I'll have this great revelation!" I thought to myself, "Right! Check's in the mail! I've spent a lot of money, taken two weeks off work without pay, and now I find out it's all for something that might happen later. Damn, that makes me mad!"

I indulged my anger for several more minutes, stomping around in the rain and muttering to myself. Giving expression to my anger gradually started to calm me down; then I began to think about all the people who had lent their capabilities and energies to me along the way. Feeling gratitude for sacrifices so many others made for me, I began to think it was okay I had this opportunity to give something back. Like my mom used to say, somebody hands you lemons, you make lemonade.

"Okay," I thought, "I've already spent the money. I'm here to participate in the program, so I might as well make the best of it. If I'm just here to assist and lend my energies to the group, I can do that."

I rolled another cigarette, replacing the one I'd sent flying away in anger, leaned back against the building, and smoked the cigarette down to the filter.

chapter 2

Pure Unconditional Love

During the first day and a half of the program, Bob and Ed were right; nothing happened. In that time our group refamiliarized ourselves with the feel of each of the levels from Focus 10 through 27. Through all these reset tapes I was awake, alert, and couldn't seem to focus on anything in particular. Little snatches of images floated by, but they were just brief bits and pieces that separated long stretches of empty blackness. Focus 27 included several groups of three or four people who appeared in front of me and then faded from view. There were lots of little glimpses of eyes peering at me, some small and some so large they reminded me of artists' renditions of the Grays, a race of alien beings supposedly seen by humans from time to time. Once in a while I got the sense of silvery, metallic surfaces with long, sweeping curves. After each of these preliminary tape exercises, my frustration and disappointment grew. Bob and Ed were right; nothing much was happening for me during this program.

Finally came the first tape exercise specifically prepared for the Exploration 27 program. At the briefing beforehand our trainers told us we were to first go to the

place in Focus 27 we'd previously made for ourselves during our Lifeline program and wait there until further instructions on the tape, given by The Monroe Institute's
(TMI's) program director Dar Miller, directed us to go to
TMI in Focus 27. To avoid confusion, I'll call this nonphysical version of The Monroe Institute TMI-There. At
TMI-There we were to look for and meet at a crystal described by the trainers.

When I followed the Hemi-Sync signals to Focus 27
and went to my place, I was surprised to find something
had changed! I didn't remember putting a lake there. As I
stood looking at it someone I couldn't see suggested that I
remember back to when I created my place in Focus 27,
and as I did, memory of how I'd created the lake came
back. I'd been trying to decide if I really wanted a mountain lake at my place after already expressing the desire
for one. It had fully formed while I wasn't paying attention, as I tried to decide if I really wanted a lake there or
not. Seeing it now, I liked the way it looked and decided it
could stay. Then at the prompting of Dar's voice on the
tape, I left my place in Focus 27 to find TMI-There and
looked for the crystal.

Suddenly, impressions of rolling hills, green grass, and
trees flooded my awareness in vivid detail, passing under
me as I headed west, thirty feet above the ground, moving
at a pretty good clip. In the fuzzy blackness I could feel
myself coming up on the institute and caught just a
glimpse of the northeast corner of the roof as I flew over
it. I had flown at least a hundred yards before I realized
I'd overshot the building, and I pulled a hard, climbing
U-turn to head back! I lined up my approach on the
tower that stuck up above the roof at the east end of the
building and accelerated toward it. Not bothering with
conventional means of entry, I flew straight in through
the roof and headed for the room where the crystal supposedly was.

The trainers had suggested the crystal would be found in the dining room. In blackness since I entered the building, I didn't bother to look around to verify its location. Instead, I just opened up my intent to locate the crystal and an impression of it, floating in the blackness in front of me, formed almost immediately in front of me. At first its image looked like a close-packed bundle of clear, transparent rods. The rods were of differing lengths, with the longer ones near the center of the bundle and the shorter ones on the outside. It changed shape several times, finally settling on a huge quartz crystal shape, very long and perhaps four feet across the flats with a dull, milky, slightly fogged appearance. Both ends of this quartz crystal came to a point, a type of crystal known technically as double terminated. As I stood there, carefully looking over the crystal, I noticed other program participants beginning to arrive.

A waving arm caught my eye and there were Bob and Ed, about twenty feet off to my right, standing near the dining room wall. I walked over to see what they wanted. They led me outdoors onto the deck and we toured the grounds. The light outside struck me first, it seemed to be coming from everything. The rolling hills surrounding this Monroe Institute in Focus 27 were lush and green. There wasn't another building in sight anywhere. The lab building and David Francis Hall seemed to be incorporated into the structure of the place. After our short tour we returned to the room with the crystal. I was headed toward it, to join other members of the group, when Bob stopped me, leaned close to my face, and I could see that devilish grin of his curl the corners of his mouth.

"Bruce, you remember standing outside in the rain, smoking your cigarette, when Ed and I last visited?"

"Yes, I remember," I replied sheepishly.

"Remember I told you that Ed and I were glad you came, and that we felt your abilities and energies would be beneficial to the program and the other participants? And that not much would happen for you in the program until later? Remember you asked, 'What's in it for me?' and I said what comes for you comes later."

"Yes, Bob, I remember. In fact I'm feeling a little embarrassed right now about the anger I felt. I thought I'd have to wait until at least a couple of weeks after I got home for anything to happen. I was feeling shortchanged and very upset."

"Well, Bruce," Bob said, "Later is now!" He was still wearing that devilish little grin of his as he gave me a smile and a wink.

Puzzling over what Bob meant by "later is now," I turned my attention back toward the crystal. Most of the program participants were standing around its base and a few stragglers were still coming in. A field of fine lines and dim colors had formed around the crystal. It looked like the field of a bar magnet you can see if you sprinkle fine iron powder on a piece of paper over one. The field extended straight out from the top of the crystal, bent down and curved around toward the bottom. The field's gentle arcs surrounded the crystal in a soft, dim glow.

As the last member of our group moved toward the crystal, I realized, curiously, that I could see myself standing among them. Three female and fifteen male participants and the two trainers were all standing in a circle around the base of the crystal. I watched, bilocated, from thirty feet away as we stood a shoulder's width apart, immersed in the crystal's field. We all joined hands and stood silently, motionless for a moment. Then, we all stepped forward with our right foot in unison. Simultaneously we bent forward at our waists and pointed our joined hands downward toward the base of the crystal. Then, raising our hands toward the top of the crystal, we each stepped back, put our right foot outside the circle, and made a sound. It sounded like "WOOO-AAAHH," starting at a low frequency while our hands were still pointing downward and rising in pitch as we raised our hands and stepped back. It was a long, smooth, joyous sound. Our hands, still clasped, continued moving with the sound, up over our heads and behind us as we arched our backs outward from the center of the circle. Our movement stopped with our hands still clasped together and extended as fully outward as possible, at the highest pitch of the sound.

From my elevated, bilocated vantage point, these hand movements made our circle look like the opening of a huge lotus blossom. There was incredible joy in the sound we were making. At the peak of its pitch soundless explosions of color and light filled the crystal and spread into its surrounding field. Beautiful, vibrant yellows, oranges, reds, pinks, and whites shot up through the crystal and cascades of sparks scattered upward into the air and showered down upon us. We repeated our movement and sound. Suddenly, the crystal came alive with color in silent explosions of tremendous power. With each repetition of the group's sound and movement, the crystal gained more power until it felt like gigawatts of energy were flowing upward through it just an arm's reach away. We continued until an ecstatic, sizzling energy filled the air around us, charging each of us with its power. It is difficult to put into words the beauty, joy, and power we experienced in our movement and sound.

As we finished this spontaneous, unplanned experience, Dar's voice came in on the tape, letting us know it was time to explore the Reception Center in Focus 27. I watched as the me in the circle placed my intent on doing so, then shot straight up through the ceiling and disappeared. In a moment I was approaching the rolling, green grass carpet of an open field from high above.

I noticed a structure jutting up into the air that looked like one of those towers that hold radio and television antennas. This structure had two very large bell shapes, joined at their small ends to the vertical tower. Looking closely at the open ends of the bell shapes, I could see the flow of something entering one and exiting the other. The flow seemed to be made up of little specks of light, millions of them flowing into the large open end of the bell shape on my left, moving through the center constriction where the two bell shapes joined, and then out the open end of the bell shape on my right. Taking this to represent the Reception Center, I pulled a hard, descending left turn, intending to land near the base of the tower.

My impressions were solid, vivid, and clear. I was standing on an open grassy field, and looking to my left, I could clearly see hundreds of people walking in my direction. Some were alone and some were walking in groups of two to four. Turning my head to the right, I could see a huge structure that resembled the opening to a stadium. Its massive, round columns looked to be at least twenty feet tall. They supported what looked like a brick structure another fifteen feet high and were surrounded at their bases by an open plaza paved in stone. The whole structure extended off into the distance in front of me as far as I could see.

Some of the people approaching this entrance to the Reception Center walked confidently with smiles on their faces. Others moved as if in a daze, just following the movement of the crowd. As I watched, two men who were dressed as paramedics and pushing a hospital bed came rushing by, toward the entrance. I could clearly see an IV bottle dangling from a pole attached to the bed. Whoever was in the bed lay motionless, covered from head to foot by something white that could have been a sheet or bandages. They flew past, through the entrance and across the plaza and disappeared in the distance beyond. Some people were walking alone; others were with friends or relatives in casual conversation as they approached the entrance. As they walked onto the stone plaza they were met and greeted by someone from the Reception Center staff. After a brief conversation, sometimes the friends and relatives of the newly deceased went with them as the staff member led the way through the entrance. Sometimes the person who arrived with the deceased would wish them well and leave as the staff member escorted them across the plaza. I figured the ones who left were probably Helpers, just volunteers who had assisted in getting the person to the Reception Center.

At that point Dar's voice on the tape suggested we ask to follow someone into the Reception Center to learn more about the intake process. Looking around, I noticed a man, dressed as a priest, who was waiting for an elderly woman who was shuffling toward him, alone. Walking over to him before she arrived, I asked if I could follow along and watch the process. As he turned to answer my question I could feel his irritation at my intrusion.

"You may follow along and observe," he admonished, "as long as you don't try to interact or intrude any further than you already have."

That agreed, I stepped back to quietly observe and turned my attention to the approaching old woman. She was very frightened, not knowing what to expect or exactly what was happening. She was worried that maybe she'd sinned too much and this wasn't Heaven she was about to enter. As she walked up to the priest I could feel a little hysteria in her voice as she babbled on about sins, Heaven, and Hell. Smiling brightly and opening his arms wide, the priest greeted her warmly.

"Are you really a priest? Is this Heaven I'm entering? Or is it the other place? I know I've sinned and I'm so worried about what's going to happen to me," the old woman blurted out, nonstop.

"Yes, my child, I am truly a priest, and you have nothing to worry about."

"But my sins, Father, I know I've sinned!"

"My child, all is forgiven."

"Are you sure, Father, are you sure this isn't the other place?"

"Yes, child, all is forgiven. This is not the entrance to Hell."

She required quite a bit of reassurance before calming down enough to speak coherently with the priest again. His priest costume served him well, as it was just what this woman needed to be assured she was all right. After she calmed down, he bent forward, placed his hands on her shoulders, and gave her one of those *no part of my body will touch you save my hands*, priestly kind of hugs. Then he stepped beside her, the two turned to face the Reception Center entrance, and they began walking together.

We crossed the plaza, past the massive columns and under the brick structure, and then emerged on the other side of the entrance. A vast number of buildings were arrayed on the grassy field in front of us. I followed quietly behind these two, as they continued talking and walking toward an outdoor cafe. The sun was shining brightly in a clear blue sky, as we approached a table and chairs. It was a fancy patio table with the umbrella extended from its center to provide a little shade. The priest pulled out a chair, motioning to the woman, and we all sat down. When a waiter came to our table, the priest suggested to the woman that she might be hungry after her long ordeal. He ordered some food for both of them, which the waiter was quick to deliver along with the glass of wine the priest had asked for. The wine was a nice touch. As he lifted the glass to his lips, a sense of relief swept through the woman. Evidently, she felt one of her greatest sins had to do with drinking alcohol. I could feel her thinking, "If I'm in Heaven and this priest is drinking wine, then my sins must be truly forgiven."

As the two of them ate and talked, I realized the priest

was doing an intake interview. He asked questions about her life and how she'd gotten here. He listened attentively, making a point of letting her know he cared about what she was telling him. With each question he was gently probing her Afterlife beliefs and using the authority of his costume to help her begin to understand the reality in which she now lived. His manner was never confrontational, he never directly challenged her beliefs or anything she said. In his conversation he laid out subtle hints about the differences between what she believed and how things really were.

While I was listening to their conversation, Dar's voice cut in on the tape, suggesting it was time to return to the crystal at TMI-There. Quietly thanking the priest, I was about to leave when he gave me a very stern look and blasted a thought to me.

"Please don't just disappear right in front of this lady. It might frighten her," he growled, as only a priest can.

"Oh, okay," I responded, feeling a little humiliated by his tone. I excused myself from the table, got up, and walked away, looking for a place I could safely disappear without alarming anyone. Within a few steps I realized I was walking into an oncoming crowd of hundreds of people. They were everywhere I looked. Every place I stopped to disappear and leave, there were too many new arrivals walking past me. Becoming concerned about how I was going to manage my disappearance without frightening folks, I stopped walking and began looking around for a way out. About ten feet away, off to my left, I saw a dark wooden door with a sign above it that read "Disappearing Room." Silently thanking whoever it was that thought this one up, I walked over, turned the knob, and opened the door. Stepping into a small room behind it, I closed the door and disappeared, leaving for TMI-There, intending to be at the crystal.

I was the last to arrive and watched, again bilocated, as I walked toward the crystal and the rest of the group gathered around it. We all joined hands again and repeated our "WOOO-AAAHH" lotus flower movement and sound, adding bursts of energy to ourselves and the crystal, until Dar's voice asked us to return to C1 (physical world consciousness). As we released each other's hands, I moved from my bilocated position into the me, stepping back from the crystal to leave. Turning, I saw Robyn, one of the women in our group, walking toward me on her way out of the building. As she approached she diverted her path and stopped directly in front of me. She smiled into my very Being, then stepped forward, arms extended for a hug. As we briefly hugged, I felt something in the center of my chest open with a popping sound. Then, moving apart, we smiled warmly at each other, and Robyn stepped past me to continue on her way to back to C1.

Turning again to leave, I noticed Bob and Ed, standing close together about twenty feet to my right. Bob was motioning "come over here" with his hand and both of them were smiling. Before I took a step Rebecca moved out from behind something, beaming happiness and delight with her smile. My heart leapt at seeing her for the first time in seven months. She moved close to Ed and Bob, and as I joined them, we came together in a group hug. It didn't feel like a physical world hug. It was more like we merged together a little at our edges with a sense of joining each other. A moment after we joined together I felt what I can only describe as a lightning bolt of Pure Unconditional Love (PUL) energy slamming into the center of my chest. I had an immediate sense it was charging my body, filling it with Love.

I say a *lightning bolt* to give you a sense of its brilliant, sudden, jolting, explosive, tremendously powerful quality. I'm certain if I ever have the misfortune to be struck in the center of my physical chest by real, physical world lightning (and remain conscious throughout the experience), I will be able to say, "Yes, the bolt of PUL had that same explosive power."

I say *Pure Unconditional Love* energy because that's what it was. No judgments, no prerequisites, nothing asked in return, just pure loving acceptance of all of me. It felt like what I would have previously described as love energy, but without my usual sexual overtones. This had nothing else in it except the pure energy of unconditional Love. Yet, if I tried to describe how it felt, the only thing in my previous experience that comes close to the actual feeling has a sexual nature. At the very peak of orgasm, during the most mutually satisfying sex you can imagine, the quality of that feeling is similar to the PUL I experienced. This joining had absolutely no sexual quality to it. I only use that example as a faint hint of what it felt like.

I could feel the PUL lightning bolt entering and filling my body. In electrical terms it raised my stored potential, charged my battery, transferred charge from somewhere else into me. I felt fuller, bigger, stronger, blissful, joyful, ecstatic—words fail me.

Just as I began to relax from the jolt of the first lightning bolt, as I was about to tell Rebecca, Bob, and Ed what had just happened, I was struck again. This time the intensity of the jolt was about the same, but its duration was longer, probably double the first one. It felt sooooo gooooood! ! ! ! I felt my entire being transformed into a smile. The PUL charge in my body felt twice as powerful as after the first bolt. My head fell back, open-jawed, in joy. I turned my eyes toward Rebecca, looking into her loving face, trying to express what I was experiencing. Then the next jolt came, same strength, lasting twice as long as the last one. My level of charge and joy were already way beyond anything I've ever experienced in my forty-seven years on this planet.

There were at least four more jolts, each doubling in duration and body charge. Then the feeling became a steady, earth-shattering stream of PUL, entering my body through the center of my chest. The intensity built up so rapidly, doubling with every beat of my heart, that I began to wonder if my body could stand any more. The steady, charging beam went on and on and on. From one heartbeat to the next, the charge throughout my being felt so strong I thought I was going to explode. Each time the bolt struck I thought I could not take one more heartbeat of buildup.

While the steady beam continued its high-rate charging, I became aware of Nancy Monroe's presence behind me. She was moving toward me, arms extended, smiling, more a cloud of light than anything solid. She stopped, close behind, and began to express her gratitude for my attempt to relay a message to Bob for her while he was still living in a physical body.

"Remember, Bruce?" she asked. In the bathroom at Bob's house? During a break from watching football? I excused myself for intruding, saying I'd avert my eyes until you were finished?

I laughed a soft, internal chuckle at the memory of Nancy's southern lady manners.

"Yes, I remember," wafted out of me like the scent of roses. "Bob was pretty skeptical with me as the messenger."

"I asked you to tell Bob I still loved him so very much, to tell him I'd wait for him, and to tell him I'd be there to meet him when he left his body for the last time."

"Yes, I remember. I don't think he believed me."

"I'd like to express my gratitude to you, Bruce, for delivering that message."

In just expressing her gratitude the total level of charge in my being, stored since the first jolt of the experience doubled again. It felt so overpoweringly, intensely joyous that it was painful. I felt my physical body suck in a reflexive, long deep breath as if attempting to remain conscious.

The cloud of Light that was Nancy then expanded, surrounding and permeating the four of us. The beam entering my chest had been about the size of a plum just before I felt Nancy arrive. Now its diameter increased until it wasn't a single beam any more. It was replaced by the sensation of being immersed in a gigantic beam, coming into me from every conceivable direction. It covered every square inch of my being, pouring energy into me at a rate ten times faster than before. I have no concepts to describe the intensity of what happened next. My poor attempt with words would be to say that with each beat of my heart, Nancy multiplied my total stored PUL potential by a factor of ten. (Engineers! I am one, and I used to think numbers and words could explain anything. I truly wish I could connect you to this experience through words and numbers.)

I have no way of knowing how long Nancy kept this up. I know at one point I was absolutely certain that at the very next beat of my heart my physical body would explode. I knew I'd burst into flames, setting my Controlled Holistic Environmental Chamber (CHEC) unit on fire and burning down the entire southeast corner of the Nancy Penn Monroe Center. But I didn't burst into flames, and she continued pumping energy into me until there was such an intense mixture of pure, ecstatic joy, and pain that I gave up all resistance. Then my heart filled with the energy of a thousand suns. A short while (or an eternity) later, I felt the cloud that was Nancy begin to withdraw. The intensity of PUL I was feeling dropped to about half of where she'd left off and it stayed at that level as I floated away from Rebecca, Bob, and Ed. I could see them all smiling at me. Then Bob moved over, very close to me, and looked directly into my eyes. I felt like a boxer, sitting in a daze on his stool in the corner of the ring with

Bob like a coach, checking my eyes to see if his fighter could go on.

"Bruce, remember how in all your previous programs my voice on the tape told you to leave the emotional energy behind?"

"Yes, Bob, I remember hearing you say that on all the Lifeline program tapes," I replied in a thick-lipped mumble.

Still looking directly into my eyes, he said with a wink, "Bruce . . . you can take this emotional energy with you."

I suddenly remembered Dar had asked us to return to C1 an eon or two ago. I shifted my attention to listen to the tape, trying to determine if it was still running and found it was. Then, like a feather the size of the Goodyear blimp, I rolled over on my back and began floating slowly downward. With no thought or concern about arriving on time, I floated, basking in the glow of PUL that filled my Being.

When I became fully aware of my physical body, it was convulsing in joy, shuddering in ecstatic spasms of bliss. Tears ran freely, dripping from my hair and face in steady streams onto the pillow below. Gradually, the convulsions calmed down to shaking, sobbing, tears of joy. I must have lain there for two or three minutes, absorbing every last drop of Love and joy I could gather. Then I got up, moved to the desk in my room and tried to fill out the information sheet for this, the first Exploration 27 tape experience. All I could manage to write down was, "A reunion with Rebecca, Bob, Ed, and Nancy. LOVE, EMOTIONALLY OVERPOWERING."

I half walked, half floated downstairs to the post-tape debriefing and I couldn't talk. As I sat on the carpeted floor, my mind drifted back to my childhood. I saw myself trudging along a lonely dirt road, kicking at rocks in my way and crying.

Walking along that road as a six-year-old boy, on a cool sunny Alaskan day, I was troubled. Powerful, awful feelings had been entering the center of my chest and blasting through my body for as long as I could remember—a confusing, dyslexic jumble of joy and pain, shame and rage, anger, love, and disgust. Some that came were so blissful my little heart floated through the air above the road without a care in the world, while others slammed me down hard, face first in the dirt and gravel, tearing the very flesh from my soul.

Walking, looking down as that child, I knew that only I could see and feel the tube extending outward from the center of my chest. I knew that tube connected me to the feelings of every other being in my six-year-old's world. I knew it was they who sent joy, love, anger, pain, and rage through the tube and into my heart. There the feelings clashed in an unrelenting, chaotic assault I was powerless to understand or deal with. The joy and love felt so wonderful and the anger and rage hurt so deeply they were more than I could bear. Nothing I had tried in my first six years of living could make any sense of this mad, chaotic jumble.

I knew the confusion and pain coming into my heart had to stop if I was to survive. I decided love and joy were not worth the pain. In one swift movement I reached out with invisible little hands and grabbed the tube in my right hand, squeezing hard to stop the flow of feelings. With momma's scissors in my left hand, a silent snip severed my heart connection to the world and ended the pain. From that day on nothing came into or out of my heart. Love, joy, anger, misery, and pain all felt the same, dull, lifeless, gray.

Bob had said, "Later is now." Something had happened. That little boy's heart was just reconnected to the world after forty-one years of feeling nothing. I realized now that by telling me nothing would happen until later, Bob and Ed had eliminated all expectations. A perfect way to relieve performance anxiety. I had Bob's word nothing would happen, so I wasn't in the driver's seat, I was just along for the ride.

When the debriefing was over, I tried to thank Robyn for her part in what just happened but words wouldn't come out, only tears of joy.

chapter 3
Ed Carter and Bob's Old Promise

Often I was one of the last to arrive in the dining room for supper, and the last two people to arrive always ended up sitting together at a table by themselves. Monday night Ed Carter was the last to arrive for supper, and after filling his plate, he joined me at the latecomer's table. We introduced ourselves and talked about our tape exercise experiences and what we did in our real lives back home. During the program I came to love this eighty-year-old man like a father.

It turned out we had engineering in common. He explained that, as a young man in the 1930s, he'd started his career as a metallurgist and was now retired. After the program I realized the old boy had sandbagged me; a mutual friend told me Ed had retired as the CEO of INCO, the biggest nickel-mining company in the world.

Ed's fascination with exploring the unknown and his way of telling a story held my attention throughout our dinner conversation that evening. I was particularly interested in what he had to say about his impressions of Focus 15. As far as Ed was concerned, Focus 15 had been misnamed. "It ought to be called "All Time," instead of the "No Time" label Bob Monroe gave it," Ed asserted.

He described an early visit to Focus 15, saying it resembled a scene on Earth. Green grass and trees filled the surrounding landscape in a place of perfect stillness. There was absolutely no movement, with everything seemingly frozen in place. Even a bird he could clearly see in the air wasn't moving. It was as if he was standing in the three-dimensional snapshot of an instant frozen in time. After looking around for a few moments, Ed had started walking. As he moved forward, things in the scene began moving too. Leaves rustled, grass swayed, and the bird flew through the air. When he stopped to look around, everything in the scene stopped moving, frozen in place again. Experimenting a bit, he discovered that things in the scene moved differently, depending on how he moved. When he walked forward, things moved as expected, but walking backward made the bird fly backwards through the air! To Ed, Focus 15 contained all the events of the scene he was in with others strung together in the proper order, so when he moved through them, time appeared to pass. But in Focus 15 there was no movement, no passing of time. For the passing of time to occur in Focus 15 as we experience it, he had to move through the events in sequence. This told him that Focus 15 contained all of the events in the sequence, or—in his words—"All Time."

I was fascinated by what this said about the nature of time. His description indicated that time was a series of events strung together like beads on a string. Thinking about the bird's flight through the air really brought this home to me. For every still-frame instant of time in Focus 15, there was a specific set of events for every aspect of the bird's flight, like a computer program in which lines of code described the length and tension of every muscle, the position and angle of every feather. Each still-frame instant of all those parameters, arranged with the proper settings, in their proper order, resulted in the flapping of wings and other movements that is the bird's flight through the air. In each still-frame instant the sequences of all other events in the scene—the wind, rustling of the leaves, and swaying of the grass—were also programmed. The bird's flight forward as Ed walked forward, and backward as he walked backward, really lent to my sense of the "preprogrammed sequence of events" nature of Focus 15. It felt like the sequence of all the interacting events was somehow preset and was just waiting for someone to move through them to give the appearance of the passage of time.

And if Focus 15 contained all the *programs* of all the sequences of events that human consciousness moved through, it contained all time. I began to understand how Focus 15 provides access to any place in time. If I knew how to land at a specific point in any sequence of events, I could move forward or backward from that point and be moving ahead or back in time. For example, if I knew how to land at a point in an event sequence in ancient Egypt, I could view the passage of events and time, from that point, in either direction. Maybe if I moved sideways I'd step into parallel events, things that happened at the same time but in a different place. I saw how, conceptually, it might be possible to move sideways through Focus 15 and see events in China or Greece that were occurring during the same time. My dinner conversation with Ed was a mind-opening experience and in the spaces between our words I began to wonder where all the programming took place. Was there someplace else, another level of human consciousness, in which someone wrote these event-sequence programs? Did someone or something string these events together like so many beads and place them in Focus 15? If so (I wondered quietly), who did it and why? We talked for quite some time.

After a while, the conversation turned to how I spent my time away from TMI programs. I told Ed that in my real life I was an engineer, and though work kept me busy, it didn't stop me from my new-found love, writing. I'd been writing articles about my retrieval experiences since the Oklahoma City bombing the previous April. When I told Ed I'd brought along my articles, an outline, and a few rough-draft chapters of a book I just started working on, his eyes brightened. He handed me his business card. Ed was vice president for planning for Hampton Roads Publishing Company, which was located in Charlottesville, about thirty miles away. He asked if he could look over what I'd brought along. Before I could tell him I'd be happy to let him look it over, the feel of Bob Monroe's voice popped into my awareness. "See why I wanted you to bring along your skimpy outline and the articles you've written about your experiences?"

When I'd first started writing, after Oklahoma City, Bob had visited from the Afterlife, encouraging me to keep writing. "If you keep on writing, I'll work from my side to get it published as a book," he'd said. I hadn't made Bob any promises, but I'd kept on writing. Now here, ten months later, was evidence of Bob's promise sitting across the table from me. I couldn't help wondering about all the sequences of events that had occurred between last April and now that led Ed and me to be sitting at a dinner table, sixteen hundred miles from my home, talking about my writing a book. It made me wonder even more about the workings of Focus 15 and who was doing the programming.

chapter 4

The Monroe Institute in Focus 27

As usual, when I reached Focus 27 at the start of our next tape exercise, I was sitting in one of the hanging canvas chairs at the table under my beach hut roof. Also, as was usual, there were people sitting in the other chairs, waiting for me. Since I had created this place with its sunny, high, rocky, mountain setting during my first Lifeline program in 1992, there had always been people waiting every time I arrived. And as usual, I could only see them from the shoulders down. Each person's face was obscured by a cloud of light. In the past I'd sometimes seen their hands as they reached for a glass of iced tea or lemonade on the table, or gestured to make some point in our conversations, but I'd never seen their faces. It had always been this way and I'd long since given up questioning why. I'd just gotten used to it.

After a little idle chitchat with someone at my table, Dar's voice on the tape requested that our group go to TMI-There to begin our next exploration. This time we were to look over TMI-There to sense its essence, examining its construction and learning what we could about what it was and how it was made. After meeting at the crystal, our group split up to look around. I went looking for the lounge area, called the Fox Den, in the physical world building and found the one in Focus 27 to be in the same relative location. I decided to examine one of the chairs I could see in the room. Moving toward it, I began getting a feel for its general size and shape, then moved my awareness into it for a closer examination. It was clearly a thought form, the mental image of a chair brought into existence in the nonphysical world.

Reaching out to sense its essence, I could feel the combination of intents that went into its construction, each one being a balance of material property polarities. Its frame was hard, shiny, and cool, as opposed to soft, dull, and warm. The seat and back were a rather odd combination of hard, cool, clear, and thin as opposed to soft, warm, opaque, and thick. They had all the properties of glass, but also appeared to be strong, tough, and curved as opposed to weak, brittle, and flat. The mixture of material property polarities spelled a chromed steel frame with a thin, contoured glass seat and back. The odd combination challenged the engineer in me. I would be afraid to sit on a chair made of such thin glass for fear it would shatter into millions of shards that my butt would meet when it hit the floor. Yet the combination of polarities also spelled indestructible, a curious combination of thoughts formed into a chair. A light fixture on the wall caught my attention. It too was a thought form fabricated from combination polarities. Warm, light, and emitting had been chosen over cold, dark, and receiving, and I could find no wires feeding it electricity.

Dar's taped voice next directed us to move outdoors for an exercise in creativity. I was to select a plant and, with its permission, alter its appearance or structure to suit my fancy. Looking down, noticing I was standing on a carpet of bright green clover, I asked for one plant's permission to play with its appearance. After getting this permission, I concentrated my attention on one stalk, and then its familiar green, three-leafed pattern filled my entire field of view. I began to wonder what it might look like with six leaves. "Never saw one like that before," I thought. As I wondered, three leaves became six, each green and shaped as clover ought to be. "Instead of green," I wondered, "what if I changed it to a deep, rich shade of blue?" Before I finished with the thought, my field of view was filled with the image of a deep blue, six leafed clover. "Pretty," I thought, "looks like a flower I've never seen before." Standing back a bit, I wondered what a field of blue, six-leafed clover would look like and the green carpet at my feet made its change to blue, answering my question. The clover was beautiful! I made choices between both ends of continuums. I'd made a choice of blue, between infrared and ultraviolet. Between zero and infinity, I chosen six as the number of leaves for my clover. As I'd thought, my choices had taken form in the reality of Focus 27. I'd created thought forms!

My blue, six-leafed clover looked every bit as solid and real as anything I've seen on Earth, and just a pretty. Pondering what I'd done made me wonder about physical world reality. Is it as solid as it seems? And who or what focuses its intent, and into where, to create it all? Gazing at my deep blue clover flowers, I became very curious about who or what created the level of awareness I live in and call real. I thanked the clover for cooperating with my practice at creation. As I thought about the clover being what it was before, the deep blue changed to green, six leaves back to three, and I was standing on the carpet of clover as it was when I arrived.

I looked up. Others in the group were still experimenting. The forest had some of the oddest looking trees and shrubs you could imagine. Each member of the group was practicing the art of creation, using thoughts and fancies to alter the environment around them. It reminded me of a forest Bob Monroe talked about in his book, *Ultimate Journey*. During an early exploration of the Afterlife, walking through a forest on his way to the Park, he'd seen tree and bird varieties that existed nowhere on the Earth. It puzzled him. He'd wondered who could have created such a place. As I stood watching my fellow Exploration 27 participants, it became clear to me that he'd seen the work of human minds at play.

Looking over the countryside, I became curious again about the light, which was illuminating everything. There wasn't any single source, like our sun. Rather, the light seemed to be coming from everything within my field of view. The clover, trees, open sky, and clouds seemed to be emitting light from within. I was suddenly struck by memory of something I'd seen in the physical world.

Staring at a tree, its green leaves motionless in the still summer air, I'd absentmindedly switched on the feeling of Wahunka, an odd altered state I'd discovered on my own. As my awareness shifted toward a stronger and stronger feeling of Wahunka's energy, the leaves of that tree had seemed to be emitting light from within. As I stood in Focus 27 now, looking at the trees and shrubs in the forest, they looked like the one I'd seen in the physical world through my Wahunka focus of attention. When our exercise was over and I was heading back from Focus 27 to C1, I was still wondering why.

chapter 5

The Entry Director

Our next tape exercise was to explore how human beings move from Focus 27 into physical lifetimes on the
Earth. I first arrived at my place in Focus 27 and talked to
the people in the hanging canvas chairs about the insights
I'd gained playing with the clover. Then it was time to
leave and meet up with my group of fellow Explorers at
the crystal. Bob and Ed were there again, standing off to
one side.

"That clover of yours was an interesting creation," Bob
remarked.

"Sure left me with some questions!"

"Good! A little something for that curiosity of yours to
play with," Bob laughed.

"Maybe somewhere along the way you'll find some
answers," Ed casually remarked.

Then it was time to leave for my encounter with the
Entry Director (ED), the guy who supposedly knew about
how humans entered lifetimes on the Earth. After taking
on a charge of energy from the crystal with the rest of the
group, I placed my intent to find the ED. I shot straight up
through the roof and into blackness. After a brief sense of

movement I saw the tower I'd seen earlier. Very tall, it looked like a radio antenna tower with two huge bell shaped objects at the top. The small ends of the bell shapes joined together and appeared to be fastened to the tower at its very top. Stopping to look more closely, I became aware of someone standing behind me.

"Are you the ED I'm supposed to talk to?" I thought out to the presence behind me.

"Well, let's just say I'm one of many who attend to the operation of the Reentry Station and I can probably answer your questions."

"I'm a member of a group in a program called Exploration 27 at The Monroe Institute back on Earth. We're all here to learn about the inner workings of Focus 27."

"Yes, I know. Your buddy, Bob Monroe, told us your group would be coming for a tour of the place. How can I be of assistance?"

"Is this thing I'm looking at, the tower with the bell shapes at the top, is that the Reentry Station?"

"Yep."

"What does it do and how does it work?"

"Look closely around the big open end of the bell shape at the left and tell me what you see," the ED suggested.

"I see a flow of something entering the open end of the bell shape," I described.

"Direct your attention to that flow and tell me what you see there."

"I see a cylindrical flow of little bits of yellowish-gold light, all moving together into the bell shape."

"Look closely at the bits of light."

I moved closer to the flow to get a better look. "They all have generally the same size and shape, and they're emitting light. They are shaped a little like cocktail shrimp after they've been cooked and peeled, kind of the shape of little cheese curls. I've seen these things before in a place I call the Flying Fuzzy Zone. These curls look the same, but in the Flying Fuzzy Zone they fly all around like moths buzzing a bright light. What are these things?"

"Focus your attention on them, what do they feel like?"

After gazing at them for several moments I got the precept, "I'll be a son of a . . . those curls are people! Each one is a separate human being!"

"And?"

"They seem to be in some kind of 'dormant' state. Not too much activity going on in them, not much thinking. More like they're asleep and waiting. Why are they like that, and why are they entering the bell shape of the Re-entry Station?"

"Come on, follow me," the ED replied, "we'll go inside the station so you can take a look."

There was a quick feeling of movement and then I was standing at the center of the area, where the small ends of the two bell shapes joined. I could plainly see the flow of curls being compressed as it passed through this area.

"This part of the station is called the Constriction," the ED volunteered.

This section seemed to be putting the curls under pressure. I asked "Why?"

"Preparation for entry into physical world reality. The awareness of each curl is compressed here to help hold it together and stay focused in one place long enough to make the transition."

"I'm getting the sense that compression also closes down its Conscious Awareness of nonphysical reality in general, including awareness of nonphysical aspects of itself. Is that a result of compressing a curl's Conscious Awareness?"

"Yes. Physical world reality is a pretty crowded, busy, chaotic place. By compressing the curl's awareness into one place, it's more concentrated. It's better able to focus—to concentrate, if you like—on its tasks and purposes once it's in the physical world. Less apt to be distracted by input overload from the high level M-band noise pressure."

"Input overload? High level M-band noise pressure?"

"At the level of physical world reality there are presently over five billion human inhabitants packed onto a very small place called Earth. Everyone living there is constantly broadcasting their thoughts and feelings into that close-quarters environment. They're like five billion little radio stations all broadcasting their own unique talk shows into the airwaves at the same time. Those thoughts and feelings are what we call M-band noise. There are so many people broadcasting at once, all pushing their thoughts and feelings out into the environment, we call it high level M-band noise pressure."

I asked if closing down a curl's level of awareness by compression in the constriction section had something to do with limiting the effect of that M-band noise, responding to impressions I was getting watching the curls pass through. "It limits the curl's ability to sense things in the nonphysical environment, doesn't it?"

"Yes it does. You see, if a curl's Conscious Awareness remained fully expanded to its normal size during and after entry into physical world reality, it couldn't function. It is being constantly bombarded by a great percentage of the M-band noise. Finding its own memories and thoughts among that blaring jumble would be extremely difficult, if not impossible. At its normal level the curl's awareness would be in a constant state of chaos, as a result of the input overload. Such overload would make progress on a curl's purpose for being in physical world reality impossible. The constriction step of the reentry process concentrates the curl's awareness into a very small area, allowing it to be less aware of M-band noise."

"So compression reduces Conscious Awareness of nonphysical reality. But doesn't that also make it so the curl has no memory of what happened to it or decisions made about its purpose before entry into the physical world?"

"Well, yes, sort of. Memory of those decisions and contact with the Greater Self, your Disk, or Monroe's I/There, is also almost completely blocked by the compression. You see, compression works on the level of the curl's Conscious Awareness. That doesn't mean those memories and contacts are removed or totally inaccessible, they're just compressed into the subconscious. They are fully accessible, but ordinarily only at the curl's subconscious levels.

"Wouldn't it be better to let curls decide whether they want this to happen or not?"

"They do decide, Bruce. Each curl understands and agrees to this as part of the reentry process. It's not a rule imposed on the curl by anyone, it's part of the preparation necessary for survival in the physical world environment. You could think of it like the old-fashioned, deep-sea diving suits. You know, the ones with the big heavy helmet and air hose hooked to a pump on the surface. To withstand the pressure and survive while exploring the ocean bottom in the old days, divers had to wear the suit. Compression at the Reentry Station is where the curl puts on that suit."

"I'm getting that M-band noise is somehow similar to the water pressure at the bottom of the ocean in your metaphor," I said, responding to incoming impressions.

"Very good! And as you go deeper toward the ocean bottom, further into physical world reality, M-band noise pressure becomes greater. Once a curl reaches physical world reality, M-band noise pressure actually helps maintain compression of its Conscious Awareness within the limits of its physical body."

"What do you mean?"

"Remember, we are talking about Conscious Awareness of the curl. If the diver tries to expand at the bottom of the ocean he has to push outward against the surrounding water pressure. If a curl attempts to extend its Conscious Awareness beyond the confines of its body, it encounters the M-band noise of all the other inhabitants. It's such a jumble of random thoughts that it tends to break up the concentration and focus required to further extend its awareness. After a while, curls generally stop trying to expand their awareness, since they so easily lose the train of thought necessary to do so. So, M-band noise pressure tends to maintain compression of Conscious Awareness. Some curls continue trying to expand their awareness into the M-band noise and the successful ones are often labeled psychotic."

"How can curls safely get through the M-band noise to expand their awareness?" I wondered out loud.

"By learning to focus their attention, not through the M-band noise, but beyond it. If the curl learns to focus its awareness at a level of consciousness where the M-band noise is attenuated or nonexistent, expansion is much easier. Meditation is a useful, time-tested method and the one you're using seems to work pretty well."

"The method I'm using?" I asked, puzzled.

"You learned to maintain your focus and avoid the jumble by shifting your Conscious Awareness past M-band noise and into states you call focus levels. Focus 10, Focus 21, and so on are levels of human consciousness with greatly reduced M-band noise."

"I see what you mean. The Hemi-Sync tool I stumbled on allowed me to remain in a coherent, focused state as I expanded my awareness past the M-band noise and into states beyond it!"

"You sound surprised! Hemi-Sync is an adaptation of a long-known technique. As for stumbling upon it, later you might want to check for filament-of-awareness connections between yourself and the guy who introduced that system," the ED said cryptically. "For right now let's get back to the purpose of your tour."

"Okay. I'm getting that compression causes the curls to lose memory of where they came from. It's the reason so few of us have any past life memories or awareness of anything that exists beyond the physical world."

"Yes, again. Compression pushes these memories into the subconscious, and by definition that means the curls are not consciously aware of them. Typically, they are also unable to extend their Conscious Awareness through the M-band noise to access 'outside' sources of the information in awareness levels adjacent to the physical. The information is carried inside the curl too, but few learn to focus inward to find it there. Curls, compressed as they are, have little Conscious Awareness of that information stored within themselves, and the M-band noise tends to cut off access to adjacent sources. Of course, there are some exceptions. In fact, here comes one now," the ED said, as he directed my attention to the incoming flow of curls.

In among the other curls in the flow was one at least ten times their size. It stood out as the biggest, brightest curl in view.

"Big Fish, we call them," the tour guide said. "What do you get from that one?"

It seemed more awake and active than the other curls. I watched as it moved through the constriction and then exited off to my right.

"It knew about the compression process it was going to go through and maintained its awareness while passing through it. I get that. After passing through the constriction, it remembered most of what it had entered with."

"Big Fish have developed the ability to be consciously aware of far greater 'volumes' of information," the ED said. They pass through the constriction, losing very little of their multidimensional awareness. They're exceptionally well suited to bringing awareness of adjacent realities into the physical world. Many Big Fish have lives in physical world reality in which they share their multidimensional awareness with others who are lacking it. By doing so they help others become Big Fish."

Something else in the flow caught my eye. Four curls, a little above average size, appeared to be connected along some kind of lighted filament. They looked like shrimp on a string with two, close together, leading the way, followed by two others, also close together, further along the string.

"Could be a family of four, or just four curls planning to act on a common purpose," the tour guide explained before I could ask. "When we see them strung together like that, we know they have a prior agreement about something that requires them to pop into the physical world in a certain time sequence."

"So if it was a family of four, the two in the lead are probably the parents and the next two will be their kids?"

"Yeah. And if it's not an actual family, with parents and children, it could be just that those four have to arrive in a specific time sequence."

"Specific time sequence? Is that group headed for Focus 15?"

"Of course. Every curl goes to 15 after they finish compression. I don't have time right now to go into all the details of what happens from then on, so don't ask. That will all be covered later in your tour. Groups like those four are usually tied into a cooperative effort aimed at carrying out individual and group purposes."

"Like?"

"Like, maybe those first two have to bring a discovery into physical world awareness that the second two will use later. In the case of that specific group, the second curl will be traipsing through a jungle when he meets the first one, a native medicine man, a local shaman. Their combined knowledge of drugs and diseases will uncover the healing properties of a certain plant. Years later, the second two curls will meet when they each deliver research papers at the same medical conference. They'll discover they've both been working independently to bring the use of that plant's properties into practical use. They'll join forces to carry on their work together as husband and wife. That's when they'll start working on the most important joint purpose for the entire group's entry."

"Most important purpose?"

"With the inflated egos those two have, it's going to be quite a challenge for them to learn to love through being with each other," the ED said, with concern in his voice. "At least they've got their love of humanity bonding them together. Working toward practical use of that plant's properties for the good of mankind is a real plus in that department."

"How do you know all that? Or are you just making it up?"

"I'm not making it up, I know because I can read curl, and because my awareness extends beyond what you're used to."

"Who decided what their purpose was and what they were going to do to accomplish it? Sounds like predestination, like they have no choice."

"Those curls made all those choices for themselves. You could call it predestination I suppose, as long as you remember they made all the decisions affecting their destinies and agreed to work as a group before they came to the Reentry Station."

"So there is predestination!"

"Of course! They decided what they were going to do, and now they're going to go do it. Call it predestination if you like, as long as you remember who planned the destinies," the ED stated flatly.

"I want to know more about that string that connects them. What effect does it have on them in the physical world?"

"That string, as you call it, is a filament of awareness that connects them and will remain in place throughout their lives. You could also call it a section of a time/event line. The string is part of the process of insertion into time frames in the physical world and the Big Clock gets used as part of that process."

"Time/event lines? The Big Clock?"

"I'd suggest you save those questions for your visit to the Planning Center. They can explain it better in the context of what they do there. Meanwhile, take a close look at the curls in the flow again. Pick out a group on a string and look real close at the filament of awareness associated with them. Here comes a group of three now. Check out the area directly behind the group."

"I don't see anything other than that they're connected together by a fine bright filament. . . . Wait a sec. . . . There's an even finer filament trailing them. In fact, now I see that all the other curls in the flow have the finer filament trailing them too. Didn't notice it before. What is that?"

"Do you remember the story of Curiosity you wrote in your first book? Do you remember Curiosity's Probes?"

"Yes, why?"

As I waited for the tour guide's answer, it hit me like a forty-foot wave crashing into a sea wall.

"Those are Probes! Those filaments trailing each curl are their connection to their Disks, the things Monroe called I/There! Those filaments are what provide transfers of awareness between the Probe and its Disk! I saw my filament and followed it back to my Disk during a vision in the mid 1970s. That's how I became aware of my Greater Self, my Disk, my I/There!"

"Glad you caught on to that, Bruce. As you continue your tour of Focus 27 during your program, I'd like to suggest you be open to learning more about who and what you really are. There's more to learn."

Looking closely at the filaments trailing the curls again I noticed something odd.

"That group of three I saw had only one filament trailing it. Some of the other groups I see have more than one filament trailing them. Why is that?"

The ED just stood there looking at me, waiting for me to get the answer on my own. Then it hit me!

"Those three curls with the single filament are all from the same Disk, aren't they!"

"And the ones with more than one trailing filament?" the ED asked.

"Not all the curls on the connecting string are from the same Disk!" I blurted out. "What are the implications of that?" I asked.

"Like I said, there's more to learn, but that's one you'll have to explore and discover for yourself."

For several moments I floated in silence, trying to get more insight into what my tour guide seemed to be alluding to. Not getting much, I decided to pursue something else.

"Wouldn't it be better if all curls who reentered physical reality lifetimes carried more of their memories in their Conscious Awareness? Wouldn't I have a better shot at carrying out my purpose in life if I knew what it was? Couldn't the compression process of the Reentry Station be modified to allow that to happen?"

"In some cases, like Big Fish, much of such memory remains intact and easily accessible. And there are things that can be done to help a curl move toward Big Fish awareness levels. Part of that process is the curl learning to feel what's going on inside its awareness, becoming aware of what's stored within its subconscious. That process also involves becoming aware of what's available in adjacent levels of awareness. That's an internal learning process all curls go through as they make progress towards becoming Big Fish. But to do that within the

M-band noise of physical reality, one must use the emotional charge and emotional impact of events in physical world reality. Emotional impact is part of the Earth school training system, part of learning to feel and become a Big Fish."

"So remembering too much would interfere with learning, Big Fish training if you will?"

"It tends to reduce the emotional impact of events that normally help a curl learn to feel what's inside itself. Think of it this way, if someone told you all the details of a suspense thriller you were planning to see at the theater, including the climactic ending, what would it do to a movie's emotional impact on you?"

"If I knew everything ahead of time, including how the movie ended, most of the emotional impact would be gone."

"And you might experience weaker feelings in response to what happened on the screen?"

"So we curls don't remember our purpose in life because it might spoil our movie?"

"Something like that. There's also the curl learning to use the filament connection to consider."

"What's the filament of awareness connection got to do with becoming a Big Fish," I asked, not seeing any possibilities.

"Becoming aware of that connection can lead to awareness of your Disk. That in turn can lead to an accelerated opening of awareness by virtue of the information available via that connection to the Greater Self. Surely, you of all people, can see the possibilities in that!" the ED said, like I really ought to have figured it out already.

"Oh . . . you mean my vision of the Disk way back in the middle 1970s. I see what you mean! Once I had some limited awareness of my Greater Self, and my connection to it, the pace of my growing opening picked up. Gee, you mean I'm in training to become a Big Fish?"

"Bruce, all curls are in training to become Big Fish," he said, taking a little wind out of my sails.

Dar's voice startled me, suggesting it was time to return to the crystal at TMI-There.

"That's my signal to go back to physical world reality, I got so involved in our conversation I forgot this is just a tape exercise in a program."

The ED said, "As you continue your tour, you're free to keep asking questions of anyone you meet and, of course, let that curiosity of yours have free rein. Feel free to come back and visit me whenever you like."

"Before I leave, since you read curl and all, can you give me anything on my purpose during my present lifetime?"

"Sure," he said as he flipped me a thought ball, "but you already know most of it, so nothing in this one should come as any big surprise."

"Thanks, ED, you put on quite a tour, and thanks for this," I said, holding up the thought ball.

"Anytime."

On my way back to the crystal, moving through blackness, I excitedly opened the thought ball, anticipating some great revelation. It said: "You entered this lifetime as a retrieving type to recover many of your Selves and those with other Disks of origin. Most of all, you wanted to learn more about the energy called Love. Beyond telling you that, I wouldn't want to spoil your movie!" It was signed, "ED, Entry Director."

chapter 6

The Healing and Rejuvenation Center

On Tuesday I decided to make a change in my tape exercise routine. Allowing the Hemi-Sync sounds to guide me to Focus 27 was beginning to feel like a waste of time. So instead, I went directly to my place in Focus 27. I enjoyed spending the additional three or four minutes just looking around, using my new-found ability to see in a full color, 3-D representation. As usual, people were waiting for me when I arrived.

I created my place in Focus 27 at the very peak of a mountain-sized rock outcropping, high above the surrounding rocky mountain terrain. Its centerpiece is a meeting place that looks like a Caribbean Gulf Coast beach hut. Its cone-shaped, palm frond roof is supported by a central pole, above a large round table. Comfortable canvas chairs hang from the perimeter of the roof. There are seven chairs, each a different color. The view from any of those chairs, looking down on the huge, solid rock mountains on one side of the beach hut table, is spectacular. The lake I inadvertently created sits on the right side of those mountains, a short walk from my meeting place.

The lake is about a quarter of a mile across and the water is warm and perfectly clear. If you're standing at the table, looking out at the mountains, there's a modern lodge set on an open green meadow behind you. Its back faces my meeting place and there's another small mountain lake in front of it. The front and sides of the lodge have lots of glass so you can see the meadow, the second lake out front, and surrounding mountains from inside. Parts of my place look like a spot in the physical world where I sunbathe and picnic in the foothills of Colorado's Rocky Mountains.

In the back of the lodge are two Holodecks, one on each side of the central hallway. The concept was borrowed from *Star Trek* and I created them during my early Lifeline programs, as I sometimes brought people there I retrieved from Focus 23. Some were still tired and confused and it seemed best to leave them in familiar surroundings with a Helper who'd come to attend to them. Each Holodeck was programmed to replicate whatever environment would be most soothing and acceptable to the person I brought there. Not long after I installed them, I discovered these Holodecks were unnecessary, since someone was always waiting at the Reception Center to greet whomever I brought. But I kind of liked the Holodecks, so I left them in place. A status symbol, perhaps, so I can brag to my friends that my place in Focus 27 has twin Holodecks!

As I moved around my place, looking it over, one of the people sitting at my table got up and started walking toward me. This had never happened before. The one walking toward me was very obviously a female. I didn't remember seeing her at my place before. Believe me, I would have remembered! She was dressed in a long, silken gown, so light, airy and translucent, it left little to the imagination. From her shoulders up, all I could see was a cloud of light that completely obscured her face.

That didn't matter at all, as from what I could see, she was breathtakingly beautiful! She moved in a way that sent signals to the male part of me that riveted my attention on her body. I could only see her from her shoulders to her feet and you'll have to take my word for it, she was absolutely stunning. As she moved close to me she extended her hand in a way that said, let's go for a walk. Speechless, I followed her lead, walking the short distance to the shore of my lake. Without her saying a word, I understood we were to go swimming.

I kept my attention focused on her as we swam out to the middle of the lake, where she surface dove beside me. I watched her legs disappeared beneath the water. Moments later, she was standing on a huge boulder, at the water's edge, half a football field away. Her beckoning hand gestures seemed to propel me towards her and then we were standing, side by side, on the flat, smooth top of the boulder. What happened next is difficult to admit to, so I'll keep it short. We made love atop the boulder in the warm mountain air. I know it could have been for only a very short time, but it seemed like an eternity in bliss as I felt my body responding to the buildup of sexual energy. Near the peak instant, the goddess I was with suggested I begin moving the energy upward to my heart and above. I can't adequately describe what came next, except to say a lightning bolt of Pure Unconditional Love energy shot through my entire Being, which is a pitiful description, but I don't know what else to say.

Floating in stunned ecstasy, I heard Dar's voice on the tape say it was time to meet at TMI-There to begin our exploration. I'd gathered my senses and looked around, but the woman was gone. The ecstatic state she had generated in me was still flowing with incredible power when I left to find the crystal at TMI-There.

Our task during this tape exercise was to explore a place called the Healing and Rejuvenation Center in Focus 27. It had been suggested by the trainers in the briefing before the exercise that we begin by returning to the Reception Center and then follow the trail of a person we'd seen entering during our earlier visit. The person covered by a sheet or bandages on a hospital bed being pushed by two men dressed as paramedics had piqued my curiosity. Standing at the Reception Center plaza, I brought that earlier scene back to mind. Everything went dark for a moment and then the paramedics and the hospital bed went whizzing by again. I took off after them, somehow knowing they were headed for the Healing and Rejuvenation Center. At the end of the plaza everything went black again and then I found myself standing in what looked like a surgical amphitheater.

The two paramedics were transferring the patient, still covered from head to toe, onto a large table in the center of the room. Powerful lighting from directly above brightly illuminated the patient's body. I could clearly see an amphitheater gallery with at least six rows of seats arranged in a semicircle. The first row was about eight feet off the floor, at the top of a semicircular wall surrounding the table. The rest of the rows were above and behind, arranged like steep stairs. Anyone sitting in the movie theater-style seats in the gallery would have an unobstructed view of the patient. While I watched, doors opened at the top of the gallery and people began filing in and sitting down. Then a door opened near the table and a man dressed like a surgeon stepped into the room and moved next to it. I felt the presence of a tour guide move up behind me and she quietly began explaining what I was about to see.

"The patient is a burn victim. He lived a few agonizing hours after sustaining third-degree burns over his entire body. The paramedics you saw were a couple of Helpers who managed to get his attention in Focus 23 and bring him here. They repeatedly bumped into his bed and got him to respond to their presence when he complained of the pain it caused him."

"How long ago did he die?" I asked.

"Just a few days ago, but the procedure would be the same no matter when death actually occurred. The Helpers were able to get him to understand they wanted to take him to a place where he would be healed and they made a big deal out of giving him a shot to relieve his pain. That's what really killed him; he couldn't stand the pain any more, so he chose to die."

"They gave him a shot?"

"Helpers can be very convincing actors, capable of doing most anything a person is willing to believe. Their offer of medication guaranteed to make all his pain go away was just what the patient wanted. So it was easy for him to believe that's what they gave him. Then, once the pain was gone, they transported him here for treatment."

The doctor near the table bent down, close to the patient's face, and spoke just loudly enough that I could hear him.

"I'm the doctor. You have your choice of being completely healed, scar free, over a period of time or instantly," he said to the patient.

"Which would you prefer?" the doctor inquired in a voice of authority.

"Instantly, of course," the patient responded laughingly, thinking this must be some kind of a joke.

I could feel the guy had no idea instant healing was possible and yet, in just moments, he witnessed a miracle.

"Very well," the doctor said. He stepped back a few feet away from the table, turned his head toward the full gallery, and nodded to the audience.

On their faces I could see smiles and feel the energy of Love building up in each of them. It approached a collective peak instant, as mine had just a short time ago on the boulder by the lake, and I could feel Pure Unconditional

Love energy filling the room. Then a beam of light emerged from each member of the audience and shone onto the patient. It happened so fast that I almost didn't see the healing as it occurred. A ball of light formed around his body and then, in an instant, the white covering disappeared, revealing a man without a hint of a burn or scar anywhere on his body. He jumped up off the table and found himself standing next to the doctor. The doctor then made a point of taking extra time to carefully examine the man before handing him a bathrobe. I could tell this was part of the act, making sure the guy watched the doctor's examination. He saw that he was completely healed, which stunned him to silence.

"He'll still need a little time to convalesce," I heard my tour guide say.

"Why is that?"

"He hasn't quite accepted or understood he is dead. By accepting the instant healing route, the worst part is over and now he'll need to adjust to the reality of his existence in the Afterlife."

"Some patients opt for slow healing?"

"Some can't believe anything else is possible. It's what they expect, so it's how they're treated. You've seen it happen here before. You wrote about it in your second book, but you didn't recognize it as such."

"I did? I wrote about being here before? I don't remember being here, much less writing about it."

"Remember George's afterlife recuperation?" my tour guide asked. "George's son, Tom, asked you to check on his father shortly after he died?"

My face must have still looked as blank as my mind felt.

"The first time you came to check on George you found him in a hospital bed sleeping . . . ? There was a woman you correctly identified as George's mother sitting at bedside . . . ?"

"That hospital room I found George in was here, in the Healing and Rejuvenation Center in Focus 27?"

"That's right! George had a long battle with the disease that killed him. At first he fought it, believing he'd beat the odds, get well, and go home. As his disease progressed he gave up hope and was just waiting to die. George was unconscious when he died, so when he regained consciousness, as far as he knew, he was still alive and waiting to die. He's an example of someone who was treated using a slower technique. His healing could only proceed at the pace he was consciously willing to accept. It took months before he changed his mind and decided he was going to regain his health and leave the hospital. You remember, he still believed he was physically alive and the last time you saw him he was just beginning to think otherwise. His realization and acceptance to the contrary were a long, slow process."

"This is amazing! I've been visiting more of Focus 27 then I knew existed."

"You were still pretty heavily into your training via retrievals and still carried quite a bit of doubt about the reality of the Afterlife at that time. Just like George, it took time for your realization and acceptance."

"Yeah, it took me three years to accept it."

"Hey, at least you got to that point! Our job here would be a lot easier if more people reached that acceptance before they arrived."

The completely healed burn victim had left the room and a new patient was wheeled in. This one appeared to be a healthy man in his late thirties, who was lying on his back, sleeping.

"This man's been in our comatose ward for a very long time. He was taught as a child that when he died he'd just go to sleep forever. That belief has kept him like this for over a century. Recently, attendants on the ward noticed some coherence in his dream patterns. After he died he could accept that dreams were possible, as they fit in with his belief about going to sleep forever and now we're going to attempt to bring him out of his coma, using the coherence in his dreams. This isn't the first time we've attempted to bring him out of it, but it's the first time we'll use this specific technique on him."

Once the man was on the table the scene in the room changed to a forest setting. It was a bright sunny day, and the man was lying naked, on his back, on a picnic blanket. A gorgeous woman, also naked, walked over to where he was lying and gently sat down on top of him. My face must have flushed red as I turned my head away from the scene.

"It's all right, Bruce, what you're about to see has very little to do with sex, except as a means of expressing Pure Unconditional Love energy. I'd encourage you to watch and perhaps you'll learn something about the power of Love."

I did as the tour guide suggested, but still felt a little uncomfortable about watching the scene. The audience in the gallery began to smile and to beam light into the scene. Some of it surrounded the man and woman, and I could tell it had the effect of bringing the total scene into his dream. Before long the man also began smiling and then some members of the gallery began beaming light into the genital areas of both people. The movements of the woman were arousing and building sexual energy, which appeared as an increasingly bright ball of light. The man, eyes still closed, raised his arms and began caressing the woman's face and body. His other body movements indicated he was joining into the activity of the dream. As he approached orgasm, the gallery members beaming light into the genital area began to push the ball of light up through his body and toward his head. I could see it energizing and awakening each chakra location as it passed through that area of his body. When it reached his head, he opened his eyes and became fully aware of the woman and his surroundings, which brought him fully conscious and out of the coma. The woman immediately began talking to him, thereby holding his attention on her presence. In a few moments they were up, retrieving their clothes from where they were scattered on the ground around the blanket, laughing and joking as they got dressed. Together, they folded the blanket, gathered up their picnic basket, and left, walking arm in arm down a path in the forest. In a short time they'd walked out of sight and the room returned to its previous appearance.

"The movement of that ball of light reminds me of something that just happened at my place in Focus 27 before I came here for this part of the tour."

"Part of your preparation so you'd be better able to understand this as something beyond a purely sexual experience," the tour guide replied dryly. "And another lesson in the power of Love within human experience."

Without much ado, the next patient was brought in and transferred to the table.

"This man was killed in a crash during an auto race. Something like the Indianapolis 500, though not that specific race. He too has begun to experience some coherent dream patterns in the coma ward. This time a similar induced-dream method will be used to bring him back to consciousness. If you watch closely, you should be able to see the dream as it's brought into being."

"Why has he remained unconscious since his death?"

"Beliefs he took on before death, the same reason the majority of coma patients arrive here. If they had some better choices of beliefs in the physical world, maybe we could start to make a dent in our backlog."

As I watched, the audience in the gallery began to smile and I felt the now-familiar charge of Pure Unconditional Love energy filling the room. When the scene around the race car driver began to change, he was sitting in a bright red car. The tour guide was right; it could have been an Indy car. He was cruising at high speed on a seemingly endless stretch of straightaway, when his car slowly began to rise into the air. At first the driver reacted with surprise and terror, but then, as he realized he could still steer the car and make it go where he wanted, he began to calm down. When he was completely comfortable flying the car, he was in a fully coherent state and, from his point of view, what happened next might have seemed strange. Once he'd taken control of his car, he flew it right into full consciousness, landing in the room as it appeared before he'd started. The people in the gallery were cheering and waving as he climbed out of the car and stood next to it. Two guys dressed like members of his pit crew ran up cheering and escorted him out of the room.

"I think I understand the point at which he was ready to make the leap into being conscious," I said to no one in particular.

"When was that?" the tour guide asked.

"Once he felt in control of the flying car."

"That's right. It was a challenge, a crack in his beliefs, for the car to fly in the first place. His desire to regain control triggered a state of hyperalertness he'd experienced during his life on Earth, while trying to avoid disasters. That hyperalert state is something he switched on, on his own, and it brought him into conscious control of his actions. All that was left was for the Helper pit crew to come in and keep the illusion going long enough for them to reach him and explain his situation."

Then, feeling a need to change the subject, I asked, "Say, as long as I'm here can you tell me what I can do to improve my own physical health?"

"The Tai Chi you do is an excellent method that facilitates beneficial energy flows throughout your body. Would you like to see what I mean?" she asked.

"Sure," I eagerly responded.

Then, like watching a movie, I saw myself doing some of the Tai Chi movements. As I watched myself go through the routine, I could see my "energy body" filling with light. It seemed to enter my feet and flow upward toward my head as, over the length of the routine, my energy body became larger and brighter.

"The energy flow you are seeing brings in massive amounts, which can be drawn on later like a water wheel in a river. When a full flow is constant, sufficient energy is available to maintain the consciousness necessary both for physical health and for energizing and bringing awareness to other levels of consciousness."

"I probably ought to be more diligent about doing my Tai Chi."

"I'm glad you said that," my tour guide replied. "I'm not fond of giving advice, and your realization obviates the need."

"Is there anything I or anyone else can do to heal a specific physical condition?"

"We could use the damage sarcoidosis caused to your liver as an example to illustrate the point if that's all right with you."

"Sure."

"The thing to remember is that what you experience as physical reality is a reflection of nonphysical reality. You already have a pretty good understanding of thoughts being things, so just combine those two knowns and the answer to your question is also a known. Without launching off into esoterics, if you picture a completely healthy liver in the place of your existing liver, you are making a healthy, nonphysical liver. Done properly, this nonphysical organ becomes a pattern that influences the physical organ to become like the pattern."

"That sounds good, but why doesn't it always work?"

"It has to do with placing your intent and any beliefs included in the way you picture the new organ."

"What's the proper way to place intent necessary to make this work?"

"That's a good question to ask the people at the Scheduling Center. I'd suggest you talk to them about it when you visit."

"Scheduling Center? I don't recall that one on the list for this Exploration 27 program."

"Then you might consider a visit there after you've learned to find your way around Focus 27, perhaps after the program."

"Oh, okay. Well, is there more you can show me about the Healing and Rejuvenation Center?"

"We've covered all the basics. To start going into more right now would take more time than you have left during the tape exercise you're doing."

"Well, maybe I'll go back to my place and hang around until it's time to go back to C1."

"Come back and visit whenever you'd like. It's always nice see you here," she said with a wink.

I turned back toward my place in Focus 27, and after a brief sense of movement through darkness, found myself standing near the hanging canvas chairs at my table. The woman I'd been swimming with earlier was sitting close by on my right.

"You're back early," I felt a male voice say.

Something about the feel of that voice was familiar, but I couldn't quite put my finger on it.

"Yeah, Healing and Rejuvenation is quite a place!" I responded. "Some of their treatment methods would be considered grounds for imprisonment back in the physical world, or at least loss of a medical license!"

"Yes, but they're effective, aren't they!"

"Yeah, they may be culturally unacceptable treatments where I come from, but they do bring people out of a coma."

I still couldn't place where I'd heard that voice before, but it was very familiar.

The woman got up out of her chair and stepped toward me. Still couldn't see her face, just a cloud of light from her shoulders up. She started walking along the short path to the lake and I hesitated to follow her. Then that same, oddly familiar, male voice spoke again.

"There's plenty of time left before you have to go back," he said. "Another swim might do you some good."

I started walking toward the lake, catching up to the woman just as she entered the water, and I swam behind her to the middle of the lake. Oddly, my movement through the water didn't cause a single ripple on the lake's surface. When we reached the middle of the lake, the woman executed a perfect surface dive and disappeared beneath the water. From my experience with her before, I start scanning the lakeshore, looking for where she went. I was slowly turning in the water when I first felt their approach.

They were too far away to see, and yet I could feel them moving toward me from every direction. I could feel complete, Unconditional Loving Acceptance of me, beaming from each of them. They swam in unison, their movements more like water ballet than just swimming through the water. When they were finally close enough to see, I counted fifteen adult dolphins, their snouts all pointing toward me on a perfect circle, and I was in its center. It felt like a ring of Pure Unconditional Love, completely surrounding me and closing in on me. As they continued slowly toward me, the intensity of the feeling at the center of that ring grew and grew. As each dolphin's snout touched my body, in the same instant of time, a bolt of Pure Unconditional Love energy shot through me, paralyzing me with its ecstatic, healing power. Then each dolphin curled around, rotating in the same direction in perfect unison, and they swam away. Tears of ecstatic joy were streaming down my face when I became fully aware of my physical body, back in C1 again. I let the pure joy of that experience saturate my being before I got up and headed for the group debriefing.

chapter 7

The Education Center

At the beginning of the next tape exercise, I followed my new routine. Picturing myself sitting in one of my hanging chairs and looking out at the sun-lit mountains below, brought me to my place in Focus 27 with a little extra time to look around. As usual, there were people who were sitting in the other chairs and who were waiting for me. As always, I couldn't see any of their faces, and what I could see of their hands, arms, and shoulders didn't give me any clues. But for some reason, I was really beginning to wonder about their identities.

"You know, I'm really curious about who you people are and why you're always here waiting when I arrive."

"We thought you'd never ask!" I heard that familiar male voice say.

Looking at the faceless body of the person sitting closest on my left, I saw the ball of light that had obscured his face begin to change. It was like watching the thick cloud of a fog bank evaporate. His face came into view. It was Bob Monroe. "Hi, Bruce. Figured it was about time you saw who we are." He motioned for me to look at the others gathered around the table. The fog lifted from all their faces, one by one. Rebecca was sitting next to Bob, in the chair on his left. We smiled warmly at each other, as I happily acknowledged her presence. Sitting next to Rebecca was Tralo.

"Tralo? What are you doing here? I've never seen you before, but I know it's you! Bob talked about you as a member of his I/There he'd found at his bowl of lights. Hearing his story reminded me of the vision of the Disk I'd seen sixteen years earlier. It gave me quite a shock when I realized the Disk I saw was my I/There, the greater part of me. Hell, I didn't even know there was such a thing before hearing Bob's bowl of lights story. It took a lot of internal adjustment to get used to the idea that I was something other than what I had always thought I was."

Tralo just nodded with a peculiar kind of smile.

"So, Tralo what are . . . you . . . doing . . . here?"

Then with a shock, the realization hit me! Tralo was on Bob's Disk, part of his I/There, and so was everyone sitting around the table, including me!! The scene around me began to quiver and fade.

"It's okay, Bruce," I heard Bob's voice say. "We just thought it was about time you knew."

When the scene came back into view, everyone around the table was smiling and nodding. From each of their faces I read the same message, "We're all in your I/There."

"That's right Bruce. You and all of us belong to the same I/There, the same Disk, the same Cluster. We are all parts of the same Greater Self that we are!"

I could feel my consciousness staggering, reeling under the impact of what I had just discovered.

"So that's why I was drawn to Bob's first book by the 'Who Are You' dream. The big guy, the one dressed in the robe, the one I saw out the window in that dream, Bob, that was you!"

"In a manner of speaking, yes, it was me," Bob replied.

"You led me to find *Journeys out of the Body* by appearing like the robed person you described seeing in your book!"

"Got you to check that book out of the library, didn't it?" Bob laughed.

"How did you do that? I grabbed your book by mistake. I could have randomly opened it to any page, but it fell open to the description of the robed person I saw in my lucid dream, two weeks earlier."

"Got your curiosity up, didn't it?" he chuckled.

"There were just too many coincidences. I had to read that book. How did you make that happen?"

"Well, you'll be learning more about coincidences later in the program," Bob said, being his usual obscure self.

"And the place I landed after flying out of the wall of the house in that dream, the place with grass and trees and the path. That was the Park, wasn't it?"

"None other," he said flatly.

"We're all part of the same Disk! Everyone here at my place is an individual member of the same Whole Being. That's why I went to The Monroe Institute for Gateway Voyage and discovered the Disk vision's meaning. That's the reason for my interest in Lifeline and my decision to come to Exploration 27 to learn more about the nonphysical world. Coming here, hoping to be reconnected with Guidance. Reconnected! Geez, this is the biggest reconnection I can imagine. Everyone around this table is me in a different body. Holy shit! And it's been Me, all along it's been Me leading me to discover I'm a part of the One who's choreographed this whole, Hemi-Sync, focus level system! And I used that system to bring that knowledge into my awareness. Now what the ED at the Reentry Station said about awareness of my connection to my Disk is making sense. That awareness accelerated my opening and led right here! Without knowing about filaments of awareness and Disks and such I wouldn't have made it here in an entire lifetime."

Everyone around the table was still nodding and smiling. I turned my attention to the seat next to Tralo and saw that it was empty. In the next chair sat someone with a familiar flattop haircut and cigar-chomping face.

"Coach . . . Coach, where have you been? When you disappeared, I went looking all over you. I felt completely lost. God I've missed you!"

"You kind of outgrew me, Bruce," Coach replied.

"Outgrew you? What do you mean?"

"We'll talk about it later."

Sitting next to Coach, and closest to me, was the woman I'd met and swam with in the lake. Now I could see her face. A goddess. That's the only way I can describe her, a goddess. It was very hard not to get lost, just looking at her. As I took in her extraordinary beauty, I began to remember. "I remember seeing you before! During that visualization at the bookstore!" I blurted out.

"Yes, that was me," the response floated out, in a voice dripping with pure, sweet sensuality, like warm honey.

I'd gone to a psychic development class about eight years ago at my favorite bookstore in Denver, the Nic Nac Nook. During a visualization exercise I'd been led to a room where I was to meet one of my Guides. Thinking the whole thing quite silly, I stood waiting by an imaginary door. It was a door that opened by sliding upwards from the floor, and the first things I saw as it did were the feet of a woman. They looked soft and smooth, pretty and sensuous. As the door rose further, I could see her legs, long and sensuously curved. She was wearing a translucent, flowing, long silken gown then too, which moved gently in an unfelt breeze. With a powerful light shining behind her, the raising door revealed the silhouette of more and more of her incredibly beautiful body through the gown. With the door fully raised I found myself gazing into the most beautiful face I had ever seen. It was framed by her long, gently curled, blond hair. As our eyes met, I became lost in them and in a feeling of total desire. Standing there, in the visualization exercise eight years ago, I remember shaking my head, trying to break free of looking at her. I'd felt certain then that no real Guide would ever look so sensuously beautiful. With that thought, the door slammed shut and I never saw her again, until I realized it was she, sitting in a hanging chair, next to me at my table.

"Who are you? And where did you come from?"

"My name is something you'll have to remember on your own. I can tell you that where I come from, pure sensuality is everything. To express one's sensuality is the reason for living. But that's the only clue you get."

"The Art of Mystery is a part of that place too, I remember that much. And no harm is ever intended or done there, but that's all I remember."

"There's plenty of time for you to remember. Something wonderful awaits you when you do."

I was racking my brain, trying to remember her name, when Dar's voice on the exercise tape suggested it was time to meet at the crystal, at TMI-There.

"For now, I think I'll call you the Woman from Sensuous," I said.

"How 'bout we go for another walk down by the lake."

How could I refuse? She got up out of her chair, waiting for me to step beside her before we started walking.

"You know, I find it very difficult not to stare at you," I said after we'd walked a short distance. "Your appearance is so alluring I catch myself gawking at you. You just seem to be dripping sensuality like honey drips sweetness from the hive. It embarrasses me to be caught gawking."

"Where I come from it is impolite not to stare. We measure the success of our effort to be ultimately, sensually alluring by the stares we get," she replied. "There's no need for you to feel embarrassment. Think of it more as a compliment to me and a way for you to take in the energy of my sensuality. That's how I view it," she said with sweet innocence.

For the most part that relieved the nervousness I felt at being in the company of such a drop-dead gorgeous woman, walking next to me in a see-through silken gown. From then on, whenever I began to feel nervous or embarrassed because I was staring at her beauty, she would stop and smile. Then she'd do something to "show off." Sometimes she'd slowly turn completely around, nonverbally beckoning me to drink in the sight of her to my heart's content. Can't say I ever really got completely used to it, but I sure enjoyed it!

When we got to the edge of the lake, she stopped and said she had something to show me.

"Watch me closely," she said.

It was strange. She was standing right next to me, on my left, and then an instant later, she was standing next to me, on my right.

"What did you see?" she asked.

"You moved from where you were standing to where you are now."

"Watch again."

This time she disappeared and instantly reappeared about thirty yards away, further down the lakeshore. Then she disappeared and reappeared an instant later, standing next to me again. "What did you see this time?"

When I told her she had moved from one place to another, the look on her face said I'd missed something. She repeated her disappear-and-reappear act again several times. Sometimes she'd be standing right in front of me and in the next instant I'd see her standing on a rock clear across the lake, waving at me. I was finally beginning to catch on.

"What I saw is that there appears to be absolutely no time between when you disappear from one place and re-appear in another. It's like you do it all in the same time-less instant. I didn't see you move from one place to another. You're either doing it so fast I can't see you move or you're getting from one place to another in a way that takes no time."

"Bruce, you're catching on! Now before you have to leave to explore the Education Center, I'd like to show you one more thing."

In the next timeless instant she was standing on a huge rock, close to the water's edge, halfway around the lake on my right *and* she was also standing near the water's edge, halfway around the lake on my left! Both of her were smiling and waving! Then both of her jumped in the lake and began swimming toward its middle. I dove in and swam out too. The two of her recombined, and then just before I reached her, she did her surface dive and dis-appeared under the water. I felt the dolphins coming again. They repeated their healing bolt of Pure Uncondi-tional Love, and I floated for a moment in its pure joy. Then it was time for me to go.

Our task this time was to explore the Education Center in Focus 27. Our group first met and charged up in the en-ergy field of the crystal at TMI-There. Placing my intent on finding the Education Center, moments later I was standing in what looked like a huge library. Shelves of books lined the walls along both sides of the long, wide corridor where I was standing. I assume the shelves went to the ceiling. They went up vertically at least twenty feet and then faded out in a kind of fog I couldn't see into. The books on the close-spaced shelves were packed binding to binding, and the corridor extended in front of me as far as I could see. There had to be hundreds upon hundreds of thousands of books that I could just see from where I was standing. Wondering how to find out about the Education Center, I looked around for someone who looked like they might work there. A likely looking prospect came walking toward me, so I thought I'd try my luck.

"Excuse me, do you work here?" I asked when the guy got real close.

"Yeah, of course I do. You know that," he answered rather abruptly.

"I'm a member of a group taking a tour of Focus 27 and I wonder if you could show me something of interest here in the Education Center?"

The guy looked at me with such a strange, befuddled look on his face, as if he expected me to know my way around. With a little hesitation in his voice, like he was humoring me, he obliged.

"Yeah . . . sure . . . something of interest. . . . Let me see," he said, as he blankly looked around. "Yeah, sure, follow me."

He was walking toward what looked like a desk in the middle of the aisle.

"This is what we call a Holodesk. You're part of the Star Trek generation, so you ought to have some idea what it is and how it works."

His tone was slightly condescending, like it irked him that he had to explain the device to me. The blank look on my face let him know he'd have to tell me more.

"You take a book off the shelf and you put it in this slot right here," he said, pointing to an opening in the side of the desk. It looked big enough to accommodate any book I'd ever seen. "Then you sit down in the chair at the desk and decide what viewing speed you want to read the book at."

We walked around the desk to where the chair was positioned.

"Okay, so put a book in the slot, select the viewing speed, then what happens?" I asked.

"The story in the book gets played out in the 3-D holo-gram, like always!" he said, with mild exasperation in his voice.

"I see. Thank you for taking the time to explain the Holodesk to me. Maybe you could point out something else of interest that I could go explore on my own. That way I won't take up any more of your time," I said, hoping to smooth over any ill feelings I might have provoked.

"Well, most of the time I see you here you're heading toward the Hall of Bright Ideas."

"What do you mean, 'most of the time you see me here'? I don't remember ever being in this place before."

"I see you here all the time. I didn't realize you wouldn't remember being here before. Geez, Bruce, you really had me going! I couldn't decide if you were playing some kind of game with me or slipping your clutch!"

"You mean, I come here often?"

"I see you here all the time."

"And we know each other?"

"Of course we do! You're such a frequent visitor, and a friendly kind of guy, we visit lots of times when you're here."

"This has got to be a joke!"

"You mean you really don't remember being here before?" he asked incredulously.

"Not at all!"

"Well, walk around. Maybe it will come back to you."

"Okay, so which way to the Hall of Bright Ideas?" I asked.

The tour guide pointed high in the air to a place behind where I was standing. When I first arrived I hadn't looked behind where I landed, and that's where the guy was pointing. I turned around and there right in front of me was a huge, arch-topped doorway. Great big letters, emblazoned around the arch said, "Hall of Bright Ideas."

"I'd suggest you follow the signs," my tour guide said dryly.

"This is where you usually see me heading when I come here?" I asked.

"Yep, most every time. You always come into the building at the same place you came in this time. Then you head in there."

"What's it for? I mean, what do I usually do in there?"

"You don't remember that either?"

"Humor me. Pretend I have amnesia and you're trying to help me remember."

"Okay, fine!" Exasperation was beginning to sound in his voice again. "The Hall of Bright Ideas is connected to the Grid, via filaments of consciousness, to all possibilities. It returns all possible responses that fit any question."

"The Grid?"

"Don't tell me you don't remember what the Grid is either?"

"No, no I don't."

"When you get to the Coordinating Center ask them to explain the Grid to you. Those guys work with it all the time, they can explain it to you better than I can."

I had the distinct impression this guy was getting a little impatient and just putting me off. Just then I heard a little commotion behind me and the jibber jabber of some familiar voices. Turning around, I saw a bunch of people from my Exploration 27 group, looking around and pointing. I moved closer to where they were standing.

"Hi guys! Quite a place, isn't it?"

It took a few moments for them to recognize me and then one piped up.

"Bruce! Have you been here long? Find anything interesting to look at?"

"Well, the Holodesk is pretty neat. There's one right over there," I said, pointing to the nearest desk.

We all walked over to the Holodesk, gathered around it, and gawked.

"Do you know what it does or how it works?" someone asked.

"Yeah, I met a crazy tour guide when I first got here and he explained it me."

"Let's see!"

"Well, first we have to pick a book from the shelves. The guy said when we put the book in this slot here, the Holodesk will show the story that's in the book."

"Maybe we should pick a story most of us already know," someone in the group suggested.

We all walked over to the shelves and after a little while we settled on a story we all knew. Something about intrigues in a medieval Spanish royal family, the title escapes me now. Back at the Holodesk, we put the book in the slot.

"Now what?" someone asked.

"The guy said that next you sit down in the chair and select the viewing speed you want to see the story at. Then the story in the book is supposed to play like some sort of hologram on top of the desk."

I sat down and saw a panel in front of me with four large push buttons. "Let's see, we can watch the story at: Savor; Informational; Relaxed; or Instant."

After a brief conversation, we came to a consensus. Since we all know the story, why not see it real fast?

"Okay, Instant it is!" I moved my hand over the button marked "Instant," and left it hovering there. "I don't know what the hell is going to happen when I push this button. Everybody watching the desktop?"

"Ready. Ready. Yeah, go ahead, we're all set," came murmuring from the group.

I pushed the button. There was very brief flash of light above the desktop. It coincided with something that felt like a silent firecracker exploding in my head. When it was over, all I knew about the story in the book was that it was about intrigues and power struggles between members of a medieval Spanish royal family. Guess we played it a little too fast.

"Anything else around here of interest?" someone else in the crowd asked.

"Well, the guy showed me a place called the Hall of Bright Ideas that looked interesting."

I explained what the tour guide had told me, as we walked over to the entrance marked by the sign above the doorway. The same tour guide was standing close by, and at the risk of upsetting him, I asked for a demonstration.

"You've usually got some engineering design question you take in there—when I've seen you here before, that is. Seems like you use the place to find solutions to unusual, complicated new product or machine-design situations most often."

"Well, if we wanted to see a demonstration right now, what product-design question would you suggest?"

"Look, it's your demonstration, you pick a design question!" he replied abruptly.

Feeling a little embarrassed at being spoken to in front of the rest of the group as if I should know how to do this, I stood there quietly, wondering what to do. Whatever I took in as a demonstration question should be something I have no previous knowledge of, I thought to myself. No fair cheating. Hmmm? Surgical scalpels!

"I don't know anything about the design of a scalpel. How about I try that?" I said, addressing the tour guide.

"It's your design, and your responsibility, so you decide!" he replied, exasperation back in his voice.

With that, I walked through the doorway into the Hall of Bright Ideas. The rest of the group stayed outside the room to watch. As I moved further into the room, its rectangular shape, defined by bookshelves along both walls, metamorphosed into a hollow sphere that completely surrounded me. It was like watching one of those fancy TV commercials where one thing magically, smoothly changes into something completely different. When the process was complete, I was floating at the very center of a hollow sphere, perhaps ten feet in diameter. The inner surface of the sphere was black and was covered with what looked like tiny little yellow lights. Examining the lights brought a sense like I was seeing the ends of thousands of fiber optic cables that extended in all directions from the outer surface of the sphere. I somehow knew these were connections to the Grid of All Possibilities the tour guide had mentioned.

"I'd like to see the design of the perfect surgical scalpel," I said to no one in particular.

There was a slight buzzing sound that bounced back and forth between two tiny lights exactly opposite each other on the inner surface of the sphere. The rate of bouncing slowly settled down until it became a soft steady buzz. I could see a beam of light between the two points of light passing through the exact center of the sphere. I reached out with my left hand and let the beam illuminate my palm. I felt something toward the extreme end of hard, along the continuum of the soft versus hard polarity. Odd way to explain it perhaps, but that's what I felt. Next, the little lights on either end of the cleanability polarity began to bounce a buzzing beam back and forth through the center of the sphere. That one settled out on the extreme end of cleanable. The polarity of smooth and rough lit up, ending up with smoothness that eliminated pits and scratches big enough to host bacteria. Then brittleness versus malleable polarity came on and caused a slight readjustment to soft versus hard.

Staring at my hand, I began to see a prototype of the perfect scalpel taking form. I realized the Hall of Bright Ideas supplied the perfect balance of every polarity required in the design of a perfect scalpel. Polar opposites of every material property were added, one at a time, and when necessary, adjustments of previous settings were made. Somehow, this place brought polar opposites into the perfect balance in a perfect combination. The scalpel design was nearly finished and I was looking closely at the cutting edge, which started out as combination of a curved section near the tip and straight section near the handle. Then the very edge of the blade began to undulate, giving it a saw-toothed appearance. A gentle sine wave began to smooth out the jagged appearance. The sine wave stretched out, starting with perhaps twenty "teeth" along the entire cutting edge. When it reduced the number to five or six "teeth," the edge slowly undulated back and forth between them, finally settling on six teeth. It was finished. The prototype was pure white, full sized, and resting in my hand. The sphere metamorphosed back into its former, straight-walled, bookshelved appearance and I was left standing in the room, holding a prototype of the perfect surgical scalpel in my left hand. The rest of my group walked in and gathered around to look it.

"What do I do with it now?" I asked, calling out to the tour guide.

"It's your design," came back sharply, "use it for whatever purpose you made it!"

"But, it was just a demonstration. I don't have any other use for it."

"You mean you don't want it?" the tour guide said, in a unbelieving tone.

"It was just a demonstration!"

"If you don't want it, then put it in one of the cubbyholes there on the wall," he replied, exasperated.

Looking at the nearby wall, I could see what looked like lots of little open mailboxes.

"You mean these little mailbox-looking things? What happens to it if I put it in there?"

"The Planning Center will get the word over the Grid that we've got a design for the perfect scalpel up here in Bright Ideas. They'll know what to do with it. And no, I don't have the time to explain all that to you. Check with someone at the Planning Center when you get there."

"Okay, thanks for your help. Sorry I don't remember being here before, but that's the way it is."

The group broke up, scattering to further explore the Education Center, and I decided to take a walk outside. A big, funny-looking box caught my eye. It was easily as high and wide as an over-the-road semitrailer, but only half as long. It was sitting outdoors, on the lawn, and the guy standing next to it appeared to be an attendant, like a ticket taker at a movie theater. I approached the man to see what I could find out about the box.

"Hi, ah . . . I'm here with a group on a tour of Focus 27. Can you tell me what this big box is for?"

"Sure, I've been expecting one of you to come by. You can probably best conceptualize this box as a Holodeck. You know, like in *Star Trek.* It's a bigger version of the Holodesk you probably saw inside. Works about the same too, except you don't watch the story, you're in it."

"I could get a book in the library, put it in the slot I see there on the side of the box, and play the book like a movie?"

"More like a 3-D hologram, but, yeah, you've got the idea. And you can pick a character in the book you'd like to play, or go in as yourself."

"Sounds like this thing is a kind of dream box."

"You could call it that, sure, and for lots of people that's how it's used."

Just then, Dar's voice on the exercise tape suggested we explore an Education Center for a nonhuman species. I stood next to the guy I'd been talking with, pondering which nonhuman species to choose. The first one that came to mind was dolphins.

"Do you know if there are Education Centers for species besides humans?"

"Sure, lots of them."

"How would I get to one if I wanted to visit and explore there?"

"You go over there," he said, pointing to a place not far away, "through the archway labeled, 'Nonhuman Section of the Center.' Then you pick the Tube of Knowing that goes to the Nonhuman Education Center you want to visit. There'll be an attendant over there to help you, if needed."

I walked in the direction the tour guide pointed and immediately almost bumped into someone.

"Excuse me, I'm trying to find the Nonhuman Section. Can you tell me where that is?"

"It's right through there," the guy I almost bumped into said, pointing to a sign over the doorway right in front of me that said, "To Nonhuman Education Centers." "If you like I can go with you and show you around."

"Yeah, I'd appreciate that, thanks."

We walked through the doorway and out into a well-lit, open field with a black, night sky. There were lots of bright yellow tubes that seemed like tunnels, going from the field every which way through the sky. Each one seemed to start at ground level at various places around the field and then head up into the darkness. There were lots of them, twisting and turning, heading off in every direction and extending far off into the distance.

"Are those things the Tubes of Knowing I've heard about?"

"One and the same!"

"What do they do and how do I use one?"

"A Tube of Knowing is like a tunnel that leads from one place to another. If you want to know about something, like if you wanted to go to one of the nonhuman education centers to explore, you get there by stepping into the Tube of Knowing that goes to that center."

"Where would I find the one that goes to the Dolphin Education Center?" I asked.

"You take that one," he said, pointing to my left.

I turned to my left only to discover I was standing right next to the entrance to a Tube of Knowing, with a sign over it that said, "NON:HU:DOLPHIN." I was beginning to get really curious why I never saw these signs until a tour guide pointed to them. I felt like something sneaky was going on, but I couldn't figure out what.

"How do I use this thing, again?"

"Just step in, the tube will take you where you want to know. That's why they're called Tubes of Knowing."

Turning toward the entrance, I looked it over. It looked like I'd be entering a solid, yellow, round tube about eight feet in diameter. Stepping back a little, I followed the tube's path up into the sky, trying to get a feel for how far I would have to travel. It looked like the tube was so long it extended past distant stars. The entrance I was supposed to step into looked like the smooth, flat end of a big, solid tube made of bright yellow plastic. I couldn't see into the tube, as it was completely opaque. Not knowing what to expect, I stepped close to the solid-looking surface; my nose was almost touching it. Feeling a little nervous about what might happen next, I just began to think about stepping into the tube and, BAM!, in the next instant I was stepping out of the tube's other end. Astonished, I turned around to look at the tube I'd just come out of. It looked the same as the one I'd thought about stepping into an instant ago, except the sign over it said, "To Human Education Center." Then I heard a voice behind me.

"Takes a little getting used to, doesn't it?"

"You can say that again!" I said, as I turned around to see who was talking. It was a dolphin! Or more accurately, a caricature of a dolphin, cartoon-like, and he was huge. The dolphin was standing on his tail and was at least eight feet tall.

"I'll be your tour guide while you're here," the dolphin said, in a moderate, baritone voice.

"First thing I'd like to know is how that tube thing works! I mean, before I stepped into the other end I thought I'd have to travel thousands of light years to get here. But in my perception, I traveled through it to here in less than an instant of time. How is that possible?"

"Well, it has to do with your concept of travel," the dolphin said. "You see, you didn't actually 'travel' through the tunnel. Did you experience any sensation of movement?"

"No, I just barely started to think about stepping into it over there, and in the next instant I was stepping out of it over here!"

"The best I can explain it to you is that when you thought about stepping into the tube, you were created here."

"Created here?"

"Yes, your experience as a human makes you think you have to travel to get from point A to point B. Truth is, getting from point A to point B is an act of creation. It requires no time or movement. One instant you're in one place, in the next instant you're created in another."

"This conversation is making me dizzy," I said.

"It's a way of Being more available here, in the non-physical world, as you call it. But tell me, what's your interest in the Dolphin Education Center?"

His question settled down the dizziness I was feeling and brought my focus of attention back to my purpose for being here.

"I'm part of a group of people exploring Focus 27. One of my tasks is to explore the Education Center of a nonhuman species and I picked dolphins."

"I'll be glad to show you around. Anything in particular you'd like to see?"

"Well . . . the last thing I was checking out over in the human section was a kind of Holodeck thing. It was a machine where people could participate in a story from a book of their choosing, kind of like a dream box. You got something like that over here?"

"You mean like this one?" he asked, pointing to big box nearby that looked like the one I'd just seen.

"Yeah! That looks just like the one over in the human section. Dolphins use this one the same way?"

"Yep. Dolphins can come here to dream as a character in a story, just like humans do. In fact, sometimes humans come over here to join into the dreams of dolphins in the Dolphin Holodeck. Mostly it's Helpers or Physicals who come to play with the dolphins. Interaction between the two species provides for some valuable learning."

"Like what?" I asked.

"Well, for example, some dolphins live so far out at sea they seldom, if ever, see a physically alive human in their habitat. By entering a dream with a human, the dolphin learns to recognize and know what human beings are. Then, if they ever do encounter a physical human in their habitat, the memory of their dream interaction lets them know the human is not a threat. Makes attacks on humans by dolphins far less likely."

"Interesting!"

"I've got to tell you, most of the dolphins who dream with you guys think humans are a pretty strange species."

"Why is that?"

"In their dreams they see you guys spending most of your time working at a job you don't enjoy, just so you can earn enough money so you can go to your grocery stores and buy food. In a dolphin's world food is freely distributed throughout their environment and the only work involved is catching it. Money is a concept for which they have no use or understanding. And your governments! That concept seems really strange to the dolphins. You guys pay some of your precious money to other guys who make rules you all have to live by or you lose lots more of your money or your freedom. Seems to them such rules ought to apply at most to just a few of your more unsavory characters, if at all. Dolphins don't comprehend the need for any set of rules that every dolphin, in all circumstances, should follow everywhere on Earth. You see, dolphins live alone or in small groups. They have no need for government beyond a few simple rules within their small groups. And there are only a very few reasons for dolphins to join even small groups, so their rules are based only on those reasons."

"For example?"

"Dolphins only join together in a group for procreation, recreation, companionship, and protection. Each reason has its own little set of rules and they only apply to the dolphins in that group while they're together for that reason."

"Hmmm. That makes sense. So if dolphins join together, like say for protection against sharks, there's a specific set of rules for interaction?"

Have you ever seen a dolphin with a completely dumbfounded look on his face? Well, I have. At my comment about protection from sharks, my tour guide's dolphin face took on that look, and the tone of his voice changed.

"Excuse me? You think sharks are a threat to dolphins?" he said, in a flabbergasted, borderline-insulted, voice. "How could anyone ever think a shark could be a threat to a dolphin? They're such a stupid, intellectually retarded, slow, dumb species! How could anyone think they could be a threat to . . . to a dolphin!" he said, the volume of his voice rising a little.

"I didn't mean any offense, I just thought that . . ."

"That would be like a normal, full grown adult human, being attacked by a retarded child! Without complete surprise, which is almost impossible for such a stupid, lower animal as a shark, they are a minor threat to any dolphin. Oh, I suppose if the dolphin was weakened by injury or disease, or if one of us was caught alone by a huge school of them, maybe. But, a shark . . . a threat to a dolphin? Preposterous!"

"What about as a threat to baby dolphins?"

"Any shark caught around baby dolphins is immediately encouraged to leave the area. If they don't take the hint and leave immediately, we just kill them. No big deal, it's easy to kill such stupid animals. Sometimes we just cripple them enough they start bleeding, spreading the scent of blood through the water. Then we just move on and let the rest of its retard-buddies find it and finish the job for us. Sharks," he said, laughing. "Sharks a threat to dolphins!" Laughing still harder, "Really, I don't know where you humans get some of your ideas."

Dar's voice cut in on my dolphin tour guide's laughter, saying it was time to return from our exploration exercise.

"Say, thanks a lot for all your help. I just got the signal that I've got to go back to the physical world again."

"Glad you came over, I haven't had such a good laugh in a long time."

"Is there a Tube of Knowing I can take to get back to TMI-There?"

"Do you really think you need one to 'travel' there?" he asked with a knowing smile.

"No, I guess you're right. It's just an act of creating myself there, isn't it?"

"That's what that gorgeous creature you call Sensuous was trying to show you at the lake, don't you think?" he said, smiling again.

"Hey. You know about the lake at my place?"

"We dolphins get around too, you know!"

"Wow! Well, I gotta get back. Just create myself there you say?"

"You got it buddy."

I stood, facing the direction that felt like it went to TMI-There. Then I just started to think about stepping into the room with the crystal and, BAM!, I was stepping out of a doorway of the building into the room.

chapter 8

The Coordinating Intelligences

Arriving early at my place in Focus 27 again before the next tape exercise, I found Bob and the others there, as usual. I noted the Woman from Sensuous's conspicuous absence and was staring at her empty chair. Bob made a sound, like clearing his throat, and my attention was pulled into the group. Then Coach piped up.

"Bruce, I see you've noticed the empty chair on my left, but you don't seem the least bit curious about the empty one on my right."

"What, Coach? Oh, yeah . . . I remember that one was empty the last time I was here too. Something special about that?"

The chair on Coach's right was indeed empty. Then I noticed, standing perhaps fifteen feet behind it, a trim-figured man, dressed in faded blue jeans and loose, tan cotton shirt. His face was a cloud of light. When he started walking toward the empty chair, I recognized who he was by his movements.

"White Bear! White Bear, it's you!" I had met him during my second Lifeline—he and Shee-un. He had taught me to sense things in the physical world in a way that was quite remarkable. When I invited him in, my walk had changed to that same, smooth gliding gait. And I remembered standing with my face not a foot away from sparrows, which were chirping and flitting from branch to branch in a tree. They never flew away! It was like they didn't even know I was there. And the fawn! I remember watching a fawn from the deck that evening and knowing its mother was close by. She was picturing the place in the forest they'd bed down for the night. "White Bear, is it really you?"

"Yes, it's him," Coach interrupted, "and he's part of the reason I'm here. After your retrieval of Joe, your *Punky* experience, something very basic in you changed."

"You're right. When I got that pet name from Joe, it verified beyond all doubt that my experiences in the nonphysical world were real."

"I remember watching you after that experience, Bruce," Coach said softly. "I remember how eliminating so many old, core beliefs at once really shook you up."

For a week I felt like the world I lived in was going to fade to black and when it faded back in I'd be in a completely different world. It was such an identity crisis I felt like I was losing my mind, or that I was going to die. I understand now that when I lost those beliefs, I lost a part of myself. It took time to integrate new beliefs, based on my Afterlife experiences, into who and what I am now. "Yeah, it was a pretty scary time. And just after Joe's retrieval, Coach, you disappeared! Boy I felt lost when you deserted me!"

"Actually, it was the other way around."

"You mean, I deserted you?"

"In a manner of speaking, yes," Coach replied. "You see, after you released all doubt, you were completely willing to accept your experiences in the nonphysical world as real. That had been my assignment, to assist you in gathering information that could lead you to that acceptance. When you did, it changed you. It altered the "frequency band" in which you and I communicated. You moved so far off the station that when you pushed the old button to find me, you were no longer communicating on the same frequency. You didn't recognize that and just kept pushing the old button. White Bear tried to connect with you on your new frequency, but there were other problems too."

"Then, it *was* White Bear who tried to communicate with me after you disappeared! I thought so! Why couldn't I get a lock on him to communicate? After the first couple of times I felt like there was someone else there, then he disappeared too."

"The change in your frequency, coupled with what you might call indulgence in grief, made communication from our end extremely difficult."

"So, I need to learn to communicate at a new frequency? I don't understand."

"That's why I'm here now. You see, White Bear's form of communication is a better match for your present capability. It's a form you seem to have forgotten."

"Forgotten?"

"When he met with you during that Lifeline program he was attempting to remind you of this method."

"That's what he was teaching me? He wasn't just showing me how to communicate with other animals in the physical world?"

"Consider what he taught you then, as a preliminary understanding of his form of communication. It can be used to communicate in any world with anything or anyone. Your best understanding of that concept at the time was that you could communicate with the other animals in the physical world. Your experience with the birds flitting around in the tree and the fawn at the edge of the forest seemed to verify that's what you were learning."

"But he was really trying to teach me a form of communication with much broader application?"

"Yes. And in order for you to be able to communicate with him, you're going to have to relearn it. My assignment is to help you do that."

"So, how will I know when I'm getting it?"

"I'm here to help you do just that. You'll know you're getting it when you begin receiving his communication."

I looked over at White Bear, now sitting in the hanging chair between Tralo and Coach. Intending to learn his method of communication, I opened my attention, waiting to experience whatever form it took. A few moments later, a soft steady tone sounded in my left ear. It was just a steady audio tone, like one you'd hear taking a hearing test. It didn't seem to carry any meaning, it was just a tone. I started wondering if the tone had anything to do with White Bear's method of communication. When I turned to these thoughts, the tone stopped. As I opened my attention, with the intent to learn again, the soft steady tone resumed. Suddenly, after half a minute or so, not knowing how I knew, I understood the tone.

"My name is White Bear," came into my mind without effort.

Turning to Coach excitedly, I exclaimed, "He's telling me his name! Somehow with that tone he's saying his name is White Bear."

The same tone sounded for a short time, stopped, and then repeated the pattern.

"'That's right, Bruce!' He just said, 'That's right, Bruce.' I kind of just know it when I focus my attention on the tone!"

"You're starting to catch on," Coach replied. "Now, focus on the tone again."

I opened my attention, the tone restarted, and I began listening to it intently. The tone began to gently warble, and as it did, I was taken back to a scene from the last day of my Gateway Voyage program, in September 1991. I was "sitting out" the remaining tape exercises after my experience of contacting Focus 21 "friends." I was sitting out on the deck, playing with the funny vibration I had felt in my head since the previous day's tape experience. Sitting there in the sun, I discovered that I could entrain words onto the vibration and send them out to my new friends in Focus 21, and I was surprised to receive a return message. It had come back entrained in that strange vibration directly behind my eyes.

Somehow White Bear's tone led me to reexperience the entire episode. I knew, somehow, that White Bear's soft tone in my left ear was similar to the fluttering vibration I'd felt during my Gateway Voyage. The basic principle was the same. In a flash, I realized that if I learned how to receive and send information using the tone, I would be able to communicate with White Bear. I decided to try. As I pulled my attention away from his tone, the remembered scene faded and I was back at my place in Focus 27.

I made up a sentence in my mind. "My name is Bruce, and if I'm getting your message, this is how I communicate with you." Then I compressed the words until they were only their feeling and consciously intended to send out a tone of my own. I actually heard my tone! It was steady, and at a slightly different pitch than White Bear's. When I finished, my tone stopped and I immediately heard one come back on White Bear's frequency. At first it was steady and then it changed to a tonal pattern that sounded like, "Whoop, whoop, reeep!" It's hard to describe on paper what the pattern sounded like. To those of you who have seen the *Star Wars* movies, I'd say it sounded very much like the pops, squeaks, and squeals of R2D2, the little robot on wheels. I immediately understood the first, steady tone to say, "Yes, you have properly interpreted the memory of your Gateway Voyage experience on the deck." The "whoop, whoop, reeep," was more like an expression of congratulations.

"Well, Bruce, that didn't take long!" I felt Coach say. "You've got the basics, boy, and from here on out, it's just a matter of practice and learning the nuances. Now if you don't mind I've got other things to attend to."

"Thanks for all your help, Coach."

"You bet! See you again some time," Coach replied, and then he disappeared from the chair.

Carrying a little sadness at Coach's departure, I headed for the crystal at TMI-There to begin our group's next exploration.

From the crystal at TMI-There the group split up, heading out to explore the Coordinating Intelligences. Intending to locate them, I found myself standing in a huge dark sphere with the feel of a hive. It was a busy place, lots going on, but I didn't see any people around.

"Excuse me . . . anybody here?"

"Yes, Bruce, we've been expecting you," said a voice that seemed to come from everywhere.

"Expecting me?"

"Of course, your buddy, Bob Monroe, was around earlier. He filled us in on your Exploration 27 program. Nice of you to drop by."

"This place we're in seems a little like the Hall of Bright Ideas sphere." It was a lot bigger, but I could see the same kind of lights scattered all over the surface of what felt like the inside of a hollow sphere.

"Similar in many ways, but we're connected to a different part of the Grid."

"There's reference to that Grid thing again. Just what is the Grid?"

"The folks over at the Planning Center can give a better overall explanation. For now, how 'bout we concentrate on our connections to it and how we use them?"

"Okay, sure. What do you guys do here anyway?"

"You can think of us as a node on the Interstellar Internet. We're connected via Knowing Conduits to all other systems on the Network."

"The Network?"

"The Earth Life System (ELS) is just one of many home worlds where cycles of lifetimes are lived out in a system of learning. The Universe is filled with many such home worlds, each with its own unique life forms and learning methods. Rumors drift through here now and again that there are other universes too. Maybe there are, maybe there aren't, all we know is, if they exist they're not connected to our Grid."

"You mean, there really are other inhabited planets in the Universe? That's for real?"

"Of course there are, Bruce. Wouldn't it seem a terrible waste of all that space if little planet Earth was the only one?"

"I see your point. I've always believed there had to be, but there's a lot of argument on that score where I come from. So what does the Coordinating Intelligences Center do with these other systems?"

"Actually, you can call us the ELSCI (el-see). Our full name is The Earth Life System Coordinating Intelligences."

"Okay, so what does the ELSCI do with other systems?"

"On the broadest scale, we share information with other nodes on the Grid, things like activity in areas of our neighborhood."

"Like what?"

"Oh, trajectories of comets, places with explosive activity, like novas, things that might be a menace to navigation. We also report on local areas suitable for habitation, and we coordinate colonizations, things like that."

"Colonizations?"

"Sure, there are systems from time to time that need to

move from their home world, and some that just need room to branch out."

"Where are these other systems?"

"Many are within our galaxy and there are lots more beyond, in other galaxies."

"Sounds like they're pretty far away. Doesn't it take a long time to transfer information from one place to another?"

"We don't really transfer it in the way you're used to thinking of it. It goes via the Grid, through the Tubes of Knowing. The lights you perceive in the inside of our sphere are the connections between the ELSCI and the Grid. You could think of it more like we just create our information at all other nodes on the Grid in the same instant of time. Information from other nodes comes to us the same way."

"This sounds like my trip to the Dolphin Education Center. I used a Tube of Knowing to get from one place to the other."

"Information we share with other systems gets here the same way you 'traveled' from one place to another. It's just instantaneously created on all nodes of the Grid, it doesn't really travel anywhere."

"I think I get it. So, what else do you guys do?"

"We coordinate contacts between systems, sort of arrange meetings between members of systems. You might call that 'Alien contact' from your Earth perspective. We also examine time/event line interactions at the interstellar level."

"Another reference to time/event lines. What are those exactly?"

"Think of our primary focus as examining the time sequence of events for movement of objects through our area of the Universe. We analyze crossover points, places in time when events occur simultaneously. Much of our work involves dealing with what you might call collisions in time. You see, movements within the physical Universe follow well-understood laws of motion. So, by looking at projected physical Universe trajectories and the time/event lines for, say, a comet, we can see what events are in its future. If the time/event line for a comet crosses the time/event line of, say, Earth, we know events between Earth and the comet occur at the same time. We examine that crossover point to determine probable outcomes."

As the voice coming from everywhere finished its last statement, something like a screen was brought up in front of me. It had white lines on a black background.

"For example, this line, labeled "ESS," represents the time/event line for Earth's Solar System within its galaxy. This other line, labeled "Comet," represents the time/event line for a comet within the same galaxy." Then, pointing at where the two lines crossed, "See this intersection of the two lines, here?"

"Yes."

"That's what we call a crossover point. It indicates a link of events in time between that comet and the Earth."

"You mean, like a collision between Earth and a comet?"

"Yes, but a collision in time is not necessarily a collision in space. Since both time/event lines continue past the crossover point, we know both Earth and the comet will continue to have events beyond the crossover. They both have futures, so to speak, but our analysis is more concerned with, futures as what?—as a comet and a planet? Or as bits of matter spreading through the system as a result of an explosive collision in time and space? To know, we must examine the crossover point more closely."

The image on the screen began to zoom in on the crossover point, magnifying it. I began to see a little fuzzy light around the point, and as magnification increased, I could see little lines of light around it that had a familiar pattern. They resembled pictures in my college physics textbook of atomic collisions in a particle accelerator. Greatly magnified, I could now see spiral lines emanating from the crossover point in several places.

"Your comparison to particle collision images is a good one, Bruce. Pictures of atomic particle collisions show physicists more about time and events than they realize."

"What are these spiral lines coming out of the crossover point?"

"Those are the probable outcomes of the events that Earth and the comet share in time. We learn a lot about the interaction between the comet and Earth by examining the probable outcome, time/event lines. By examining events in the continuation of the Earth time/event line, we can see how they are affected. In this case our analysis of Earth's events shows it continues on through time without events that would indicate a physical collision takes place. But there is an alteration in the time/event line trajectory. See how the line bends away from its trajectory right at the crossover point? That indicates an alteration in events-in-time, a change of events on Earth that's associated with the comet/Earth interaction in time."

"You guys have any idea what effect this change of events will have?"

"That's where the potential outcome trails come in, those spiral lines you see emerging from the crossover point. Notice how the outcome lines spiral inward and end? Notice that the time/event line of the comet ends long after having passed the crossover point? This particular comet is primarily frozen gases and water. That indicates the point at which it ceases to be a comet. In other words, the point in its time/event sequence where it has completely evaporated."

"I see. So those spiral lines are probable outcomes that indicate the end of the Earth?"

"They could, or they could indicate the end of events triggered by the crossover. If one of those spiral lines, probable outcomes, led to the end of the Earth, then the end of the line would indicate the end of the Earth, just like the comet. But you can see the Earth's line continues on; this event will not be the end of the Earth. If you looked very closely at the crossover, you'd see the bend, or deflection, in the Earth's line occurs in the same area the spiral lines emerge. Here at ELSCI, part of what we do is to analyze all the probable outcomes and interact with the ELS in ways that favor our best choice for the actual outcome."

"You mean there are things you guys can do to alter the course of these time/event lines?"

"Of course, Bruce. What would be the sense in knowing all about this stuff if you weren't going to use the information?"

"Okay, I get your point," I replied.

"You'll get more detail about influencing outcomes at the Planning Center. It will be easier for you to understand at the level they work in. Suffice it to say, we can lay in time/event lines at our level to influence the probable outcome selected."

"How do you know when you've accomplished such an influence?"

"One way we can tell is by the number of spiral lines we see as our influences take effect. In our first examination of this crossover point, there were many more spiral lines representing many more probable outcomes. Our alterations have brought them down to four probables and the deflected probability, which is firming up as the actual outcome."

"So, there's no actual collision between this comet and Earth?"

"That's what our analysis shows, yes. They pass very, very close to one another—very, very close—but there's no physical collision event in either of their sequences."

"Is this stuff you've been showing me an example from the past, or in Earth's future?"

"It's happening now. This crossover point is in your present time."

"There's a comet approaching earth right now? I haven't read anything about that in the news."

"Keep checking your newspaper sources. Actually, it's already been discovered, the information just hasn't been released to the general public on Earth yet," the tour guide said.

"Thanks, I'll keep my eyes open. How did the ELSCI come into existence?"

"We were formed as a result of the experience of humans and grew into our interstellar Internet node status as that experience expanded."

"So you kind of grew into the Earth home world connection to the other home world systems?"

"Yes, as human awareness grew to encompass more and more of the unknown, there came a time in which that awareness included knowledge of other home world systems. We are that human awareness that grew. Each system has its own Coordinating Intelligences, and we have Grid feeds to the level above all of ours."

"You mean, there's a level of coordinating intelligence for the physical Universe, above the one you and the other home world groups make up?"

"Yep. We're not really sure what that one does. We feed everything we collect to Knowing Conduits on that part of the Grid, but we don't get much back from it. Maybe you can explore that one too some time. If you do, come back and tell us what you find out."

"Where would I look?"

"Around here we refer to it as the Planning Intelligence, but we don't really know much about what it does."

Dar's voice on the exercise tape cut in and suggested I ask about other functions of the Coordinating Intelligences.

As a means of remembering to ask specific questions, this method was used on all the Exploration 27 exercise tapes. As usual, her suggestion this time diverted me toward a different path of questioning.

"Okay, thanks for the tip. If I find out anything, I'll let you know. Now what about other things you guys do?"

"Well, we coordinate transfer of loaners between systems."

"What's a loaner?"

"You have one in your . . . your . . . Disk, I believe you call it. The one you call Tralo. Tralo's a loaner. A part of your awareness that was transferred to another system and lived its lifetime cycles within that system. We coordinate such transfers."

"What about Earth school system graduates? You guys do anything with them?"

"Earth school grads have lots of options. The ones we see are usually taking transfers to other systems as diplomats or teachers. Once in a great while one will transfer to another system to experience lifetime cycles there. That's pretty rare, though. Most other systems don't seem to offer enough reward for the effort."

Dar's voice cut in again, with another suggested question.

"Can you tell me something about the next steps in Earth's evolution?"

"In general, an accelerated pace of individuals graduating in preparation for great reductions in physical life experience opportunities. Many individuals are accelerating toward graduation by moving through, or experiencing, collapse of the ecosystem because of greed."

"A lot of folks are making that claim. Can you tell me more about this collapse?"

"Check with the Planning Center guys. We're interstellar; they're much closer to the situation and can give you more of the details."

Any further interrogation of the voice from everywhere was cut short by Dar's voice on the tape requesting we finish up and return.

"That's my signal to return, so I've got to go. Thanks for all your help, you've given me a lot to think about."

"Glad to be of service. And I was serious about you coming back if you get anything on the Planning Intelligence. If you find anything, we'd like it if you would share your information."

I left for my place. When I arrived, I was standing next to White Bear on the path that goes to the lake. His whole body seemed a little fuzzy, like it was partially obscured by a thin cloud of light. I heard him start to tone and focused in to pick up his communication. It was a mixture of short steady tones and R2D2 squeals and squawks.

"Bruce, I thought I might explain a little more about why you had such a hard time communicating with me after your *Punky* experience," I felt coming from the tone. "You and I are so much the same, so much alike. That's part of why it is hard for you to see me and why it was so hard for you to hear me after *Punky*. Coach is a little more 'different' from you, so that contact was easier."

I toned back, "Kind of like, it's easier sometimes to see a trait I have in someone else than to see it myself?"

"Sometimes the hardest thing to see is ourselves," he toned back.

chapter 9

The Planning Center

I was extremely tired at the beginning of the next tape exercise. I had been up late the night before, talking with other participants in the program over popcorn, chips, and fruit juice, and I probably didn't get to bed until after 2:00 a.m.

White Bear was sitting in his chair again. I heard a tone I recognized as on his frequency and then the chirping, squealing patterns began. It was a request that we take a walk down by the lake.

As we walked there, and then along the shore, I practiced toning conversation with White Bear. It still felt strange, having to assemble my thoughts into words, compress them into a feeling, and then send a tone. It felt very cumbersome and slow. Gradually, I began to learn that when White Bear asked a question, I could just "feel" my answer nonverbally and send a tone that was automatically imprinted with it. With practice, it was becoming second nature. White Bear wanted to show me what he called leaping.

We walked to the water's edge. He explained I could learn much by practicing this "leaping" as often as possi-

ble and then he demonstrated. From a completely relaxed, standing position, he bolted straight up in an arcing
trajectory, out over the lake, and went in, feet first, forty
yards from shore. He toned his request that I do what he
just did. I crouched down, and then sprang up off my legs,
catapulting myself up into the air. Aiming close to where
White Bear had gone in, I tried to mimic his landing. My
entry into the water was by no means a perfect dive.
When I stopped going down, he was next to me, underwater. I was heading up for the surface when White Bear's
penetrating squawk grabbed my attention.

"Relax, Bruce. No need to hold your breath or to
worry about how long you're underwater," came toning
to me.

He was right. Just before I'd splashed down, I'd in-
haled a deep breath in anticipation of going under water.
I was feeling quite a bit of tension about not having
enough air and I wanted to surface for more.

"Relax. Let the tension go," White Bear toned.

It took a bit of control to do that, but after a short time it
felt as natural and relaxing to be under water as above it.

"Okay, now let's leap back from here to the shore and
try that again," he toned.

I watched White Bear shoot straight up through the
water. Then I kind of rose up slowly, until my body was
above the water, and skittered across the surface to the
shore. Standing on the shore again, I watched White Bear
as he bolted from his relaxed, standing position up into
the air, out over the lake, and into the water. After several
tries I could leap into the air without relying so much on
my legs to propel me, but entry into the water was still not
very pretty. White Bear was very patient. Before I left to
explore the Planning Center, he suggested I practice leaping as often as I could.

When I got to TMI-There, Bob Monroe and Ed Wilson were waiting for me.

"Ed and I just wanted to tell you how well we feel you're doing," Bob said, as I walked up to them.

"Bob's right," Ed chimed in, "and as a physician—both Ed and Bob burst out laughing—as a former medical doctor, I'd like to recommend you get to bed early tonight. Your energy's low and a good night's sleep is just what this doctor orders."

"Seriously," Bob added, "it would be best if you were more rested. There's a lot to do yet and you'll do better if you sleep at night instead of during tape exercises."

Then it was time for the group to gather around the crystal and take on a charge of energy. After a couple of WOOO-AAAHHs, we were ready to explore.

Entering the Planning Center was like walking into an air traffic control center. There were several rows of what resembled radar screen workstations with someone sitting in front of each one. I could see a few people walking around in the facility. One approached me.

"Hi, glad to see you made it! You're Bruce, aren't you? From the Exploration 27 program and here for a tour of the Planning Center?"

"Yes, I am. How did you know that?"

"This is the Planning Center, it's our business to know times and events. I'm your tour guide and I'll be happy to show you around. Feel free to break in and ask anything you'd like at any time."

"Well, for starters, just what is it that the Planning Center does?"

"You've already visited the Coordinating Intelligences area, so you know a little about the way they handle things at the interstellar level. We work in a similar way, but at what you might call a more local level. The Planning Center coordinates activities for the Earth Life System (ELS), which includes all of your focus levels from C1 to Focus 27 and some local areas beyond. Most of our activity involves managing time/event lines in the local

Time Grid, what you call Focus 15. We analyze crossover points, determine probable outcomes, and plan for them by laying in time/event lines at the crossovers. Sometimes we lay in a completely new time/event line to pickup a probable outcome—those spiral lines you saw over at the Earth Life System Coordinating Intelligence—and encourage it to be the chosen, actualized outcome."

"Whoa . . . whoa! I need to know a lot more about what a time/event line actually is before I can understand what you're telling me."

"Sure, okay. You and your friend Ed Carter talked over dinner the other night about Focus 15 being mislabeled as 'No Time,' when it was really 'All Time,' remember?"

"Yeah."

"Ed's on the right track. When he first landed in Focus 15, everything he saw was completely still. Think of what he was seeing as a single, still photograph of all the events in the scene. As he began walking, things in the scene appeared to move, like seeing a series of still photographs. An event line is just a series of events strung together in a sequence. As Ed walked through Focus 15, he was moving through time, along an event line. You could say, he was walking a time/event line."

"You said something about laying time/event lines into the local Time Grid. Several tour guides have mentioned the Grid, but I don't understand what it is."

"The Grid is a way of describing Conscious Awareness. Maybe if I use the scalpel you designed in the Hall of Bright Ideas as an example, that will help explain it. It's pretty typical of the process we use to introduce new ideas into physical world reality."

"You guys do that?"

"That's part of our function."

"How?"

"When you placed the prototype in the cubbyhole,

you placed it on the Grid. Its existence was entered into Conscious Awareness."

"Whose Conscious Awareness?"

"For now, let's just say *the* Conscious Awareness. Now, at the Planning Center we have Knowing Tubes, conduits of awareness, connected to those cubbyholes." We walked a short distance to one of the workstations. "This workstation operator monitors awareness of those cubbyholes on the Grid. When you put the scalpel into the cubbyhole, it came into the awareness of the operator at this workstation. Everything that comes off the Grid at this workstation is within the Conscious Awareness of the operator. Requests for inventions are also placed on the Grid and come to this workstation. So the operator is consciously aware of all available inventions and all requests for inventions."

"Who places the requests on the Grid?"

"Anyone. In the case of your scalpel design, there are two men on Earth who have recently been thinking about a better scalpel design. Both of them work for companies that manufacture surgical scalpels. As they began to express their desire to improve scalpel design, their thoughts came into the awareness of the operator via the Grid."

"So these guys are connected to the Grid too?"

"Everything capable of Conscious Awareness is connected to the Grid. Now, the operator here was aware of their requests for a better scalpel design when you were wondering what to use as a demonstration for your friends. You placed a request for something to design on the Grid by wondering. The operator sent the request for a scalpel design into your awareness. That's why you picked a scalpel as your demonstration. As you did your demonstration, everything that happened was brought into the awareness of the operator. In a sense the operator recorded a time/event line of the entire design process.

When you put the scalpel thought form into the cubby-hole, the operator connected it to the Conscious Awareness of those two men."

"Only those two?"

"No. Actually once it's on the Grid, it is available to everyone and everything capable of Conscious Awareness. Since those two men expressed a desire for an improved scalpel design, their connection with it is more solid."

"So they are both aware of the perfect scalpel design now?"

"Well, it's there for them to become conscious of, but when they do that is up to them. We can provide some encouragement toward that by a little time/event line management, laying some event lines into Focus 15 , and in doing so affecting the probable outcome."

A screen then popped into view and the tour guide continued. "This diagram represents what we do. The line labeled Inventor is the time/event line of one of the two men, and the one labeled Scalpel is the one we generated and laid into Focus 15. The Inventor line is the sequence of events in one of the men's lives, the Scalpel line is the thought form of the scalpel. That thought form contains every detail of your design process. It has all your thoughts, in the sequence you had them, as well as the final thought form of the prototype. We assemble the scalpel time/event line as a repetitive sequence of your design process. It's like an audio loop tape that plays the announcement in your old-style telephone answering machines. It plays the same event line pattern over and over and over. Now, notice how the Scalpel line meanders back and forth across the Inventor line?"

"Yeah, are those the crossover points?"

"Precisely! Those are points at which an event in the man's life sequence will occur at the same time as an event in your design process sequence. For example, this fourth crossover occurs during a machinery sales convention he's planning to go to. There's a special machine on display at that convention that is capable of grinding extremely sharp, scalloped cutting edges, like the ones on your scalpel. The crossover point occurs in his sequence when he sees that machine. The scalpel design sequence event line will be at the point where you watched the undulating cutting edge. Both events will be in his awareness at the same time. If he focuses his attention on the scalpel time/event sequence at the crossover point, he'll pick up our desired probable outcome. He'll see the completed prototype and then the entire design process from start to finish from the undulating cutting edge point of your design process."

"He'll have the light-bulb-come-on-in-his-head experience, an inspiration, a breakthrough!" I exclaimed.

"Or as we say, he will have downloaded awareness from the Grid."

"What if he doesn't focus his attention on the scalpel time/event line at the crossover?"

"Several things are possible. Since both the special machine and scalpel design were in his awareness at the crossover point, they are connected by association in his memory. Every time he sees or thinks about that machine, the scalpel sequence will come into his awareness too. So he may become consciously aware of it later by association within his stored memory. There are also several other events he has already planned that present opportunities for crossover points. The event in the scalpel sequence, selected for those crossovers, will be keyed to trigger on a similar event in his experience."

"What if the guy doesn't happen to see the special machine? Can that happen?"

"He's constantly making decisions that affect his experience from minute to minute. He's altering his own time/event line constantly by making freewill choices. But if his desire for the scalpel design is strong, he'll keep making choices that will lead him to see it."

"How do you know if he's going to get it?" I asked.

"We don't know, but by looking closely at the cross-over point, we can examine potential probabilities," he said. "If you look closely at the four crossover points, you can see the probability lines."

The image of the crossover zoomed in. Now I could see the little spiral lines emanating from where the two lines crossed. It looked a lot like the one I'd seen during my Coordinating Intelligences tour.

"By examining these spiral outcome lines, we can determine probable results and make a choice as to the best outcome. Basically, we just select the spiral with the highest probability of successful scalpel design transfer and then add a triggering event to increase the probability. We bring the triggering event line in tangent to the selected spiral in an attempt to get the actual events to follow the new course."

"And this same process is going on with one other man at the same time?"

"Two more, actually. There's the one who also works for a different scalpel manufacturer, and a janitor in Ohio with an interest in knife blade design."

"What are these triggering events you might generate?"

"We could make use of the Holodeck over at the Education Center. For example, we might lay in a time/event line that brought the man who will see the special machine into the Holodeck. The folks over at Education could prepare a book to be played in which the guy goes to a machinery sales convention and sees the special machine in a dream. Memory of the dream then becomes the triggering event we use in that case. Education could include the scalpel design sequence, so he would associate the two together. If the guy was consciously aware during the dream, like you were in the Hall of Bright Ideas, he'd get the whole enchilada right there in the

Holodeck. The invention would be transferred into the physical world through that dream and that part of our job would be finished. If not, it would be stored in his sub-conscious memory, waiting for the fourth crossover point, at which time the dream would be the triggering event to bring the scalpel design into his awareness."

"Hold on a second . . . I'm getting something . . . When the triggering event occurs he might perceive it as a déjà vu experience! Since he saw the whole scene previously in a dream in the Holodeck, it might seem familiar when the crossover happens!"

"Previous dreams, unremembered, are very often the source of déjà vu experiences and are great triggering events. That déjà vu may bring him back time after time to look at that machine while he is still at the machinery show, and each time your scalpel design time/event line will cross over his. The crossover event will occur as many times as he sees that machine, because the two events are connected in time. People's curiosity is often piqued by a déjà vu experience, and as you know, curios-ity is a powerful force. If he didn't make the mental jump to the scalpel design at the convention, just wondering later about the déjà vu experience would become poten-tial triggering events for the transfer. Either way, the oper-ator at this workstation would be laying in time/event lines to provoke as much memory of the dream as possi-ble."

"Like what?"

"Like, maybe an old friend of the man, who also plans to be at the machinery show, would have been included in the Holodeck dream. Maybe these guys haven't seen each other in ten years, but the shared dream could get them to thinking about each other before the crossover. Time/event crossovers could be laid in that bring both men together at the special machine at the same time and, presto, another triggering event."

"The déjà vu would contain the coincidence of the two old friends meeting," I offered.

"And help trigger memory of the Holodeck dream experience to increase the probability that the man's attention would jump over to . . ."

". . . Picking up the scalpel design sequence, time/event line," I realized out loud. "The roots of coincidence! Holodeck dreams can be the source of coincidences!"

"Coincidences, déjà vu, presenting answers to questions during dreams or daydreams, these are just good time/event line management techniques," the tour guide said, as if everybody knew this stuff.

"This is amazing! There's actually a place where coincidences are planned and set up. I'm flabbergasted!"

"Bruce," the tour guide said, "feeling flabbergasted by coincidences is just another good time/event line management tool."

"What do you mean?" I asked.

"Do you remember a certain dream in which you were screaming, 'Who are you'?" he questioned.

It took a moment for me to realize what he was referring to, then all came back clearly in a flash.

"Of course! My first lucid dream! The big guy I saw in the robe with the strange facial features! The Norwegian/Oriental!"

"And you remember feeling flabbergasted later by an event connected to that dream?" he asked.

"Two weeks later I was at a library, looking for a book on hypnosis. I reached for it but grabbed the book next to it by mistake, Bob Monroe's *Journeys Out of the Body*. I opened it at random and started reading a description of someone Monroe met in one of his out-of-body experiences who looked just like the big guy in my dream."

"Encouraging a random book opening to a particular page is an example of very detailed time/event line management. Remember feeling flabbergasted?" the tour guide asked, a sly look on his face.

"Yes! I couldn't believe it! I kept wondering about all the coincidences that led to grabbing the wrong book. I remember thinking this was one of those coincidences that meant I'd actually grabbed the right book."

"And how did the feeling of being flabbergasted affect the probable outcome?" he asked.

"I took the book home, read it cover to cover, and began to practice out-of-body techniques," I replied.

"And that event led you to be here with me now, wouldn't you say?"

"Yes, it altered the course of events in my life. It sparked and fed my curiosity to know what lies beyond physical death. It led to my attending the Gateway Voyage and Lifeline programs at The Monroe Institute. And to my attending the Exploration 27 program I'm in right now! Say, I'll bet you guys used the Holodeck dream stuff to set me up for that!"

"Just another fine example of time/event line management we do here at the Planning Center," my tour guide said, smiling.

For a few moments I was caught up in reverie, gathering insights into how the Planning Center was involved in transferring ideas into physical world reality. In awe, I gathered my wits, returning my attention to the tour guide.

"What if there's a desire on the Grid for a design that's not already in one of the cubbyholes? What do you guys do then?" I asked.

"We might bring one of the Receivers, someone capable of conceptualizing the design, to the Hall of Bright Ideas when that person's desire is strong. It could be one of the inventors. They would directly experience the invention of that design as they themselves did it there. Later we could bring them to the Holodeck to set up déjà vu or coincidence to trigger memory of their inventing it. We might catch them in a daydream state, staring out the window at work, and run a recording of their design process through their awareness. There are lots of techniques. A Helper living in Focus 27, with the necessary conceptual talent, might go the Hall of Bright Ideas, record the invention sequence, and place it in the cubbyhole. Lots of old-time inventors living here enjoy spending their time in the Hall of Bright Ideas to create things. Then likely Receivers might be brought to the Holodeck to play the role of the inventor in the story, as a way of bringing it into physical world reality. For really critical inventions, the Planning Center pulls out all the stops, laying in time/event crossovers in so many potential Receiver's paths that the idea is almost guaranteed to be transferred very quickly."

"I'll bet that's the reason so many inventors come up with the same new invention at the same time," I thought.

"Of course! For critical inventions we arrange crossover points to transmit the idea to as many people in physical reality as we can find who have the capacity to receive it and to be a part of bringing it through."

"I'm curious," I said. "The tour guide at the Coordinating Intelligences Center said the Planning Center coordinates contacts between aliens and humans?"

"There's another workstation here, connected to the Grid for that activity, yes. The operator there has, within her awareness, all the humans on Earth who have interest, capability, or need of contact with people from other home worlds. She is also aware, through Coordinating Intelligences, of requests, or intended contacts, from other home worlds. She lays appropriate time/event lines in Focus 15 to assist and facilitate those contacts. The same tools, such as the Holodeck, déjà vu, coincidence, and others, are available for use in her facilitating preparations."

"Seems like a lot of responsibility, adding events into people's lives." I remarked. "What qualifies someone to be an operator at one of these workstations and to make decisions about other people's lives?"

"The operator has to be capable of holding millions of things in Conscious Awareness simultaneously. As for making decisions affecting other people's lives, nothing is ever done without the affected person's prior permission. That permission may come directly from the person 'represented' by the one living in the physical body. These are almost always in the form of direct requests they've placed on the Grid. Sometimes that permission comes from the Higher Self, your Disk or I/There, as the action is in line with the person's purpose or mission in life. But *the* primary qualification is that every act by an operator, is an act of Pure Unconditional Love."

"Takes a lot of trust for me to accept that one!" I exclaimed.

"As your friend Rebecca says, trust is always the first issue. Oh, by the way, you had a question I am supposed to remind you of, something from Reentry, over at the Reception Center."

"Yeah, thanks for reminding me! I watched four curls, connected to each other by a filament of awareness. The Entry Director said you could explain more about what it meant that they were strung together, and something about the Big Clock."

"That filament of awareness is encoded with an event sequence, a time/event line, which we'll lay into Focus 15. The events in the sequence will lead each of those curls to meet each other as physical human beings. The filament provides an awareness of each other's presence and activities within the physical world. Depending on their levels of Conscious Awareness, they may be led to each other consciously or subconsciously. Being strung together by a filament of awareness is a much stronger influence than ordinary crossover points on one's time/ event line. These people will be in continuous communication, conscious or subconscious, as they work together to complete their shared and individual purposes. Even if they are barely conscious of their connection, they'll experience the feeling of fatedness when they physically meet. That feeling is a powerful force that can draw people together."

"So, you'll place them in Focus 15, they'll be born in a certain sequence, meet, and carry out their purposes. And whatever the Big Clock is has something to do with the timing of their entry into the physical world, like with their birth dates? So, what is the Big Clock, and how does it work?"

"Someone later in your tour can give you the real details of the inner workings of the Big Clock. You'll need to know more about Earth history and Spirit Gravity to understand how the thing really operates. The Big Clock is just something we use to synchronize the timing of events between Focus 15 and physical world reality. I can give you the basics of how we use it, but you'll need to understand more to really comprehend how it works."

"Who should I ask?"

"When you hear a tour guide mention Spirit Gravity, that's the one who has the information for you. I can see that, by the way, because I'm aware of a crossover point on your time/event line that is simultaneous with the mention of Spirit Gravity. I don't know exactly what time it will happen but it's when those two events coincide."

"Is that why it's so hard to get timing of events from a psychic? They can see the events but the actual timing is not yet determined?"

"Precisely. Now as for the Big Clock, let's say a crossover point needs to happen at a particular point in physical Earth time. It has to occur before another crossover can take place, so the events must be synchronized in physical Earth time. That's an occasion when we would use the Big Clock."

"How?"

"For simplicity's sake let's say the first crossover had to happen to you, early this coming Friday morning. Again for simplicity, let's say the crossover point event was that you were supposed to meet a certain person. Now the time/event line of the planet Earth's rotation about its axis is a very precisely repetitive pattern. Physical laws of mass and momentum ensure that. To synchronize the timing of the crossover point, we would examine the time/event line for your location on the Earth, Friday, say a little after sunrise. Then all that's left for us to do is connect your time/event line, and the other person's time/event line so that they cross over each other at your Earth location's time/event line a little after sunrise on Friday. There are now three time/event lines crossing over each other at the same physical Earth time. We've used a portion of the Big Clock, the Earth's precisely predictable rotation about its axis to bring these events into physical reality at a specific time. We could then use the same method to synchronize the second crossover to a specific time if necessary. By the way, are you meeting anybody special a little after sunrise this coming Friday morning?" the tour guide asked innocently.

"Not that I know of. Why do you ask?"

"Just checking awareness levels, I guess."

"So if I understand it right, Earth's rotation on its axis and maybe its rotation relative to the Sun is the Big Clock?"

"More like a couple of the hands on the Big Clock. Any guesses about the other hands?"

"I get it! It's called the Big Clock because it's the size of our solar system. All the planets in our solar system are like hands on very large clock!"

"Precisely. That's the idea. But actually the clock is bigger. We can also use positions of stars, comets, galaxies, moons, any celestial body with predictable movement. Any of these can be used to synchronize the timing of time/event line interactions. This work is done in Focus 15 and we refer to it as Interweaving of Events, since we're actually producing the fabric of time."

"In physical world reality, time appears to move only in one direction. It may appear to speed up or slow down, but it almost never appears to move backward. Why is that?" I asked.

"It has to do with the interweaving of events within physical reality. It's a product of using the Big Clock to manage time/event lines in the physical world. The physical laws of mass and momentum are interwoven with the time/event lines of activities in physical world reality. It might be more accurate to say physical world time moves in the direction given by predictable movements of masses within the system. This gives the appearance of time always moving in one direction. Planets, after all, seldom stop and move backward in their orbits."

It was here that Dar's voice on the exercise tape cut in to suggest a question that had to do with something called the Big Plan for the Earth. So I asked.

"I've got a little change of the direction in my questions. Can you give me any information about the Big Plan for the Earth? You know, near future stuff?"

"In general the Earth's near future is preparation for large population reductions. This will reduce human impact on the ecosystem. There's been a steady buildup of too many time/event line crossings, which is driving toward ecosystem collapse."

"What's the cause of this?"

"The primary cause is indulgence in the emotional energy of greed. Consumption of Earth's resources has been accelerating, primarily not for direct use, but rather for accumulation of wealth. That, coupled with an extremely large human population, is pushing the ecosystem toward collapse."

"That sounds like the same stuff I got at my Coordinating Intelligences visit. Is the Planning Center involved in these preparations for population reductions?"

"Oh yes. We're been working with this for quite some time."

"In what ways?"

"A lot of our work involves preparing support for the huge volume of people trying to finish out their ELS degrees."

"Finish out what degrees?" I asked.

"Just a manner of speaking. Many who are near completion of their Earth school training want to graduate while there are still lots of incarnation options. After the population reductions, there will be far fewer people living on Earth, so the total number of births worldwide will drop to an extremely low number. It will take Earth's population a very long time to build back up, causing a long-term shortage of available incarnations. So we're very busy here with time/event line management for the huge population as a whole as well as for all those who are working to graduate during their present lifetimes. Many of these are working to mitigate the ecosystem situation."

"What makes these population reductions necessary? Isn't there another way?"

"First, let me say the reductions result from many forces coming together, which by their nature lead to such reductions. Don't get the idea that someone has decided to exterminate large numbers just because it would be better for the ecosystem. But, ecosystem recovery will be easier, since there will be fewer resource consumers. Humans are by far the biggest consumers, so population reductions in that segment will have the biggest ecosystem benefit."

"So the Planning Center is planning mass murder?"

"Bruce, everybody dies. Everybody who transfers from here to there transfers back at some point. It's all a matter of timing of the transfers."

"Still sounds like mass murder to me," I replied.

"Let's just say that everyone who decided to enter physical world lifetimes during this time frame made an informed decision. No one who decided to live on the Earth during these population reductions entered without full knowledge of this situation."

"The thought of so many people dying at once is just hard for me to get used to," I replied sadly. "So many of us are ill prepared to make the transition back here without getting stuck in Focus 23. And there will be fewer people left in the physical world who know how to do retrievals to help out. It's just so sad."

"The retrieval angle is one that is near and dear to your heart, I know," the tour guide said. "You went in as a retrieving type. It stands to reason that part would bother you. In fact, that's another part of the preparations we're working on."

"You mean retrievals?"

"Yes, of course. Much of our work involves bringing awareness of the Afterlife into physical world reality. You and all the Lifeline graduates are a part of that, both in the retrievals you do and in spreading the knowledge that what comes after death isn't an unknowable secret. The writing you've been doing is part of this effort."

"Writing is such a slow process. I've finished a few articles, and I'd like to write a book, but working full time as an engineer doesn't leave much time to make any real progress. Sometimes I feel like I should quit my job and write full time, but if I do that, there won't be any money to pay rent or buy food."

"Don't worry about that. Help is already laid into Focus 15."

"That's hard to trust. I'd have to quit my job and write full time for at least a year!"

"Don't worry about it. Help is already laid into Focus 15."

"How's it going to happen?"

"Now, now . . . you don't expect me to spoil your movie do you?" he chuckled.

"I sure wish you guys would give straight answers!" I said, brightening. "What other preparation work is the Planning Center involved in?"

"We've got some special projects, like AIDS," he said matter-of-factly.

"AIDS? You guys are responsible for AIDS?" I asked incredulously.

"AIDS is just a new form of the disease processes spawned by overpopulation. Earth has seen it before in things like the Black Plague and other types of diseases. Many who decided to enter during this time saw AIDS as an incredible opportunity."

"An opportunity?"

"Certainly! Look at the factors involved. Detection of the virus is possible many years before any symptoms show up, so the certainty of death is there long before the actual event. Many who decided on the AIDS route understood the value of facing certain death. Facing it for years gives lots of opportunities to break through the fear. And it has embedded within it the opportunity for those not facing the certain death of AIDS to advance their ability to experience and express unconditional love."

"What do you mean?" I asked.

"Look at the population segment where AIDS first showed up—in homosexuals. Now there's a group even good Christians can hate. That's a real incongruity in a religion based on a God who said you must love your neighbor as yourself. Such incongruities can cause Christians to question their beliefs. And such questioning can lead to changes in beliefs that are more consistent with 'love your neighbor as yourself.' That incongruity is an opportunity to incarnate into a lifetime as a Christian to learn about Love."

Dar's voice on the tape cut off further conversation with my tour guide at the Planning Center with her request that we return to C1 consciousness. I left with lots of things buzzing around in my head.

chapter 10

The Earth Core Crystal

White Bear was waiting for me at my place in Focus 27 when I arrived at the beginning of our next tape exercise. After exchanging greetings he suggested another walk to the lakeshore, and we conversed in the new tonal form he was teaching me.

"There are many variations to the leaping exercise I have shown you. Much can be learned by practicing as often as you can."

"What is it I'm supposed to be learning from jumping up into the air?"

"The answer to that question is part of what you may learn by practicing."

"Wouldn't it be easier if you just told me what I'm supposed to learn, so I could focus on learning it?"

"No. There is no other way to learn what leaping can teach you."

"Okay, okay, I'm ready to learn."

I felt White Bear smile, then he catapulted up into the air, out over the lake, and entered the water feet first again. I stood at the water's edge, completely relaxed and concentrating on not moving a muscle. Then, with the thought of leaping, I shot up into air, arced out over the lake, and aimed to land next to where White Bear had gone in. I found him waiting for me under the water.

"Your takeoff has improved, but your landing still makes quite a splash!" he said. "Now, let's leap back to shore from right here."

"From underwater?"

"Why not?"

"Well, for one thing I'm not standing on anything. Floating in the water like this, there's nothing to spring up off of."

"Hmmm . . . Oh well, let's try anyway."

With that, White Bear shot straight up through the water and disappeared from view. I wasn't sure exactly what to do next, so I pretended I was standing on a big rock and then relaxed. With the thought of leaping, I rushed upward through water, broke the surface with a gigantic splash, and flew through the air, landing next to White Bear on the shore.

"No fair cheating, Bruce! I didn't have to stand on an underwater rock to leap here. This time, try it without the rock, and let's leap together."

When he leaped up, I followed and we both entered the water, feet first, side by side.

"Now, no rock this time. Do it the same way you do it from shore, but from a completely free-floating position. You go first."

I relaxed, allowing myself to be floating, and then, with the thought of leaping to shore, I was rushing upwards through the water. When I broke the surface, White Bear was right beside me and we landed together on the shore.

"Very good! You're ready to try something new. Watch closely, and do what I do."

This time after leaping into the air White Bear landed feet first, standing on the surface of the water. With the cloud of light surrounding his face still beaming a smile, he stood there, waiting. I just started to think about leaping and I was flying through the air toward White Bear, but I must have lost concentration. I hit the water on my back, made a huge splash, and stopped three or four feet underwater. When I swam to the surface, White Bear was standing there, laughing.

"That was a pretty good takeoff, but your landing still needs a little work! Lucky for me I know how to stay dry. That was quite a splash you made."

It wasn't until then that I realized that when White Bear leaped and dove into the water in our previous exercises, there had been absolutely no splash. There hadn't been even a ripple. As I thought about this, White Bear began laughing harder.

"See what I mean? Lots of things to learn. Now let's see you take another shot at it."

"Why wasn't there a splash when you dove into the lake before?"

"More to learn. Hey, you're catching on quick! Now, let's see it again."

While he stayed out on the lake, I made several more attempts. The best I did was to land, feet first, next to him and stop moving downward when I was waist deep in the water. I still splashed each time I landed. Looking down at me, White Bear had the feel of mischief about him and looked like he was about to explode with laughter. When he couldn't hold it in any longer, he bent over and slapped his knee as he burst out laughing.

"When you can dive in without splashing and land without sinking, you will have learned much, Grasshopper. Stop back here after your exploration tape exercise and I'll have a few more pointers for you."

After thanking White Bear, I headed for TMI-There to begin our next exploration. As I entered the room with the crystal, I notice Bob Monroe and Ed Wilson standing near a wall. Bob motioned for me to join them. When I got there, he started talking, but what he said all seemed like idle nonsense.

"White Bear's got quite a sense of humor, don't you think?" Bob asked.

"Yeah, although it seems his laughter is at my expense."

"Well, he's really great at helping people learn more about who and what they really are," Bob replied, dryly.

After a little more idle chitchat that seemed to be totally irrelevant, Ed turned his head and pointed with his chin at something beside him. Turning to look where he was pointing, I noticed a man, standing, facing me, about two feet from my right shoulder. I turned back to Ed.

"Ed, who is that?"

Ed, just smiled and stood there without saying a word. I turned and looked at the guy on my right again. He had medium length, coal-black hair surrounding an expressionless face. I turned back to Bob.

"Bob, who this guy?"

Bob kind of shrugged with an expression on his face like, "Don't you know? Heck I thought he was with you."

Taking a really good look at the guy again, I searched my memory for his identity. He had long sideburns, almost mutton chops; he was maybe five feet, ten inches tall. No beard, no mustache, dark brown eyes, average weight, and a complexion that was perhaps Mediterranean. But whoever this guy was, I'd never met him before.

"Come on, Bob . . . Ed . . . who is this guy?"

Neither one gave me a clue. Bob just kept blabbing on about what seemed like rambling nonsense. Then it was time to rejoin my group of fellow Explorers to find out about Mother Earth Consciousness and something called "the Earth Core Crystal." (See appendix A for information about the science of the Earth Core Crystal.)

We began our exploration by sensing the energies of the mineral, plant, and animal kingdoms. As I concentrated, information flowed to me in a series of Knowings. I've organized and written down, as best I can, the information that just came to me.

The energy of each kingdom had reproductive cycles and a sense of life as well as the levels of freewill choices available in each. Each kingdom seemed a step from something raw and unorganized to something more organized in the evolution of Consciousness.

It was clear from observing the kingdoms of physical world reality that each physical object and Being is the expression of some form of nonphysical awareness, focusing itself into the physical world, projecting a thought form, if you will. I got a feel for how life came into being within the physical world.

In the case of the mineral kingdom these thought forms were highly organized patterns of nonphysical energy. In a sense nonphysical awareness projected a specific pattern into something we could think of as raw, unorganized consciousness. The thought form pattern served to organize bits of this raw consciousness into forms that became the components of atoms of various chemical elements. By focusing the pattern of, say, an electron, into the raw, unorganized consciousness, it was "organized" into the form we recognize and drawn together as the "components of consciousness" that make up the electron. So these thought form patterns, or templates, can be thought of as components of consciousness, which became the physical world's subatomic "particles." Each thought form template organized raw state consciousness with certain properties. The electron, for example, has both mass and charge. Protons, which also are created by projecting a thought form pattern into raw state consciousness, also have mass and charge. The mass and charge properties of these components cause them to interact with each other and to behave in predictable ways.

By combining several components of consciousness in more complex thought form patterns and using the properties imbued in each, large assemblages can be formed—atoms. More complex patterns can then be projected, using the properties of atoms to form larger assemblages—molecules. Carrying the process further brought minerals into being, as atoms and molecules of different thought form patterns combined according to the inherent properties of each. These minerals were really just raw, unorganized consciousness, given form by the focused awareness of nonphysical consciousness. In that sense these were a form of living Beings, all members of the mineral kingdom, and the first creation of physical reality. Nonphysical consciousness found a way to be expressed in physical reality in the form of atoms, molecules, and minerals.

With the building blocks of consciousness the mineral kingdom provided, nonphysical awareness began to focus itself into the physical world with more complex thought form patterns and templates. Now, instead of drawing tiny bits of raw unorganized consciousness into these templates, the mineral kingdom's already organized bits of raw consciousness provided the raw material. As more complex forms were created, some were found to be "inhabitable" by simple nonphysical intelligences. Living within mineral kingdom creations, some of these were able to manipulate their outer forms through intent. Drawing to themselves the mineral kingdom components they desired, they discovered they could directly alter their form and function from within their physical world existence. First as tiny, single-cell creations they implemented patterns and templates that were self-replicating. No more than crude assemblages of mineral components, for the first time living Beings fit one of the most basic requirements of their definition: they could reproduce themselves.

As with the mineral kingdom before it, the plant kingdom evolved with simple single cells as the building blocks to larger and more complex expressions of nonphysical consciousness within physical reality. Each new variety sought to adapt to its surrounding supply of mineral components to grow and reproduce. In doing so the simple atoms and molecules of the mineral kingdom became capable of providing a "home" for sufficient levels of awareness to become autonomous and self-replicating Beings, but now in a form we would recognize as plants.

In the pattern of their ancestors, the plants, these tiny single-cell creatures, were drawn into ever more complex and capable collections of conscious intent. Templates grouped cells together into living Beings with more freedom to sample the delights of physical world reality. Continuing to build on all that came before, some plant forms manipulated themselves into mobile creatures. No longer bound to the earth by roots, they were free to roam their environment, gathering from other plants and minerals the components of consciousness they needed to fill templates projected by nonphysical consciousness. The animal kingdom was born.

As the only member of the animal kingdom that records its past activities, we human beings consider ourselves the greatest and final achievement of this process. I feel certain evolution toward total freedom within our reality is still an ongoing process. I wonder what patterns and templates our awareness is being organized into. I wonder where this evolution of nonphysical consciousness, which gives form to our reality, leads from here.

When we completed our exploration of the mineral, plant, and animal kingdoms, our next task was to explore something the program trainers called the Earth Core Crystal (ECC) and the focus level called Earth Core Focus 27 (EC F-27). From recent geological studies of the Earth's core by scientists, it's suggested that conditions are right for growth of a crystalline form of iron. The ECC is supposedly a huge iron crystal at the center of the Earth. New Hemi-Sync sound patterns had been created that supposedly assisted one in accessing the EC F-27 level of consciousness. This is a nonphysical level of consciousness at the center of the Earth. A little skeptical about all this, I decided to play along and let my imagination run the show. After following the Hemi-Sync sounds to EC F-27, I opened my awareness to my surroundings. At first I just seemed to be in a black, formless void. Then I bumped up against something hard and smooth. It had the feel of rough-surfaced, black granite and I began to perceive it as a flat plane. While trying to get impressions of what it was, a door in the surface suddenly opened. It was like in a cartoon, when one of the characters draws the outline of a door on a wall and then opens the door. I saw the outline drawing of a door form, complete with door knob, on the smooth black surface, and the door opened, inward. There was a person standing inside the solid structure.

"Hello, I've been expecting you," the person said, "I'm your tour guide here at EC F-27 and the Earth Core Crystal."

"It looks like you're standing within solid rock; you expect me to come in there with you?"

"It's an iron crystal, actually," he said. "And don't worry; since you're nonphysical at the moment, it's no great trick to enter."

I move into the crystal and the tour guide closed the door behind me.

"Let's go more toward the center of the crystal. The effects are felt the strongest there," the tour guide said.

As we began moving, I started to feel what I can only describe as alignment along an axis. It felt like every molecule of my nonphysical body was rotating into alignment with a powerful field, like a molecule of iron must feel inside a huge, powerful bar magnet. The field had an incredibly powerful aligning force along its central axis that gave the sensation of stretching me lengthwise. I could feel the flow of tremendous amounts of some kind of energy moving through the crystal.

"Am I feeling the effect of a magnetic field?"

"While there is a magnetic field present, what you're sensing is the field and flow of nonphysical energy resulting from the ECC's nonphysical structure. There is a physical structure present also, which is responsible for Earth's magnetic field observable in the physical world. The magnetic field is actually the result of nonphysical energy field alignment induced by the crystalline structure."

"What does the field around this crystal look like and what does it do?"

"It looks much like the field around a bar magnet in the physical world. This field's flux lines extend out into space, far beyond Earth's surface. On the nonphysical level, space here means the superdense field of energy that your scientists call the Zero Point Energy Field. The ECC's function is to draw energy into the Earth Life System (ELS) from the surrounding Zero Point Field. The energy drawn in by the crystal sustains the ELS at levels of awareness you'd define as both nonphysical and physical states of consciousness."

"So the field induces a sort of organizing influence of the surrounding Zero Point Energy Field?"

"Yes, you could think of it as a polarizing influence that organizes consciousness."

Either this was a fairly short exercise tape, or I had lost a lot of the information I received. In any event Dar's voice came in on the tape, requesting that we all return to The Monroe Institute There (TMI-There). I took a quick diversion to my place in Focus 27 and found White Bear waiting by the lake. Our tonal conversation resumed.

"So, you said you'd have some tips for me about what I can learn from leaping."

"They're hints, questions for you to ponder over, as you're so fond of doing. There isn't time for you to do this right now, so consider it a task to work on in your spare time. First, ponder the question, 'What is the lake?' and then consider, 'What am I?'"

"Easy, the lake is a body of water, and I am me."

"That's a start, but I suggest you spend a little time later, back in the physical world, being open to understanding more. There's a lot more to know."

With time in the tape exercise running out, I thanked White Bear for his help, headed back to TMI-There, and then returned to C1 consciousness.

Our next tape exercise continued exploration of the Earth Core Crystal.

"Come up with anything?" White Bear asked when I arrived at my place in Focus 27.

"No, the lake is just a body of water. I created it, a little unconsciously, here at my place. It's just a lot of water, puddled up to look like a lake. And I'm a Conscious Awareness, which isn't much different from saying, 'I am me.' I suppose I could take a line from the affirmation and say, 'I'm more than my physical body.'"

"That's an improvement, but I'd suggest you keep working on it in your spare time," White Bear chuckled. We've got a few minutes before you have to leave and re-join your group. How 'bout a little leaping practice?"

He didn't give me time to answer, he just shot up into the air, still chuckling, and landed fifty yards away on the lake. I had the brief impression he'd landed on the hardwood floor of a gymnasium. He just stood there on the surface of the water, waiting. I relaxed, cleared my mind, and then started to think about leaping. That's all it took to immediately catapult me into the air. This time I landed as I was supposed to—feet first, standing next to White Bear.

"So what was different this time?" White Bear asked. "Your landing was much better. You didn't even get your shoes wet. How come it worked this time?" he asked, with a genuine sense of puzzlement.

"Well . . . I don't know. I remember thinking there was something odd about how it looked when you landed, like you landed on a gym floor instead of water."

"So, you were thinking I landed on a gym floor? Maybe somewhere in there is the reason you did so well. Let's try it again."

White Bear leaped to the shore and I followed. I didn't have much problem landing properly on the shore, and once there, he leaped out on to the lake again. I thought about White Bear landing on a floor, even though I could see the lake under his feet, and I landed perfectly again.

"Hmmm," White Bear toned, "I think you're on to something. When you get back here after your tape exercise, let's play with this some more."

His timing was correct. Just as I started to question him, Dar's voice came in on the exercise tape requesting that we all head for the crystal at TMI-There. "Okay, more when I get back," I said, looking over my shoulder as I left. Then it was off to our task of forming a connection between the crystal at TMI-There and the ECC at EC F-27.

We started by learning a faster technique to reach the EC F-27 level—the one-breath method. We learned to bypass all the intermediate focus levels during one long exhale and to go directly to either Focus 27 or EC F-27. While practicing this method, I began to notice changes as I shifted from one place to the other.

As I shifted toward EC F-27, my visual field became darker and darker. As I entered EC F-27, I'd begun to feel the strong, low-frequency vibration of the place. That vibration built up tension in every muscle of my physical body to the point that I began to lightly, physically shake. It felt like the frequency of this shaking was in the range of four to ten cycles per second. Every time I entered EC F-27, my body vibrated and shook. It wasn't painful, but it wasn't all that pleasant either. The vibration was accompanied by a strong sense of the forces of attraction and repulsion within the ELS. These were the kind of forces that lead to mating of individuals and group dynamics. A primitive driving force that subconsciously drives the activities of all beings within the physical world.

Shifting toward the crystal at TMI-There in Focus 27 by using the one-breath method, my visual field became brighter and brighter until it had a golden, pinkish glow. As soon as I began to move away from EC F-27, the muscle tension and body shaking subsided. The frequency of the vibration gradually increased and my body shook faster and faster, until the shaking was so fast I felt it not as shaking in the physical body, but more like the sensation of warmth or heat. Approaching Focus 27, my body began to feel lighter and lighter, less "physical." I also noticed something very odd. It was easier to move in one direction than the other. Shifting from the crystal at Focus 27 toward the Earth Core Crystal, at EC F-27, resulted in a gentle, floating downward feeling. Shifting from EC F-27 toward Focus 27 required effort. It felt like there was a force, weaker than, but similar to gravity, resisting my movement away from the ECC at EC F-27. After a few practice trips back and forth, I met someone from our Exploration 27 group at the ECC.

Denise was one of three women in our program's group of eighteen participants. Although she and I hadn't talked in detail about our experiences during the exercise tapes, I had the feeling they paralleled each other. Now, from a separate, bilocated position, I was watching as she and I danced and played like a couple of children. Then it was time to begin our task of establishing energy cord pathways between the crystals at Focus 27 and EC F-27.

The program trainers hadn't really explained why we were to do this. Now I had the feeling we were establishing pathways for some kind of energy flow between the two crystals, a way to provide awareness of each focus level within the other and awareness of all the focus levels in between. I wondered why, if this was necessary, it hadn't been done already by those who lived in the non-physical world. An answer floated back to me.

"It's a little like performing retrievals, in that those still living in physical bodies have an advantage over non-physical Helpers. This task will forge a link between physical and the nonphysical world reality."

"Who said that?"

"I'm your tour guide in EC F-27. I said it."

"Can you explain what you said in terms I can better understand?"

"Remember the image of the Earth Core Crystal's field surrounding Earth and extending into space? If it was a magnetic field, what could you say about the field strength or field density in general?"

"I'd expect the field to be strongest nearer the crystal and progressively weaker the farther from it you get."

"You've noticed that when you move from the ECC to Focus 27 it seems to require a little effort?"

"Yeah, it's almost like a weaker form of gravity that acts on my nonphysical awareness."

"And you understand that your nonphysical awareness is a form of consciousness, and so is the crystal's field?"

"Yes, but what are you getting at?"

"What force do you suppose holds individuals in the different focus levels after death?"

"The crystal's field?"

"You're getting warm."

"The crystal's field density has something to do with it, doesn't it?"

"Getting warmer."

Then all of a sudden it hit me.

"Spirit Gravity, the field is Spirit Gravity!"

"You're getting hot!" the tour guide exclaimed.

"Each focus level is a range of crystal field density, a range of pull on the spirit body by Spirit Gravity! The rings Bob Monroe spoke of in his books are arbitrary divisions of the strength of pull of the ECC on the nonphysical bodies of the dead. Now wait a second. The nonphysical bodies of the dead are somehow like hot air balloons. I'm getting that from somewhere. The density of a nonphysical body is variable. If it is less dense it floats higher, more dense it floats lower. Hmmm . . . I've got it! The more a person considers itself a physical world Being, the more dense it is and the lower it floats. So a ghost is a person who still thinks it's living in the physical world, so it's in Focus 23, close to physical world reality. A person who's conscious of being more of a Spirit Being floats higher, Focus 26 or 27!"

"You've got it!" the tour guide said with a smile.

A screen came up in front of us with the image of the ECC in the center of the Earth and lines representing the crystal's field surrounding it.

"Here's an image of the field. The rings Bob talked about are labeled with their focus level numbers."

"By changing what I consider myself to be, I can change my density! If I think of myself more as a spirit body, I become less dense and float upward toward Focus 27. If I think of myself more as a physical body, I become more dense and float downward toward physical reality. The focus level I'm aware in is determined by how physical I consciously or subconsciously believe myself to be."

"You've just discovered an aspect of Spirit Gravity and the duality nature of the ECC."

"Duality nature?" I asked.

"The ECC's polarizing influence lends a duality nature to the surrounding environment. Your description of floating between the pulls of physical and spirit realities is an example of the duality nature induced by the crystal."

"There's more to it than this, isn't there?"

"Of course, and when you hear the term 'Spirit Gravity' from a tour guide in the near future you'll have the opportunity to learn more. For now I'd like to suggest you continue with your energy cord pathway task. It will help build awareness within each of the focus levels of the larger reality they're a part of."

"Thanks, I'll do that. By the way, the vibration I feel at EC F-27 is very strong and very low frequency. What is the frequency of that vibration?"

"Right at this moment it's 7.46 cycles per second."

"Thanks again."

When I looked around, Denise was gone. Using the one-breath method, I flashed up to Focus 27 to look for her. I didn't see her there, so I flashed back down to EC F-27. She came into view as I arrived.

"Geez, Bruce, you took off out of here like you were shot out of a gun! How 'bout we go a little slower so we can work together on this?"

We flew at a more leisurely pace together up to TMI-There and followed the instructions on the tape to establish the energy cord pathways. After gathering energy from the crystal, we returned to EC F-27, each trailing a thin fiber behind us all the way. At EC F-27 we followed Dar's instructions to anchor our fiber in the center of the ECC. These fibers glowed with an inner light that suggested the flow of information from my previous experience with them. After Denise and I had anchored our fibers in the ECC, we followed one of them upward toward Focus 27. A kind of elevator car formed around us. It was round, maybe six feet in diameter, with a solid floor and a waist-high railing completely surrounding its perimeter. The fiber we had anchored in EC F-27 was taut and straight and passing through the very center of the elevator car. As we rode upward we could see other fibers in the distance, with open-topped elevator cars similar to ours. Each car contained people from our Exploration 27 group, who were looking out at the scenery as they rode up or down. We went slowly back and forth in our elevator between EC F-27 and Focus 27 before Dar's voice on the tape requested we return to the TMI-There. I headed back to my place. White Bear was, of course, waiting by the lake when I arrived.

"So, how was your trip?" he asked, with a devious smile in his tone.

"Great. I learned a little about Spirit Gravity and its effects on the experience of nonphysical people, based on the extent to which they believe they are a physical body."

As my tone ended, White Bear shot straight up and did backflips through the air all the way to his spot on the lake. I didn't understand why he did that at first, then the realization slowly overtook me. That's what my leaping lessons were all about! Catapulting myself upward, with the thought of standing next to White Bear, I executed a perfect flight and landing.

"This lake is not a lake," I toned to White Bear, who was beaming a huge smile at me. "This lake is the thought form of a lake. I created it here at my place in Focus 27. This is not my physical body I see here on the lake. It is the thought form of my physical body. I, the Conscious Awareness of myself, created this thought form body here also."

"Your trip was very productive," he toned, beaming joy into me.

"The reason I had so much trouble, like feeling panicky underwater, was because I was thinking of myself as a physical body in a physical world lake. At a subconscious level, identifying myself as a physical body expressed as a strong desire to breathe air to stay alive. When you dove into the lake, there was no splash. When I did, there was. In the physical world, I expect a lake to splash when I dive into it. Here, I project my expectation of a splash into the lake thought form, and a splash is formed. My expectation creates the splash!"

"Very good, Pardner!" White Bear toned, still beaming joy.

"My physical world existence has conditioned me to expect things to behave in certain ways. Here in the non-physical world, I project these expectations into my surroundings and create them. I might not be consciously aware of doing it, but I'm creating what I expect to see, all around me, all the time."

"You call them human forces of habit," White Bear toned. "Some are very subtle, and they all limit your ability and perception here in nonphysical reality. Even calling this place nonphysical reality imposes limits on your awareness."

"And leaping is a tool that makes me aware of projecting my subconscious, physical body beliefs and expectations into my surroundings! It's a way to uncover my beliefs about being a physical body."

"That has been an underlying theme of your exploration, *beyond the physical body*, since you began it years ago."

"I see what you mean by an underlying theme. In my first Lifeline program I kept trying to see with my eyes and hear with my ears, and I ended up perceiving nothing. Only when Rebecca suggested that what I was trying to perceive were very subtle energies, did I begin to perceive anything. She helped me make a breakthrough by pointing out that I was trying to use physical body senses to perceive nonphysical things."

"Leaping is my way of bringing more of your self-imposed, physical-body-thinking limitations directly into your awareness," White Bear said solemnly.

"This is great! Thank you so much! Whoops, there's Dar's voice calling us back, time for me to go."

"Keep practicing your leaping, there's more it can teach you," White Bear toned as he disappeared from view.

chapter 11

Portals—Earth History

A little tired at the start of the next tape exercise, I took the lazy man's route to Focus 27, following the Hemi-Sync tones. That didn't leave any time to visit at my place there, and so after charging up at the crystal at TMI-There, I headed off to explore the assigned topic, early Earth history and evolution. At the Earth Core Crystal (ECC) I met a very friendly tour guide, who offered to show me around.

"I'm here to learn about how the Earth was formed and its evolution since."

"Glad to help out, just relax for a second and I'll have it for you," the tour guide replied.

In a few moments I felt like I was floating in space, watching a 3-D movie documentary of Earth's history from formation to the present day. The following summarizes what I saw.

With sufficient mass collected, gravitational forces caused compressive heating of the core. The Moon's rotational speed, which was much faster than it is now, contributed to violent movements of Earth's mass through both gravitational and magnetic field interactions. This transferred a portion of the Moon's rotational energy to Earth, contributing to heating through movement of mass and electrical currents in conductive materials. After a time the molten core extended almost completely to Earth's surface. Material continued to be added from surrounding space, as huge meteors, asteroids, and comets plunged through Earth's thin crust and into the molten mass. Gases and water vapor were released into Earth's growing atmosphere as the material from space melted. Iron, being one of the most abundant, heavy components, gathered at the center of Earth's core.

Earth's mass continued to grow. When sufficient core temperature and pressure had been attained, a huge iron crystal began to form and grow along Earth's rotational axis in the central core. Gravitational and rotational forces combined to cause preferential crystal growth along the axis. When mass imbalances or incoming material impacts caused a shift of the rotational axis, the crystal dissolved near the core of the Earth and then began to regrow along the new axis. Nearer Earth's surface, end portions of previous crystals remained and, over millions of years, formed a generally spherical shape surrounding the molten core. These crystal remnants remain to this day in many places. Larger such remnants continue to cause localized energy flows. Today, these are identified as "power points" in metaphysical circles and some are large enough to influence Earth's magnetic field poles during times of field reversals.

The largest crystal is aligned very close to Earth's present rotational axis. The field of this crystal extends beyond Earth's surface and its visualization is similar to that of a magnetic field. Field lines also emerge from Earth's surface from some of the larger crystal remnants aligned with previous rotational Earth axis. These field lines can be visualized as overlaying the main field to form a grid pattern with intersecting lines.

Once Earth reached a particular size and cooled sufficiently, it became inhabitable. The crystalline structure of the huge Earth Core Crystal, with its precise alignment and pattern at the atomic level, acted as an organizing influence on the surrounding consciousness. The field of the main crystal acted like a form of nonphysical world gravity that drew nonphysical beings to the Earth. At that point the earliest beginnings of organized consciousness began to be introduced into Earth's environment. Working with mineral kingdom forms, plant kingdom forms were evolved and introduced in the process described during an earlier tape exercise. Animal kingdom forms evolved from these plant kingdom forms of organized consciousness.

When the final scene of the 3-D documentary presented by my tour guide came into view, I saw Earth as it looks today. I could see the main crystal's field lines surrounding it and power point field lines of earlier crystal remnants emerging from the surface, forming an intricate crisscross pattern. Then the scene faded and the tour guide came back into my awareness.

"I know you have some questions about the Spirit Gravity aspects of the crystal. I'd like to start by taking a brief trip to the Moon," he suggested, as if trips to the Moon were a commonplace occurrence.

"Okay . . . I am curious . . . so if the Moon is a good place to start, let's go," I replied, wondering if this was really happening.

After a short sensation of movement, the Moon came into view and then disappeared as we moved into it.

"Notice anything familiar?" the tour guide asked, prompting me to open my awareness to my surroundings. I began to sense an organized structure near the Moon's core.

"There's a crystalline structure here in the Moon's core also! It has a different feel to it. I can't quite put my finger on it, but it feels different than the Earth Core Crystal."

"Very good!" my tour guide said, encouragingly. "Earlier you saw that when the Moon's rotational speed was much faster, some of its rotational energy was transferred to Earth, which generated heat. Heating also occurred here, causing the growth of a crystal within the Moon. As time passed most of the Moon's rotational energy was transferred to Earth, until field interactions between the two caused a rotational synchronization to occur. The field lines of the Moon now interact more smoothly with those of Earth. The Moon's crystal has slightly different characteristics and operates within a different band of energies. Its crystal's field lines overlay Earth's and cause predictable patterns of interaction between the Moon's band of energies and those of Earth."

"I'm getting that there's some connection to astrology," I said.

"Yes, the energies of the Earth and Moon crystals could be thought of as portions of the spectrum of emotional energies. Certain angles between the two sets of field lines tend to combine these energies at a nonphysical level. Some of these angles can evoke specific emotional states. Astrology is an ancient science based on observation of human response to these field interactions. Of course, humans are not the only ones affected, but astrology is, after all, a human science."

"All the other planets in our solar system also have crystals, don't they?" I said, prompted by whatever it was that was entering my awareness.

"As does the local star, our Sun," replied the tour guide. "It, and each of the planets, has a crystal that operates within a different band of the emotional energy spectrum. Astrology is based on physical world, human understanding of the interactions of the fields of each planet's crystal with that of Earth. In fact, that brings us to another topic you're interested in, the Big Clock. I believe you were curious about synchronization of timing between Planning Center activities in Focus 27 and physical world reality?"

I felt something pop and then realized it was a thought ball containing questions left unanswered by a couple of previous tour guides. That thought ball was what I'd felt pushing itself into my awareness, prodding me to ask more about the Big Clock.

"You're right. There are some aspects that I'd like more information about," I replied nonchalantly. "I understand that in Focus 15, time/event lines can be interconnected to the predictable positions of planets to synchronize things like birth times and places for people entering the physical world. But I have the feeling there's more to it than just timing—like some sort of astrology connection?"

"Let's take the example of the four curls, strung together, that you saw passing through the Reentry Station. They were entering together for a specific group purpose—discovery of a jungle plant's medicinal properties and introduction of its healing properties to physical world use. You remember?"

"Yes, and I remember something about work on the group's most important purpose starting after the last two curls in the string meet," I replied, a little fuzzy about the details.

"Good, and do you remember why or what that work was?"

"Let's see. I remember they meet at a medical convention and discover they've both been doing research on the same jungle plant. I think I remember those two get married, and that has something to do with the group's most important purpose," I slowly recalled. "But that's all I remember."

"Do you remember the Entry Director saying that with the inflated egos those two have, it's going to be quite a challenge to learn to love each other?" the tour guide queried.

"Yeah, I think I remember something like that. What's that got to do with the Big Clock?" I asked, trying see how it fit together.

"Their inflated egos? Where do you suppose their inflated egos came from?"

"I'd guess they're both just inflated ego types to start with, that they carry those traits into physical existence with them, but there's more to it, isn't there?"

"Yes, there's more to it. Think about not only the timing characteristics of the Big Clock, but the astrological aspects as well," the tour guide prompted.

"Okay, let me think out loud for a minute here. Hmmm . . . If the emotional energies of the Big Clock, at the instant of a person's birth . . . defined an inflated ego type personality, it might form some sort of passageway for a person who already has an inflated ego to enter physical world reality. Hmmm . . . That's what I'm getting, but it doesn't feel complete," I responded, still puzzling over the question.

"You're pretty close. What do you suppose a person planning to enter the physical world could do if they didn't have an inflated ego personality, but needed one to work on some purpose? Think of it in terms of your understanding of the Disk or concept of I/There," he suggested.

"All the personality components needed to assemble an inflated ego type would be available on the Disk from previous life experiences. So, Curiosity, the Disk, could assemble a Probe with the proper mix of personality traits that could be generally defined as an inflated ego type. Hmmm . . . And if that mix matched the Big Clock's emotional energies pattern, that might provide some sort of passageway for the person to enter physical reality. Am I getting warm?"

"You've already said the answer to the question, you just don't see it yet," the tour guide replied. "Maybe if you think about the Big Clock's emotional pattern and the instant of birth, maybe that will do the trick. What does the instant of birth define, in terms of nonphysical and physical realities?"

"Well, it's the point at which a person leaves one reality and joins another. In astrology the Big Clock's emotional energy pattern is called the Birth Chart, or Natal Chart. It's viewed as the personality a person is born with."

I floated quietly for a short time, trying to feel the connection, trying to understand how all the pieces fit together. The tour guide very patiently waited all the while. Then suddenly it all flooded in.

"I see it! I see it! It's like a time stamp! Like an imprint of emotional energies at the nonphysical level onto the person just as that person enters the physical world. It's the physical world persona. If the person needs an inflated ego personality to work on a purpose, it's assembled long before birth. The personality traits required are sort of encoded and embedded in the curl prior to placement in Focus 15. The emotional energies, just the right balance, are stored in the curl's pattern of consciousness. So it's not just the physical locations of the planets that are used as the Big Clock, it's the emotional energy patterns as well. The Big Clock's personality trait patterns are constantly changing as the planets move. When just the right pattern exists in the Big Clock, the one that matches the pattern embedded in the curl, the curl resonates to it. It's energized by the Big Clock pattern, and like a seed, sprouts and grows with that pattern as its beginning as a physical world being! The resonating of the curl with the Big Clock energy pattern brings it to awareness within the physical world. In fact, the energy pattern might actually pull or draw the person into physical reality!" I felt excitement as the realizations and insights continued flooding in.

"Very good, Bruce!" the tour guide replied. "The Big Clock is used not only for time synchronization between the physical and nonphysical world, but also for insertion of specific personalities. And it's all based on the specific bands of energy of each core crystal in the Sun and each planet in the solar system."

"There's more to understand about this. I can feel it," I said excitedly.

"Yes there is. You've got the basics, and in the interest of spending our time together most productively, I'd like to suggest we move on for now and you ponder more about the Big Clock later."

"Okay." And shifting gears quickly, I said, "I am kind of curious about remnants of previous Earth Core Crystals. Can you give me more information on them?"

"One of the largest remnants is near what is now Bimini Island. We could go there if you like." (I began to feel a sense of warm ocean surrounding me.) "A line drawn from Bimini Island to the center of Earth defines an ancient rotational axis of the Earth. Deep below the island rests one of the largest Earth Core Crystal remnants in existence. This area was a polar region before an almost ninety degree shift of the rotational axis brought it nearer the equator."

"Where is the other end of the axis?"

"Come on, I'll show you," replied the tour guide, and we started moving toward the center of the Earth.

We continued moving and then popped up at the ocean's surface. I did a slow three-sixty, scanning for the feel of any land. There was nothing nearby. I could feel a large land mass beyond the horizon to the east, and a much larger one, much further away to the west. All I could feel in my immediate vicinity was vast, open ocean.

"Your sense of direction is correct, Bruce. Australia is east of here, Africa much further to the west," the tour guide volunteered. "The nearest major land mass is the western coast of Australia." (See appendix A for a reference to magnetic pole reversal and western Australia.)

"Isn't Bimini Island near the area known as the Bermuda Triangle? Is there any connection between the crystal remnant and supposed disappearances in that area?" I asked.

"Yes, to both questions, and there's a connection to the planet Uranus in this solar system."

"What's the connection?"

"Earth revolves around the Sun in roughly the same plane, called the Great Ecliptic, just as all the planets do, including Uranus. For a moment visualize extending a line into space along the ancient Bimini axis. This is a simplified explanation, but it will give you enough to go on as you think about it later. Now, because of the tilt of Earth's rotational axis, relative to the Sun, at certain times of the year the Bimini axis passes through the Sun and is parallel to the Great Ecliptic. This is where Uranus comes in. Its rotational axis is parallel to the Great Ecliptic."

"I remember that one of the deep space probes launched by NASA sent back photographs of Uranus. The rotational axis of Uranus was pointed out as being very peculiar, because it points at the Sun."

"That's right. Now, because of the tilt of Earth's axis, relative to the Sun, there are times when the line extended along the Bimini axis points directly at Uranus. The crystal axis of Uranus, and the Bimini crystal axis are on the same line. This opens a nonphysical world pathway between Uranus and the area around Bimini Island. This alignment of the Uranus and Bimini crystals is the basis of the Bermuda Triangle events."

"That's interesting. Those events sure fit with the astrologically identified traits of Uranus—sudden, unexpected, and bizarre change," I remarked.

"When the two axes are aligned with each other, the opening of the pathway is triggered by the position of Earth's moon."

"Any way to verify this information?" I asked, thinking I'd get some brush-off answer.

"If you investigate the timing of all the actual Bermuda Triangle events as well as when the axes were in alignment, you'll see a statistical significance that lends proof. A word of caution, though. Some supposed Bermuda Triangle events are just ordinary disappearances at sea."

"Do these same kinds of strange events occur on the other end of the Bimini axis, off the west coast of Australia?"

"There's less shipping and air traffic in that area, and it's so far out to sea the few disappearances there aren't considered strange. Unusual dolphin activity out in the open sea of the area can be observed and will mark the spot," he replied.

"What happens to the people who disappear in these Bermuda Triangle events?"

"They and other physical world objects, like ships and aircraft, can be transported to Uranus," he said, flatly.

"You're not serious!"

"There are aircraft, ships, the bodies of birds, people, and fish on the surface of Uranus."

"You are serious!"

"Yes I am, it's not that peculiar when you understand what the opening of such a pathway is," he replied, like this sort of thing was normal.

"Do other crystal remnants have similar effects?"

"Most are physically much smaller in size than the Bimini axis remnant and therefore have smaller effects. The Earth power point locations of these smaller remnants do have pathway opening effects, but the results are less spectacular. Still, they do provide openings for communication between physical and nonphysical levels of consciousness."

"Are there other effects of the crystal's field that are detectable in some way?" I asked.

"Those of us who work here at the Earth core gather information about distortions of the field due to tectonic plate movement. Analysis of such distortions yields information about things like earthquake activity, which we put on the Grid for the Planning Center."

"You guys can predict earthquakes?"

"Of course. Field distortions occur over long periods of time and the patterns of such distortions are reliable predictors for earthquake activity. In fact, many human beings who are physically alive on Earth have awareness of the field distortion patterns that occur just before an earthquake. Many other animals are also aware of them and react with characteristic behaviors that humans can use for earthquake prediction. Most of this is already well known, albeit little understood, by humans."

Dar's voice cut in on the exercise tape at this point, requesting that our exploration group begin the return to C1 consciousness.

"Well, thank you for everything you've shared with me. Some of this stuff is borderline believable for me. But thanks, I've got lots to think about."

"I understand your reluctance to take everything I've said as fact, and frankly that's just as it should be. Enjoy the rest of your exploring, there are some great things coming up."

The scene surrounding me faded from view, and I returned my awareness to my CHEC unit, via TMI-There.

For some reason I got confused about Dar's instructions regarding our return to C1 consciousness. Maybe I clicked out for a moment and missed something that she said before I came back in. When her voice came in the first time to suggest going back, I was at EC F-27, in the Earth Core Crystal. I'd become aware of the strong, body-shaking vibration of the crystal and was still feeling it as she and the Hemi-Sync tones assisted my shift toward C1. Somewhere around EC F-15 I must have clicked out and the next thing I heard her say seemed to indicate we were at Focus 12. In my confusion, I paid little attention to the rest of her instructions. When I arrived at C1, I could still feel the powerful, low frequency vibration of the Earth Core Crystal in my physical body. I don't think that was supposed to happen.

All through our debriefing I could feel the vibration, invisibly shaking every molecule of my body. After the debriefing there was time for a short break and I felt a tremendous desire to go outdoors. Once there, I found myself pacing back and forth on the sundeck like a caged animal. The sensations I was feeling were not all that unpleasant, but they carried a raw, animalistic charge that felt very unfamiliar. Pacing didn't seem to attenuate the feeling, so I decided to try a grounding exercise. I'd inadvertently carried nonphysical energies into my body before during programs and had been taught several techniques to help drain it off. Sometimes pulling out of a focus level too quickly or not completely had left me with a spacey, disconnected feeling. What I was feeling now was in no way spacey or disconnected. It was more like an incredible level of whatever the opposite of spacey is. With an animal's single-minded determination, I threw off my sandals and started making my way across the rain-soaked ground, heading for the nearest tree. Hugging a tree had always worked before to drain off a spacey feeling. I waded into a prickly evergreen, oblivious to the scratching branches. Finally reaching the trunk I discovered hugging it had no effect. If anything the, pacing-animal-feeling vibration was stronger!

Like an animal, trying to shake a sprung trap, I backed away from the tree and lumbered toward a grassless patch of mud. If grounding was what I needed, pushing my bare feet into the gooey mud and visualizing a connection between my body and the center of Earth should have done the trick. Nada! Again, if anything, the vibration I felt in my body was stronger. If I'd thought it would do any good, I'd have stripped off my clothes in full view of the other participants standing on the sundeck and rolled naked in the mud. Modesty, and my lack of success so far, intervened and I headed back to the briefing room to await the beginning of the next tape exercise. From my previous experience I decided the vibration I was feeling must have occurred because I had pulled out of the Earth Core Crystal focus levels too quickly. So I figured the problem was not with being too spacey, but with being too grounded. Like there was some sort of spectrum of energies between Focus 27, with its spacey, light, airy feeling and EC F-27, with its strong vibration. It felt like I had come out of the last tape exercise too far from my accustomed null point and the vibration was becoming unnerving.

I was sitting on the floor, alone in the room, when one of the women in the program walked in. Bless her soul! When she saw me sitting on the floor, her first words were, "Boy, you look like you really need a hug!"

I stood up, still feeling like a caged animal, shaking and pacing inside. The instant we hugged, the vibration stopped! I explained what was going on inside me and we tried an experiment. We stepped back from each other and the vibration I was feeling came back immediately, full force. The instant we hugged, it disappeared again! Then Denise, the participant I met at the Earth Core Crystal earlier, entered the room and I overheard her telling Franceen, one of the trainers, that she was experiencing the same kind of energetic vibration. When she and I hugged, the vibration disappeared for both of us. When we stepped back from each other, it resumed. Together we decided to experiment to see if there was any difference in the hugging effect between males and females. Since we had both a male and female trainer, we decided to use them as guinea pigs. After several trials we determined that the vibration only stopped in opposite-sex hugs. When Denise hugged the female trainer, and I hugged the male, there was no diminishing effect on the vibration. When she hugged the male and I the female, or we hugged each other, the vibration stopped! By hugging for several minutes, the vibration we both felt subsided somewhat when we stepped apart. By the time the briefing for our next tape exercise began, the vibration was still there, but down to a tolerable level. As I sat listening to the trainer's briefing, I began to wonder about the polarizing effects of the Earth Core Crystal. What Denise and I were experiencing seemed to indicate that Earth core energy was capable of driving opposite sexes together with a reward of feeling comfort and relief from a constant internal pressure. I sat musing through part of the briefing for our first exploration beyond Focus 27.

chapter 12
E. T. Contacts

In Bob Monroe's second book, *Far Journeys*, first published in 1985, in a chapter entitled *The Gathering*, he described an area now called Focus 34/35 in the Exploration 27 program. According to Bob's description, Beings, or Intelligences, from many other locations within the physical Universe are gathered around the Earth to witness what has come to be called the Earth Changes. Bob learned of this while exploring out-of-body techniques after being led to the Gathering by a being he called his INSPEC. His experience, related on pages 230–232 of *Far Journeys*, might prove interesting to readers in light of my extraterrestrial (E. T.) contacts described below.

After our briefing by the trainers, just before our first attempt to reach the Gathering, our group was asked to stand in a circle. As we assembled and worked at making our circle more round than oblong, Tom, one of the participants, began clowning around.

In a singsong voice he said, "You put your right foot in, you put your right foot out . . ." making reference to a teenage, sock hop dance called the Hokey Pokey.

He was standing close to me and my mind was suddenly yanked back to a memory from the first tape exercise of the program when I'd first seen our group gather around the crystal at TMI-There in Focus 27. We'd gathered, nonphysically, standing silently in a circle around the crystal and had all joined hands. Then, we'd each stepped forward, in unison, into the circle, with our right foot, as we reached our joined hands downward, toward the base of the crystal. Then we'd raised our hands, stepping back in unison, each moving our right foot outside the circle. Our clasped hand movement continued, upward and outward until, from above, we looked like a huge lotus blossom. While raising our hands and stepping back, we'd made a sound. And with the joyous sound of our "WOOO-AAAHH," the crystal had come alive in silent explosions of incredible power. Vibrant energies in yellows, oranges, reds, pinks, and whites had shot up through the crystal and showered down on all of us. Memory of that scene begged that we repeat it in the physical world. My voice stumbled out as I explained the scene to our group that I'd seen during our first tape exercise and asked that we do it right then. After showing everyone once what the body movement looked like, they all joined me in unison. They moved and made the sound as if we'd practiced for hours. It was absolutely incredible! By the second WOOO-AAAHH I could feel a tremendous column of energy the size of our circle shooting straight up out of the floor. By the fourth sound my entire body began to heat up, like a full body fever of 104, with pure joy the only accompanying feeling. After eight or nine WOOO-AAAHHs, we all stopped, again in unison. There were several comments about feelings of energy and heat running through people's bodies. With that finished, we all headed for our CHEC units to explore the Gathering for the first time.

After resonant tuning and the affirmation, I went

directly to the crystal at TMI-There to wait for the rest of our group to gather. One by one, everyone walked in and formed a circle at the base of the crystal. When we were all assembled, we repeated our WOOO-AAAHH, lotus blossom movement, and sound. Colored light and sparks cascaded up into the air and showered down on everyone, charging each of us with Pure Unconditional Loving energy from the crystal. Then, following instructions on the exercise tape, we used a slingshot method, suggested by the trainers, to reach Focus 34/35. I first shifted to the Earth Core Crystal with a feeling like stretching a long rubber band. It became darker and darker as I approached the heavy vibration of EC F-27. Then, letting go of EC F-27, I felt myself accelerating through all the focus levels toward the crystal at TMI-There in Focus 27, as my field of vision became lighter and brighter. Flying through the brightness of the crystal at TMI-There, I shot past it and entered a vast expanse of empty blackness. I continued to feel a sense of movement through the blackness, until the Hemi-Sync sounds stabilized at Focus 34/35. Without any way of knowing if I'd actually arrived at the Gathering, I opened my perception to my surroundings, trying to sense whatever was in the vicinity.

There seemed to be nothing but blackness at first, then things lightened up and I sensed something moving through my field of view from above to below. Focusing my attention on the movement, perceptions of strange shapes began to form in my imagination. Rolling clouds, a huge snail shell-looking object, and then a long cylinder. The cylinder appeared to be several thousand feet long and had what looked like a dish antenna on one end. Occasionally, I heard strange gurgling sounds. Then, something that looked like a huge mushroom went by, a large flat cap and stalk that reminded me of images of the Disk from my vision more than twenty years previously. Then an odd-looking shape like a giant puffball came into view and I had the sense it contained intelligence of some type. I decided to try to make contact with it.

"Hello? . . . excuse me? . . . anybody home?" I called out tentatively. There was a funny gurgling noise and then I could feel something moving inside the puffball. It seemed to be sort of pulling itself into a form separate from the rest of the form. It felt like the inside of the puff-ball was filled with a sort of conscious gelatin and a por-tion of it was separating and organizing itself into a form that could communicate with me. A little ball of this con-scious gelatin sort of oozed out of the rest of the mass and popped into view. My sense was that it was a shy sort of Being and not exactly sure how to communicate with me.

"Hi, my name is Bruce and I'm here on a tour with a group from Earth. We're here to learn about the Gathering. Is that where I am?"

I could feel the little gelatin ball in front of me working up the courage to begin speaking. When it did, I almost burst out laughing at the sound of its voice. It was a fast, very high-pitched, squeaky voice, higher and faster than Walt Disney's *Chip and Dale* cartoon chipmunk voices, but with a similar sound. It spoke in repetitive, fast-paced sentences.

"Yes, this is the Gathering, you're in the right place, this is where many are gathered to observe the Earth school. Sorry it took so long to get started, not used to act-ing as a separate individual, apart from the main body, took a while to separate this form from the whole to be able to communicate with you, can you understand my communication?"

"It's a little fast and high-pitched, but yes, I under-stand. This is not your native form of being is it?"

"Oh no, my form is more that of a whole, conscious on my many levels simultaneously, you seem to need a nar-rower band, smaller fraction of the whole, less than all levels available at once, to receive my communication, hence the separation. I'm just a small portion of what's available, more at once would appear to be too much for you to comprehend, overload your switchboard, probably jam your circuits."

"I heard a funny gurgling sound just before I felt you begin to separate from the whole."

"Yes, we tried to communicate as a whole at first, but it was obvious from your response that you weren't getting it, no comprendo, nada, over your head."

The high squeaky voice was comical, cute, and effective.

"Can you tell me why you're here?" I asked, prompted by Dar's voice on the tape to ask the question.

"We're here to witness the Big Event and report back to our home world. We're an information gathering unit. Like a news crew, you know, live from the scene, cub reporter, film at eleven, now back to the studio. We send reports of events as they unfold here back to our home world. We're from a different galaxy than yours."

I must have worded my next question poorly. All I intended to ask was a friendly "where are you from" kind of question, like you'd ask any stranger, just to make polite conversation. When I did, the little blob I was talking to stopped abruptly and was quiet for about two seconds. I expected he would point to a distant star and say something like, "Our home world is over that way." That's not what happened . . .

"I'll show you, come right this way," it said in a determined, squeaky little voice.

I had the impression we both turned to the right and then the little guy pointed into space with something. After that, everything happened so fast, it will take longer for you to read the next sentence than it took for everything to happen. A bright yellow tube, like a Tube of Knowing I'd seen earlier, leaped forward and in an instant traversed thousands of light years of space. The tube's straight line course then bent at an angle and leaped forward another couple of thousand light years. It's hard to believe what happened next. The little guy and I zipped along the first section of the tube in one or two milliseconds, turned, and flashed across another couple thousand light years of space in the next millisecond or so. The whole while I could clearly see the stars and blackness of space ahead of us and feel a sensation of speed that is beyond comprehension in any physical world context. Each time we came to a place where the tube bent and went off in a different direction I could feel a slight sideways acceleration through the turn. While we were moving I could see the tube continuing to form in straight line sections extending past the farthest stars I could see. At various, oddly spaced points the next tube section would shoot off at a different angle, then continue in a straight line past the distant stars, only to repeat the cycle again. I have no way of knowing how far we actually traveled, but it had to be multiple millions of light years. Then I saw the tube had stopped forming up ahead, and when we reached the end, we stopped.

"There it is, my home world, where we live, where we send the film at eleven," the high pitched, squeaky voiced little blob said to me.

I looked down and realized I was looking at a planet. It had swirling cloud patterns and its surface appeared to be mostly in blue and tan colors. We stayed for perhaps half a second.

"Well, seen enough? Well, okay then, time to go," my little buddy squeaked out.

We started moving backwards and the planet quickly became a pinpoint of light in the distance and then disappeared. My impression was that we came back along the same route we'd taken to get to the little guy's home world. We flew backwards the entire time, again at a speed beyond the meaning of the word. Along with the sensation of moving backwards, I could feel the bumps each time the tube changed direction. Visually, I could see star fields that were stable images for a few milliseconds, and then with each bump I could see a different field with stars in different positions. When we came to a stop, we were back where we'd started, floating next to the giant puffball shape. My impression was that the entire trip took two, maybe two and a half seconds at the outside. I know in physical world terms such a trip, traveling millions of light years in seconds, is impossible. I also know I experienced it. It was very long trip, we moved very fast, and we did not travel in a straight line. I floated quietly for five or six seconds, reviewing images of our trip and trying to restabilize my thinking. The trip left me with a feeling of mental shock like being hit in the psyche with a baseball bat.

"You okay?" the little guy squeaked, with a feeling of concern carried on his voice.

"What? . . . I think so . . . that trip seems to have jumbled me a little, but it feels like I'm coming back around." I needed several seconds before my head cleared and I remembered where I was and what I was supposed to be doing. "Yeah, I'm okay, no harm done. You said earlier you're here to observe the Big Event, can you tell me what it is?"

"Sure, the core crystal of your planet is moving into alignment with a very distant object. It's an alignment at an intergalactic level," the little guy said, flatly.

"What's the object the core crystal is aligning with?" I asked, curious.

"The Big Guy, head honcho, Mister Big, the main man, center of the Universe, the beginning, the grandfather of all grandfathers, get it?" he replied.

From his redundant answers an image formed in my awareness. It was similar to the Uranus/Bimini axis alignment, except it was the main Earth Core Crystal and some very distant object. There was a sense that this alignment would make a pathway through which some kind of energy would enter and be infused into the Earth Core Crystal. Whatever this energy is, it would become a part of a new "consciousness environment" for Earth's inhabitants, both physical and nonphysical. My sense was that this was not yet perfectly in alignment, but very close. Close enough. Earth's inhabitants were already feeling the effects from just the fringes of the distant object's energy. The effects would continue to intensify as perfect alignment approaches.

"How soon before this Big Event takes place?" I asked.

"It has already begun. Complete alignment will occur very soon," the little blob replied.

"What happens at complete alignment?" I asked.

A visual image formed in response to my question. It bore a strong resemblance to the final scene from the movie *2001: A Space Odyssey*. An image of the planet Earth shone brightly against the blackness of space and distant stars. A ball of bright light emerged from the Earth and rose upward. The ball of light was the size of the Earth and inside the ball I could see the fully formed body of an infant human. Its eyes were open and it was looking around.

"So, when the Earth Core Crystal and this distant object are in perfect alignment, there will be a birth of some kind?" I asked.

"Yes, a birth, a human birth would be a way to describe the Big Event," the little guy replied.

"Why are you here to witness this birth?" I asked.

"We are all here at the Gathering to witness it because the change it represents may affect us all. We're recording the event to try to better understand the effects it may have upon all of us. There's also the aspect of a desire to record it so we are better prepared to deal with this change should it occur on our own home world," he replied straightforwardly.

"What emotional effect will this have on Earth's inhabitants?" I queried.

"Emotional effect? That doesn't translate to anything I'm familiar with, sorry, can't help you there, maybe try someone else in the area," the little guy squeaked back.

"Oh, okay. Well, thanks for your help, I'll check around a bit," I responded.

With that, I sensed the little blob I'd been communicating with oozed back into the puffball shape and merged back together with the rest of itself. Opening my perception to a wider field, I watched as the puffball drifted away and several more odd shapes floated past. Then Dar's voice on the tape suggested that we try to contact an Earth school graduate if there were any around us. I decided to give that a try.

"Hello? . . . is there an Earth school graduate in the area I can communicate with?" I asked, sort of casting my bread on the waters. A deep bass, very low frequency voice came rumbling back in response.

"Yes, I'm here, how can I be of service?" the lower-than-James-Earl-Jones voice asked.

"I'm curious about the emotional effect the Big Event will have on Earth's inhabitants. Can you give me any information on that?" I asked.

"Hmmm . . ." came back, sounding like the lowest note possible being played on a pipe organ. "Emotional effects . . . ? It's been so long since I've experienced emotional effects I don't seem to be able to remember enough to give you a meaningful answer," the deep voice replied.

Not getting an answer from a supposed Earth school graduate made me immediately feel suspicious. How could someone who went through the Earth school profess not to remember about emotional effects. It felt like I was dealing with an impostor!

"Let's try this," I heard the deep voice say, with a deep, vibrating rumble.

Then something grabbed my attention. To say it was a vibration doesn't really describe it, but that's as close as I can get. I began to feel a definite sense of acceleration within the vibration. It kept moving faster and faster, carrying a feeling of hyperalertness into my awareness. Then the feeling faded.

"That's the best I can do to describe it. I realize from your perspective, it's not much, but it's the best translation I can give you. Hope it's been helpful," the deep voice rumbled out.

"Well, I felt something. And it had a definite sense of acceleration of something, but that's all I got," I responded.

"You'll be getting more, soon," boomed out to me.

"Okay . . . well . . . thanks for your input," I replied. Then I moved away to explore a little on my own. A short time later Dar's voice cut in to request that we all return to the crystal at TMI-There. I arrived early and found Bob and Ed waiting for me.

Addressing Ed, Bob said, "Told you his energies would be beneficial to the group!"

"Never doubted it for a moment," Ed replied with a chuckle.

Then, addressing me, Bob went on, "We had to prime the pump a little with Tom's Hokey Pokey dancing, but you caught our intent right away after that. I just can't tell you how important it was for the group to perform that little ritual before this tape exercise. By the time you guys were done, everyone in your group was positively glowing with energy. It made the leap to the Gathering so much easier for everybody."

"Bob's right," Ed added. "This is the best shot at conscious exploration of the Gathering, by the largest number of people we've seen since the beginning of the program. Your group is doing extremely well. Everybody working over here on our side is just thrilled with how well this Exploration 27 group this is doing."

"And just wait," Bob said excitedly. "There's more; there's a lot more."

"Geez, Bob, you're going to give me a case of performance anxiety if you keep talking like that," I laughed.

"Nonsense, we took care of that in the beginning, remember? Nothing is going to happen until later? Well, later is still now, just relax and let come what comes, you'll do just fine," Bob replied. "Looks like almost everyone is back. I'd suggest you rejoin your group and have fun!"

Indeed, everyone had returned and we all joined hands in our circle at the base of the crystal and repeated our WOOO-AAAHH exercise until it was time to return to C1 consciousness.

In the debriefing that followed this exercise the energetic effect of the physical world WOOO-AAAHH we had performed just before embarking was very apparent. Almost everyone remarked about the strong sensation of body heat they'd felt throughout the exercise. Most had to kick off the blankets they usually needed to keep warm in their CHEC units. Some had opened the privacy curtain of their CHEC unit and a few had to remove clothing in an attempt to cool down. From my previous experience with such body heat sensations, I knew this indicated tremendous flows of energy. Such energetic flows greatly facilitate maintenance and focusing of awareness. Like putting additional batteries in a flashlight, it has the effect of increasing brightness of the mind. Body heat is one of the telltale signs.

I was still pondering my first experiences at the Gathering later that evening when I headed down to the dining room for supper. Arriving a little late, as usual, I found myself sitting at a table alone again with Ed Carter. I guess we were both a little slower than the rest of our group when it came time to eat. Ed had looked over the articles, rough draft chapters, and skimpy outline of my first book. We talked a little about what I'd written and what we'd each experienced at the Gathering.

During our dinner conversation, Ed mentioned he'd invited a man named Frank to join us for breakfast Friday morning. Frank is a partner in Hampton Roads Publishing Company, located in Charlottesville, Virginia, a half-hour drive from TMI. Ed said he thought Frank might be interested in what I was writing, and meeting him over breakfast would be an opportunity to have someone in the business assess the possibility of publishing it as a book. I felt a little excitement at the prospect of meeting him, but then Ed's and my conversation turned to what we'd experienced during the day's tape exercises, and thoughts of books and Frank faded into the background.

chapter 13

2ndGathgroup, First Contact

Thursday was the last full day of the program. Our first tape exercise task was to return to the Gathering at Focus 34/35. We were to make contact with the intelligences there again and continue to explore both their reasons for being there and whatever we could find out about the so-called Earth Changes. Bypassing the Hemi-Sync sound guidance, I shifted to my place in Focus 27 once again, immediately after resonant tuning and the affirmation. White Bear was waiting at the lakeshore as usual.

"One more leaping exercise I want to show you," he toned, in a series of squeaks and squawks. "Elements of this one should keep you busy for quite some time."

"Okay, let's see what you've got for me this time," I replied boldly.

"The first element we need to talk about, before we get started," White Bear toned, solemnly, "is your focus of attention. In our exercises so far, where has your focus of attention been?" he asked.

"I'm not sure what you're asking me," I replied.

"Put it this way, where have you been watching yourself from? Where's your vantage point been? What have you seen during our leaping exercises?" he questioned.

"Well, now that you mention it, I realize I've been seeing myself leap up into the air from the outside. I've been watching my body go through the air and land on the lake. Then I kind of rejoin it while we're talking. Why, what's important about my point of view?"

"Up until now you've been watching a body fly through the air. If I say it hasn't really been you doing the leaping, do you understand what that means?" White Bear toned, a sense of serious inquiry emanating from him.

"I think I get it. This has something to do with seeing myself as a physical body, doesn't it?"

"Couldn't have said it better myself," he replied, chuckling. "I'll wait quietly now, while you explore this element."

I stood there trying to understand what White Bear was getting at. I kept hoping he'd give me a hint, but none was forthcoming. Then it began slowly seeping into my awareness.

"The lake is a thought form I've projected into Focus 27. The splashes when I dove into the lake were responses of that thought form to my expectations, based on my belief in being a physical body. But, I remember I saw those splashes from my vantage point here, at the edge of the lake. The body I saw leaping, diving, and splashing I saw as separate from the me observing the experience. I was projecting a thought form of my body into Focus 27, and then watching it! I wasn't actually leaping! I was watching the body thought form that I was projecting, as it was leaping!"

"And what," White Bear toned, "do you suppose is the next lesson in leaping?"

"To actually do the leaping! Not watch my projection of a thought form of myself doing it, from a separate location, but actually do it myself!"

"You catch on quickly! There's a special form of leaping you are to use for this exercise. Watch me closely."

With that, White Bear shot up into the air along his usual trajectory, but he was doing forward somersaults from the time his feet left the ground. He was bent forward at the waist, with his knees tucked up against his chest, and his hands gripping his ankles. Just before he landed, his body stretched out like an Olympic gymnast finishing a perfect ten floor exercise routine. Landing on his toes, he brought his arms down from above his head and straight down along his sides. When he finished, his tones beckoned me to repeat his movement.

I immediately found myself off to one side, watching my body attempt the leaping somersault I'd just watched White Bear do. I had all the basics, with an awkward, amateur form, and I landed with my legs still tucked up against my chest. I made a very big splash.

"Bruce, where are you?" I felt White Bear tone. That's when I realized I was still standing on the shore, looking at myself and White Bear on the lake.

"Whoops! I was supposed to do the leaping, not watch a thought form of my body leaping," I toned back with embarrassment.

"This can be a difficult exercise. It takes tight focus of attention. Watching yourself instead of being yourself is a common trait for physical humans. Let's try it again," he toned, with a sense of encouragement.

For the next several attempts White Bear stood on the shore and watched as I attempted this new form of leaping. He suggested that as a beginning exercise I could just try to stay in the body thought form I was projecting as it was leaping. I was astounded at how difficult this is to do. Once or twice I managed to be in my body thought form for a short portion of the leap. When I did, it felt like I was flashing back and forth between my standing position on the lakeshore and my head over heels flying through the air. For the brief snatches of time I was actually in my leaping body, I could feel the sensation of somersaulting through the air. Dar's voice on the exercise tape cut my leaping exercises short with her request that we all meet at TMI-There.

"For brief moments you are leaping properly. If you focus your attention on feeling the bodily sensations as you somersault through the air it will help you develop the tight focus required. Know that successfully experiencing these bodily sensations from the beginning to the end of your leap is only in intermediate step toward what leaping can ultimately teach you. Don't get hung up thinking you've mastered it at that point. All it means is you're just beginning to learn," White Bear cautioned.

"What can leaping ultimately teach me?" I asked, knowing beforehand what he would say.

"You will discover it when your leaping teaches it to you," White Bear laughed.

"Can't blame me for trying to find a short cut," I laughed back.

"I think you will find that all such attempts at short cuts are really long cuts," he barked back. Then it was time to join the group at the crystal.

Before this exercise began most everyone had expressed some excitement and interest in further exploring the Earth Changes. To be sure, each of us viewed our contacts at the Gathering through our own unique sets of filters. What we perceive is always colored by our past experience and the contents of our personal library of images and beliefs.

So, with all our baggage and preconceived notions we were ready to explore and gather first-hand information once again. We used the same slingshot method to reach the Gathering at Focus 34/35. From darkness at EC F-27, at the Earth Core Crystal, I rocketed through the light at the TMI-There crystal and into the darkness beyond. When the Hemi-Sync tones began to stabilize, I opened my awareness to the lightening surroundings and waited for an impression to form. Several odd shapes floated into and out of view. The large, dark, mottled snail shell-looking thing came into view again above me and floated downward out of view. Next, the long tubular structure with the large satellite dish shape on one end moved by and faded from view as it moved from my right to my left. Then I could feel something very large directly in front of me, giving off impressions of hard, shiny, metallic, and curved. I couldn't see it yet, but there seemed to be many individuals grouped together inside and they were busily working at various activities. I took this to be one of the intelligences at the Gathering and so I opened my intent to communicate with them. I'll refer to this intelligence as the "2ndGathgroup" because they were the second group I contacted at the Gathering. 2ndGathgroup isn't a name they gave me to call them. They might have had a name they called themselves, but it didn't occur to me to ask for one. So, we're stuck with 2ndGathgroup as their moniker.

As it turned out, there was a purpose in White Bear's teaching me his tonal language beyond just being able to communicate with him. During my first encounter at the Gathering, ordinary verbal communication had been sufficient. 2ndGathgroup didn't have a verbal language capability. They spoke in the same *Star Wars*, R2D2 beeps and squawks as White Bear did. If he hadn't patiently prepared me to communicate in this way, contact with 2ndGathgroup would have been impossible. To emphasize the way we communicated, how it sounded to my nonphysical ears, I'll try to describe the sound of it, at least for a little while. I discovered White Bear was right, the method he taught me is a universal language. Still, you'll probably have difficulty understanding what I mean when you read, "I turned to the 2ndGathgroup Spokesman and said, 'Shreeeep, wop, wop, rerrrr, pop, snap, nurt, nurt." It's completely unintelligible squeaks and squawks to the ear, but the sounds carried more information in two squeaks than do several paragraphs of text. Floating there in Focus 34/35, I faced the large, metallic object I could feel in front of me and opened my intent for contact.

"Hmmmmmm, meep, meep," I toned out to them, indicating I was an Explorer from The Monroe Institute's Exploration 27 program, who was interested in communication.

"Screeep, pop," came back, indicating it would take a moment for one of their group to separate himself from the rest and act as a liaison or spokesman. After a short wait I had the impression that one of their group moved out to my immediate vicinity, distinctly apart from the massive craft I could feel nearby.

"Ommmm, beep," I toned out to him, asking him to tell me who he was–and now we'll drop the tone language sounds. He said (in effect) "We are a telepathic race, all connected to each others' thoughts in an instantaneous manner. We are a group consciousness. It was somewhat difficult to separate myself from the group to communicate with you, but here I am. As a telepathic group, all other members of the crew can listen in on our conversation through me. What is your interest in communicating with us?"

"I'm exploring this region of space to learn about something we call the Gathering," I replied. "I'm one of eighteen people participating in a program to explore beyond physical Earth existence and to learn what I can. What is your interest in communication?"

"We've come to this region to witness events taking

place on the Earth. Specifically, the Great Event that is happening here to the Earth school. You know anything about that?"

"We call it the Earth Changes but there seems to be lot of confusion about exactly what that means," I responded.

At this point Dar's voice came in on the tape and suggested I ask a question. I focused my attention on the 2ndGathgroup spokesman and toned it.

"I've noticed there are many other groups gathered here also. What is your relationship to those other groups?"

"We are mostly all members of an intergalactic group. You might call it a federation. There are also some loners here who came on their own to observe these events. They are not members of our federation but are welcome to be here to observe. As federation members, we are part of a network that shares information in a cooperative effort to learn more about each other and the unknown. Every member of the federation with the capability has a contingent here to observe and we share our information with other members who haven't the capability," he replied.

Dar's voice stated the next question, "What proportion of those gathered here are Earth school graduates?" I passed it on to the 2ndGathgroup spokesman.

"Their actual numbers are very small, perhaps five or six percent, but their power is great," he replied.

"How do those gathered here identify themselves and their current locale," I asked my host, prompted by Dar's voice on the tape.

"As a network of aliens, or other home worlders, if you prefer. We each have our own home world in the physical Universe. Each home world has sent a contingent here to observe the Earth Changes, as you call them. We are located here where you've found us, in relatively close proximity to the Earth. But we are just a small group of astronauts here on a mission from our home world. It's our understanding that one of the potential results of the Earth Changes, as you call them, is that Earth will be joining our federation."

"What is the focus of your interest in your observation of the Great Event, as you call it?" I asked, rephrasing the question Dar's voice suggested on the tape.

"We are here to try to gain some understanding of the energies involved in the Great Event," he replied. Calling my attention to the interior of his ship, he said, "As you can see we have brought the most sophisticated equipment available from our home world to record this Great Event."

As I looked around the interior of their ship, my impression of the control room was that of a NASA moon shot—row upon row of computer monitors, technicians, sensors, control consoles, recording equipment, and other assorted gear. It felt like there was close to a football field size area in their ship filled with technicians and equipment. Quite impressive.

"What sort of energies are you interested in recording?" I asked.

His answer came in a series of squawks and squeaks that translated themselves into images. The first one was an image of Earth that looked about two or three times the diameter of a full moon. As I looked at it I wondered if this gave some clue as to the distance from Earth to 2ndGathgroup's ship. I could see the huge crystal within the Earth aligned to the axis of rotation. At one end, near the north pole, a ring was placed around the crystal. The word "LOVE" was engraved on the ring. In response to my question about the nature of the energies 2ndGathgroup was here to record, the ring slid from the end of the crystal to the center. With the images of the crystal and Earth superimposed, the ring moved to the core center of Earth.

These images then translated themselves into the following information. The energies are about a change in the duality nature of the Earth school. When they're infused in the Earth Core Crystal, some of the confusion we Earth people have about this duality nature may be cleared up. The crystal symbolized the polarizing nature of the Earth school where everything can be described in terms of opposites. Polar opposites like hot and cold, wet and dry, tall and short are just a few examples. Moving the ring labeled LOVE from one end of the crystal to the center symbolized a change in which we in the Earth school would now recognize our confusion. We would have the opportunity to understand that Love does not have a polar opposite called Hate. That is a confusion, caused by the duality nature of the Earth school. As a result of the ongoing Earth Changes, the true opposite of Love would be revealed to be No Love, or lack of Love.

As I watched the images and listened to the translations from the 2ndGathgroup spokesman, I noted his flat tone and clinical description of the Earth Changes. I realized he had absolutely no understanding of what he was describing at an emotional, feeling level. At a mental level, the spokesman and his group reminded me of the Vulcan character, Mr. Spock, from the *Star Trek* television series, totally incapable of experiencing anything at an emotional, feeling level. Not a single member of this telepathic race had the slightest inkling of what Love felt like. To them, Love was just an energy like heat or light. It might be more useful to them if Love's energy came in the form of a wooden log. At least then it would provide heat when burned in a fireplace. It would have some reason for existence. Any actual use for energies such as Love was inconceivable to them. They were completely without any ability to perceive from an emotional, feeling perspective and lacked any means of emotional expression of such energies.

Responding to my query about any messages he might have for Earth's inhabitants, the 2ndGathgroup spokesman replied. "Many of your people will make the leap to your Focus 27 soon and will have to exist there for a very long time. There will be great reductions in overall Earth population. Do what you can to prepare your people for this event."

"Can you give me a sign that will help me validate the information I've received from you?" I asked, again prompted to do so by Dar's voice on the tape.

In response I was shown the image of a comet with a very large, tear drop shape. Existence of this comet would be a surprise to the general population of Earth. My mind flashed back briefly to my tour of the Coordinating Intelligences. Then, as I watched the comet approach Earth, in the background I could hear the line from a sixties tune that goes, "This is the dawning of the age of Aquarius." From that information I interpreted that the comet might come out of Aquarius in the zodiac or might indicate the "new way of thinking" nature of Aquarius. I also noted that Uranus is Aquarius's planetary ruler, meaning the energies of the two are similar. So, this comet might in some way be linked to events consistent with that energy which tends toward sudden, unexpected, bizarre changes, usually uncomfortable in some way.

Next I had the impression of something very far distant, millions or billions of light years away. Whatever this was would align with Earth's rotational axis on the north pole side. This alignment would allow connection with some form of energy that would enter Earth's energetic system. The approaching comet would provide a triggering event to establish this energetic connection. At the end of the image sequence I was shown a crab, by which I took to mean there is some connection between the comet and the zodiac sign of Cancer, which is energetically similar to the Moon. The moon's energies deal with the emotions, the distant past and the feminine principle.

(As a side note, I was a little flabbergasted after returning home to read in the *Rocky Mountain News* about the sighting of the previously unknown comet Hyakutke, discovered by an amateur astronomer in Japan on January 30, 1996. Astrologically, January 30 occurs when the Sun is in the sign of Aquarius in the zodiac. I was further floored by the projected path of the comet, which was provided in an illustration accompanying the article in the newspaper. Its path viewed from Earth, the article disclosed, would bring it very, very close to the North Star, Polaris. Polaris is the one star that is aligned to the Earth's rotational axis on the north pole side of the globe. The article stated that comet Hyakutke would pass within 9.3 million miles of Earth in late March of 1996 and then continue on, around our sun. As I was reading the article the hairs were standing up on the back of my neck as I remembered the images from my 2ndGathgroup contact. I'm still very curious about the meaning of the crab in those images. Whatever it all means, I feel like the appearance of comet Hyakutke gave me some level of confirmation of the information I received.)

Another of Dar's voiced questions on the tape asked, "What will be the emotional impact of the Earth Changes on human beings." When I asked that question, my earlier suspicions about the feeling nature of 2ndGathgroup were confirmed. My host could not use his normal tonal language to respond to my question. Instead, he attempted to tone back to me the sound in our English language that caused him confusion. Nothing in his tonal language equated to the energy of the word "emotional." He could only try, with great difficulty, to repeat back the English language sound of my word.

"EEEE . . . MMMM . . . OOOOOOOH . . . SHAAA . . . UN . . . ALLL impact?" was his response, spoken in very broken tonal English, followed by a huge question mark.

"Yes emotional impact, you know, feelings. For example, if you were on Earth when this Love energy entered the core crystal, what expression would you give that energy as an individual?" I toned back to him. By the dumbfounded look on his face I could see this guy was clueless.

"We are a telepathic race and as such have almost no understanding of what it means to experience anything as an individual. We are all connected in an instantaneous access fashion and all of us experience everything as a collective unit. A member of our race, acting as an individual, causes great disruptions in the flow of information among the rest of us. It does happen occasionally, but it's greatly discouraged. We've had to develop a form of group consciousness that is relatively cooperative and uniform. This cooperation emanates from the group as a whole and is controlled by the group as a whole."

Now I was the one feeling a little dumbfounded, trying to conceive of and understand the implications of being a member of a telepathic race. I kept asking myself what it would be like to live as a member of such a race, where all minds are connected. What were the implications of each member's thoughts being freely, instantaneously perceived by all others? On Earth that would mean the thoughts of an aboriginal native in the Outback of Australia would be running through the mind of a New York stockbroker. The thoughts of a suicidally depressed woman in China would be drifting through the mind of the queen of England. The thoughts of a Muslim soldier engaged in a holy war in Baghdad would be flooding through every other mind in the world. It would be the complete and utter chaos of listening to five billion different radio stations, all broadcasting through the single radio receiver of my mind. For me to function at all as part of such a group, there could be no cultural, sexual, religious, ideological, or nationalistic differences whatsoever. Such an existence is inconceivable to me. Yet, 2ndGathgroup's telepathic existence had to deal with all these individual differences in order to function. Now I was the one drawing a blank. I was the one with the clueless look on my face.

"We in the Earth school perceive ourselves to be individuals, separate from the rest of our group," I responded. "Most people here operate as if their thoughts can be held in complete privacy. I don't personally believe that myself, but that's what most Earth people believe and live by. Reep, rang, rang, wacko!" I toned to the spokesman, meaning, "The implications of your telepathic existence for the individual mind in the human Earth school are incomprehensible. Such telepathic connection does occur for some individuals here, but it is definitely discouraged. Here, we call those kind of people insane. Not too many years ago we burned those kinds of people at the stake as witches."

"If individual thoughts were not tightly controlled," the spokesman continued, "with our telepathic ability our consciousness would be jammed by the simultaneous reception of all of the individual thoughts of the billions of inhabitants in our race. No one could possibly exist or think in such a jumble of random thoughts."

"And yet," I toned to the spokesman, "that's exactly how we in the Earth school live our lives, but without conscious telepathic connection."

"This is beyond our comprehension!" exclaimed the spokesman. "We've always thought your way of living was impossible."

"Yeah, I think your way of living is impossible too! We in the Earth school evidently took a different evolutionary route to Conscious Awareness. Our adaptation was to close down our awareness of others in our group to survive and function as individual beings, separate from the whole."

"We, conversely, have evolved a way of thinking our thoughts as a telepathically connected whole," the spokesman declared. "When you mention existence as individuals, we become more interested in communication with you. We want to learn how it is you Earth schoolers manage to exist as individuals. This is one of the things we have come to observe and record. As for that other sound you made, that EEEE . . . MMMM . . . sound, we have no contact, zero understanding, no comprehension, nothing on file. Whatever it is, it is not in our language or awareness in any form. But as Explorers we understand that many times great understanding comes from probing that which is unknown. The thing you refer to with your EEEE . . . MMMM . . . sound definitely qualifies as an unknown. Is this thing connected in some way with learning to feel?" he asked.

"Yes, emotional impact and feeling are very closely related in Earth school reality. They are sort of two ways of communicating about the same thing," I told him. "Some of us view emotion as an energy and feelings as the impact of emotional energies."

"Really! This is great! The major goal of our mission here is to learn about feeling. That's why we brought all this equipment and these technicians here from our home world. Our primary mission is to observe and record whatever we can about this feeling thing, whatever it is."

"I see, and that's a lot of fine-looking equipment you have here too. Look, I hate to be the bearer of bad news, but I'm pretty certain all your instrumentation and hardware is going to be useless to fulfill your primary mission," I toned to the spokesman.

The very next thing I heard sounded like the voices of a thousand individual turkeys screaming at the top of their lungs and echoing around inside a huge, hollow tin can.

"Squabble . . . squabble, squabble . . . squabble, squabble, squabble exploded from the control room of the

2ndGathgroup's ship. They had temporarily lost control of their group mind, in the logical incongruity they saw in my remark. In the feel of the sound, as hundreds of the crew members shouted out in their thoughts, I heard things like, "What that earthling is saying is impossible. Our technology is so far ahead of theirs, he doesn't know what he's talking about."

It took a good ten seconds or more for the squabbling sound of the thousand turkeys in the big tin can to quiet down. I immediately knew I'd just witnessed an example of what happens when there is strong, individual expression within the group mind of a telepathically connected race. Utter chaos erupted in their thinking process, as they reacted to the logical impossibility of my statement. After a short struggle, they got themselves back in the groove of their normal form of consciousness, and then the spokesman connected with me again.

I continued, "In my opinion, as an Earth school student, in order for you to fulfill your mission, you won't be able to rely on your hardware."

The sound of a thousand turkey voices screaming in a big tin can erupted again. "Squabble . . . squabble . . . squabble, squabble, squabble, squabble, squabble," flew around like a zillion ping pong balls, bouncing and ricocheting off everything and everyone inside their ship until the crew regained control of their individual thoughts. It quieted down more quickly this time.

"As you've probably noticed, there is some disbelief on the part of most of our crew on that point," the spokesman said, "could you explain more please, about our . . . ah . . . hardware inadequacy."

"Not so much inadequacy as unsuitability," I replied. "The only way I know to observe and record the feeling or emotional impact of an energy such a Love is for me to be the instrumentation. I think to complete your mission, you'll have to become the detectors and recorders yourselves. It will require that you use your body as the hardware. Your other instruments might pick up something, but it will most likely not fulfill your mission to understand the meaning of feelings."

Such an idea had obviously never occurred to these guys. I heard a minor bit of squabbling off and on during an extended silence, as the 2ndGathgroup pondered the meaning of what I was saying.

"Since the energy of Pure Unconditional Love is involved in the Great Event we are here to record, is there any way you can demonstrate to us what you mean, by using that specific energy?" the spokesman asked.

Now it became clear to me why Robyn, one of the women in our group, had suddenly appeared nearby just a few moments ago. I'd caught her arrival and wondered why she had showed up.

"Just a moment please," I toned back to the spokesman.

Then I turned my attention to Robyn. "Shereep, nanck, grreeech, grreeech," I toned to her. Thereby, she took into herself, understood, and remembered the entire story from my first point of contact with 2ndGathgroup, to just after she'd arrived. I ended my toning to Robyn with the question mark, "Can you help me with a demonstration for these guys?"

Robyn took it all in and immediately toned back, "Sure, let's give it a try. This could be a lot of fun!"

Then turning our attention to the spokesman, Robyn and I indicated our willingness and readiness to demonstrate.

"Just a moment," he said. "We want to do an instrument check to make sure everything is ready to record." Then, after a few moments, "Okay, go ahead and begin your demonstration."

Robyn and I stood face to face a few feet apart. We gazed deeply into each other's eyes, smiling, and allowing a feeling of Pure Unconditional Love to build up in both of us. We each let our individual expression of Pure Unconditional Love energy generate our own, unique tone within us, separately. My tone sounded so real to me, I was sure a physical world tape recorder could have picked it up and played it back. We let the power of our tones build up and each projected ours to the heart of the other. When we did, our hearts were joined together in expression of Pure Unconditional Love.

Our tones were at slightly different frequencies and in their joining I could both hear and feel a beat frequency! I probably shouldn't have been surprised, but I was! Joining our tones, two separate, individual expressions of Pure Unconditional Love, behaved just like Hemi-Sync sound. The resulting beat frequency carried a feeling like a combination of deep gratitude and totally loving acceptance of everything and everyone. Absolute bliss! Robyn and I let the beat frequency's power build up between us for about ten seconds and then diverted a portion of its energy toward the 2ndGathgroup spokesman. We held it there for five or six seconds and then both switched it off, simultaneously. After stopping, I looked around inside the ship to get an image of what the technicians were doing. They were all busily checking the readouts at their workstations.

"Jabber, pop, pop, snap," came back from the spokesman. "Our instruments registered something, but it makes no sense to us. Some sort of time anomaly we think."

Robyn and I waited for the minor squabbling sound in the background to quiet down.

"Well, it's great that your instruments registered something. But like I said before, to complete your mission of observing and recording the feeling and emotional impact of Pure Unconditional Love energy *you* must become the data gathering devices."

They were very confused again by this statement. "Squabble, squabble . . . squabble," broke out in minor pockets of the crew, bouncing around from one area to another. It made me think of what would happen if scientists here in the Earth school were trying to learn about Love by using oscilloscopes, sensors, and other physical world hardware. They might be able to sense the smoke, but they'd never feel the fire.

Just then Dar's voice came in on the tape informing us it was time to return to the crystal at TMI-There.

I toned to the spokesman, "Sorry, we have to return to our . . . uh . . . base now. I hope that demonstration helped."

Without waiting for a reply, Robyn and I turned to leave, heading for TMI-There. Looking back as we left, I saw a rather puzzled look on the 2ndGathgroup spokesman's face. I can only assume our sudden departure was another form of logical incongruity to him. I had the distinct impression he just couldn't logically fathom why we'd leave right in the middle of his important experiments.

We went to TMI-There, gathered with the rest of our group around the crystal, and basked in its energy for a little while. Feeling fully recharged, we all left for our CHEC units and C1 consciousness at Dar's request.

chapter 14

2ndGathgroup,
Second Contact

The next tape exercise was the last of the program. It had been such an exciting, interesting experience that I approached its end with a bittersweet feeling. Bypassing the Hemi-Sync guidance to Focus 27, I arrived at my place to find all the hanging chairs occupied, except one, where I sat down. Everyone around the table was all smiles. Bob, Rebecca, Tralo, White Bear, Coach, and the Woman from Sensuous all sat beaming at me. Bob was the first to speak.

"Well, for a program in which nothing was going to happen until later, it's been quite a ride, hasn't it?" he remarked. "I can tell you now. There's even more that comes later. I'm looking forward to working with you in the future. For now, we all just want you to know how much we appreciate what you've done, for us, for your group, and for your Self. This has been the best Exploration 27 program yet and you've helped to make that happen."

"And the progress you've made toward learning the meaning of Love," Rebecca said, "Bruce, I'm so pleased and happy for you! It's just marvelous!"

"When the program is over, and you've gone home," White Bear toned, "come here whenever you like, and we'll continue your leaping practice. You've got enough of the basics to keep you busy for a while. Remember, leaping can teach you much!"

"I remember the early days, Bruce," Coach chimed in, "your struggle to find Rebecca at the flowers, our first meeting. Son, you've grown so much in so little time. I know your curiosity will drive you on to places you can't even imagine right now. I'll always be nearby, watching and cheering."

"And as for me," Sensuous said, in a voice dripping with honey, "I'm looking forward to the time you remember where we were once together. Until then, look for me in your dreams and surrounding you in the environment of your waking hours."

With that, it was time to go to TMI-There and meet my group at the crystal. Before I left, everyone around the table stood and applauded. I get choked up just remembering the scene. When I arrived at the crystal, Bob and Ed were waiting for me off to the side. Bob motioned me over and I walked to where they were standing.

"One more thing before you go," Bob said. "Blah blah . . . blah, blah, blah."

Blah, blah isn't exactly what he said, but whatever he was saying seemed like idle nonsense. Then I felt someone standing to my right, two feet away. I turned and looked to see who it was and it was the same guy I'd seen a day or so earlier, when Bob was talking nonsense. The same unknown guy.

"Bob, that same guy is standing here again, who is he?" I asked.

Bob went on blabbing like he hadn't heard me. I turned to Ed.

"Ed, who is that?"

Ed just smiled and stood there without saying a word.

This was really puzzling behavior and it was frustrating not to get an answer. I looked at the guy again. It was the same guy, same medium length, coal black hair. Same neutral expression on his face. Same long sideburns, almost mutton chops, maybe five feet, ten inches tall. No beard, no mustache, dark brown eyes, average weight and a Mediterranean complexion. I turned back to Bob.

"Come on, Bob, who this guy?"

He just shrugged and said, "Isn't he with you?"

"Come on, Bob . . . Ed . . . Who is this guy?"

Feeling frustrated, I walked away and joined my group at the crystal. Before beginning this tape exercise I had decided I wouldn't go to Focus 34/35 this time to explore on my own. Instead I intended to see what I could do to assist other members of our group. During our debrief sessions between tapes it was apparent some of them were having a little difficulty in their exploration at the Gathering. Since I was having such an easy time and had already received more information and insight than I thought possible, I decided to help some of my buddies. After we performed our lotus blossom WOOO-AAAHH a few times, I held back a little when everyone else took off for Focus 34/35. After I started moving in that direction my plan was to look for any stragglers from our group. I was just about to place my intent on assisting them when I felt a very odd, very strong pull, as though some kind of strange gravity was pulling on the very top of my head. I had no idea what this strange force was, or why it was pulling, so I did what seemed reasonable. I let the force pull me to wherever it wanted me to go. After a brief sensation of movement through blackness, I found myself standing in front of the 2ndGathgroup spokesman again, inside his ship

"Sorry for the intrusion, but you left before we really gathered anything from the demonstration experiments. This is very important to our mission here and we want to continue. Could you demonstrate the EEE . . . MMM impact of Pure Unconditional Love energy for us again?" the spokesman asked. "We didn't really get anything we can use from your last demonstration, but we're pretty certain whatever it is you did has something to do with why we're here to observe and record."

"Of course, I'd be happy to," I replied.

Then, looking around inside their space craft, I noticed two of the 2ndGathgroup's crew, standing face to face on a raised platform in the control room. They were positioned between the spokesman and me, and standing stiffly on the platform.

"Yes," the spokesman said, "these two from our ship have volunteered to participate in the experiment. Since you said we would have to be the sensing and recording devices, two of our crew members have volunteered to allow you to demonstrate, using their bodies. We've selected a male and a female for the experiment, since in your previous demonstration a male and female of your race were present."

The image of those two volunteers still stands out in my mind. They stood at attention, military style. They were both dressed in uniforms that made it difficult to determine if males and females of their race had any visible, distinguishing features. Also, they were either wearing some sort of helmet or these guys have very large heads. Their heads seemed disproportionately large for the rest of their body size. Both had volunteered for a mission all of 2ndGathgroup considered potentially dangerous. Like a couple of gung ho Marines, they'd volunteered, understanding full well it might cost them their lives. These were dedicated, professional Explorers who understood the concept of risk versus gain. Knowing they might be killed didn't deter their logical understanding that someone must volunteer to fulfill the overall mission of the group. The potential gain for their race was a necessary risk.

As I was looking over the two volunteers, Robyn came into view again. I acknowledged her presence and let out a "Sqweeeeeek, beep" to her, bringing her up to the present. With this communication she got everything that had transpired.

"Sure, I'm game. Let's demonstrate it again for them," was Robyn's response to their request. "These two volunteers are so serious! Think we should tell them it isn't going to hurt?" she laughed. "Naw, let's let them find out on their own," she said, punctuating her statement with a devilish giggle.

Standing back about ten or fifteen feet from the two volunteers, both Robyn and I looked them over carefully.

"I don't know, Robyn. Which one is the male and which is the female?" I toned to her, trying to keep a straight face.

Her giggling response was, "Hmmm, that's a good question, Bruce. In those suits it's really hard to pick out any recognizable, distinguishing features, if their males and females have any, that is."

"Ya, I'd really kind of like to get this right, you know," I giggled back to her. "Hmmm, I think the male is the one on the left."

"Ya," she responded, "I was thinking the one on the right was the female. Let's just go with that."

We each flew over to a position very close to, and behind the volunteers, Robyn stood behind the female, I behind the male. The volunteers were somewhat transparent to my vision and looking through them, I could see Robyn's smiling face, superimposed over the less visible body of the female volunteer. I nodded to the spokesman, indicating Robyn and I were ready to begin the demonstration.

"Just a moment," he said, "let us check to make sure all of our instrumentation is ready to record."

I glanced at the technicians in the control room. All eyes were glued to their monitors and readouts.

"Okay, you may begin when you're ready," the spokesman said.

I turned to look directly into Robyn's eyes. She was smiling confidently, happily. So was I. A feeling of Pure Unconditional Love began to fill each of us. We both let the feeling build up for a moment or two and then we stepped into the bodies of the volunteers from behind. We stood there, gazing into each other's hearts, allowing the emotional expression of Love to build for perhaps three or four seconds. I took a quick look at the technicians in the control room. They all looked completely stunned, frozen in place. Even the spokesman was affected. Not a single one had the intense focus on their monitors and readouts I'd seen just seconds before. Instead, blissful, ecstatic smiles were just beginning to form on some of their faces. I suddenly realized that since these guys were a telepathic race, they were all experiencing what the volunteers were experiencing. I looked back at Robyn and she and I both stepped back in unison, out of the bodies of the volunteers.

The control room became a flurry of frantic activity, as the technicians snapped out of their stunned stupor to check readouts on all the instrumentation. Not a single one had maintained consciousness during our demonstration. In Monroe Institute parlance they had all "clicked out."

"Ah . . . MMM . . . This is very unusual," the spokesman said. "I assure you this has never happened before! We seem to have experienced some sort of total malfunction of every piece of our equipment. System clocks show approximately three of your Earth seconds elapsed during the experiment, but not a single other instrument registers anything! I apologize for any inconvenience, but would you mind demonstrating again?"

I glanced over to get Robyn's okay and was surprised to see her gone. Instead, Rebecca was standing in her place, behind the female volunteer. Rebecca smiled and nodded her agreement. I turned back to the spokesman.

"Believe me when I say, it will be my great pleasure to repeat the demonstration for you again," I toned to him.

"Very well, we'll need a few moments to recheck our instruments and reset all our recorders."

"That would be fine with us. Please take all the time you need to be certain all your instrumentation is ready," I replied.

Turning back toward the female volunteer, Rebecca and I stood, beaming radiant smiles to each other, waiting for the go ahead from the spokesman. I had to suppress the urge to giggle as I said, out loud, "We're ready when you are."

After a moment the spokesman nodded, indicating they were ready. Looking directly into each others' hearts, Rebecca and I simultaneously stepped into the bodies of the volunteers. We let the feeling of Pure Unconditional Love that was building between us continue to rise in power for perhaps six or seven seconds this time. I took a quick survey of the control room to check on the technicians. Their silly, goofy-looking, love-struck smiles had started again. We continued until most of them had their heads leaning back over their chairs, in a completely relaxed position, an expression of open-jawed bliss on all their faces. They were all completely and totally clicked out, totally unconscious. Then Rebecca and I stepped back in unison, out of the bodies of the volunteers.

The technicians had more time to relax their bodies into the Pure Unconditional Love feeling during this demonstration. They had slumped into their chairs in deep relaxation and some got quite a jolt when we abruptly stepped out of the volunteers' bodies. Their physical bodies jerked violently back into the positions they had been in just before we started. It registered with several of them that their body position had changed during our demonstration. We may even have caused a case or two of whiplash if these people have necks like ours. Most had just suddenly catapulted themselves back to the body positions they'd been in just before we started, without realizing anything out of the ordinary had happened. The control room became a flurry of activity again, and when it settled down, the spokesman addressed me.

"I apologize," he said, "this is highly unusual. We seem to have had another malfunction with our equipment. This time our system clocks show approximately seven of your seconds elapsed. And this is odd too. None of our crew has any memory of what occurred during those seven seconds. We're experiencing a loss of time during your demonstration. I know it might be an inconvenience, but would you mind demonstrating again?"

"Not at all," I replied, "it will be our great pleasure."

This time Franceen's smiling face greeted me as I turned back, expecting to see Rebecca. Franceen had taken Rebecca's place and we were both doing our very best to suppress a severe case of the giggles.

"Whenever you're ready," I called out.

The spokesman nodded after their instrument check, signaling they were ready to record our next demonstration of the emotional impact of Pure Unconditional Love energy. This time Franceen and I allowed the feeling to build up for perhaps twenty seconds or so. I was floating in a warm, cozy sea of Pure Unconditional Love, a bliss I could have stayed in forever. Smiling from ear to ear, I turned to look over the control room technicians. We'd held the state long enough that a few of them were beginning to regain some level of consciousness just before we stepped out of the volunteer's bodies. A few of them were just beginning to catch the faintest whiff of the feeling. The rest, almost all of them, hadn't regained consciousness and again lurched violently forward to their predemonstration positions. None was quite sure what was going on, but there were a few who were almost conscious of the feeling.

"Squabble . . . squabble, squabble . . . squabble, squabble, squabble, squabble," erupted in chaos in the control room.

"This is completely unexplainable!" the spokesman blasted, after the screaming turkey sounds subsided in the ship. "We've experienced the same malfunction of our equipment again! A little over twenty seconds this time! But this time, some crew members claim something happened during the missing time. Nobody is able to describe what happened in terms the rest of us can understand. We're postulating you're demonstrating some sort of control of time. It appears you Earth school people are capable of making time disappear by rendering us all unconscious. If our system clocks are correct, you're somehow able to remove our awareness of the passing of time, and we are unable to resist. Some crew members view this as a potentially dangerous threat to our security. All the squabbling you heard was required to restore order and get the entire crew's agreement and consent to continue these experiments. All have agreed to do so, because of the importance of our mission, but we must also consider our security. Are we getting close to a logical point at which to terminate further experimentation?" the spokesman asked.

"Your perception of missing time is most likely the same thing we call 'clicking out,'" I replied. "Some in the Earth school understand that when we experience something completely beyond our ability to comprehend, unconsciousness is often the result. Clicking out is a common experience for Earth people too. It means 'unconscious to the experience.' We'll try it again and I think this time you'll get it. Let us know when you're ready."

I looked over and saw Robyn had returned, taking Franceen's place. She was beaming an absolutely radiant, loving smile from every molecule of her Being. Bright pinks and yellows filled the space surrounding her. I realized, as I was looking at Robyn, that her place had been taken by Rebecca and Franceen to communicate the impersonal nature of Pure Unconditional Love energy. It had been done to demonstrate that this was not restricted to only one pairing of humans. It demonstrated that Pure Unconditional Love can be shared between any individuals.

We waited for the signal from the spokesman, and then stepped into the bodies of the volunteers again. This time I checked the control room guys right before we stepped in and followed their progress throughout the demonstration. Many of them were no longer bothering to pay any attention to their workstation consoles, monitors, or readouts. They were leaning back in their chairs, relaxed, and waiting for the demonstration to begin. As we stepped in, the lovestruck expressions returned to their faces, telling me they were again stunned by the power of the experience. Robyn and I let the feeling build higher and higher until it was reminiscent of my experience during the first tape of the program. It continued building until it felt like it had when Nancy Monroe enveloped Bob, Ed, Rebecca, and me in a cloud. It felt like I was going to burst into flames again. Robyn and I held that level for over a minute and a half. We held it so long our bodies disappeared and were replaced by a single, soft ball of gently swirling pastels. Warm gentle currents of soft, loving beauty wafted through the single orb in which Robyn and I had become One Being, loving itself. We glowed with the fire and power of the Sun.

Somewhere after the first minute or so of holding that feeling, some of the technicians in the control room regained enough consciousness to begin moving their bodies. We continued to hold the feeling of ecstatic bliss. A few technicians were able to stand and move around the ship. A few of them consciously took in the full force, ecstatic blast of the glowing ball, Robyn and I had become as the expression of Pure Unconditional Love energy between two human beings.

The blissed-out joy in those few technician's faces, as they looked at one another in the control room, clearly indicated they were acutely aware of the feeling. We held the feeling long enough to ensure that those who were conscious would retain memory of the experience. Once we were certain of that, Robyn and I gradually let the feeling subside, separating back into our individual selves. Then, slowly, we turned down the feeling until it flickered like the flame of a candle. As we held the feeling, low and flickering, a few more technicians began to move around the control room. The gradual reduction minimized the shock to the crew when, at last, we stepped out of the volunteers' bodies. As we stepped out, and the energy level dropped for the 2ndGathgroup, I felt an immediate, collective yearning coming from the few conscious members of the crew. They had experienced the feeling of Pure Unconditional Love at a powerful, emotional level and wistfully yearned to experience it again. A wispy feeling of missing that energy floated from the few crew members who'd felt it.

As the rest of the technicians regained consciousness, I could sense the feeling of Pure Unconditional Love moving from those who had become conscious during the demonstration to those who had not. Before the demonstration I hadn't even considered this possibility. The memory of the experience, firmly imprinted in the minds of just a few members of the crew, quickly spread throughout the ship. Thoughts were no longer the only things communicated telepathically between them. Now the feeling of Pure Unconditional Love passed between them too. Immediately following the feeling's spread through the remainder of the crew, the collective yearning to feel it again, coming from the entire crew this time, washed over me like a gentle, twenty-foot roller out at sea. There is such a bittersweet longing in that feeling.

Without realizing it would happen, without any thoughts about the consequences, all of 2ndGathgroup had just experienced the emotional impact of both Pure Unconditional Love energy, and its true polar opposite, its absence. The sense of yearning dropped a little over time as we all stood in silence but remained in the background energy of the entire crew as we continued.

I looked over at the spokesman, "I think you got it this time," I said. "Judging by the looks of your crew and the feeling of yearning I sense coming from them, I'd say you guys definitely got it this time."

"Yes . . . yes . . . something . . . very . . . unusual . . . has happened . . . we're not sure what to make of it yet," he slowly replied. "But we can all recall from our collective memory something . . . something beyond our ability to express it in words. Is that what you call a feeling?"

"Yes . . . yes, that was a feeling. And although we on Earth label our feelings with words, feelings are something far beyond the ability of words to express. They are the experience of an emotional energy within ourselves, as Pure Unconditional Love energy is now for you," I replied.

We all fell silent again for a little while, letting the impact of the experience soak in. During the silence, two other members of our Exploration 27 group flew in and hovered together, nearby. I'll call them Julie and Rollo. As program participants, these two had been falling in love with each other over the past several days. I wasn't surprised at all that they were hand in hand, exploring together.

Then, suddenly shifting gears, I addressed the spokesman, "Say, listen, my friend and I have some other things we must do now and we need to be moving along."

"Is there any way we can have another demonstration of that feeling?" 2ndGathgroup's spokesman toned.

The two volunteers were still standing on the platform, ready to continue their mission in another demonstration.

I looked over at Rollo and Julie and toned, "Screeeep, bip, bip, whoosh, whoosh?"

In those few sounds they were given the complete story of what had happened since the beginning of my first encounter with 2ndGathgroup. It ended with a question mark, because I was asking if they would mind taking our places in another demonstration.

They turned to look, starry-eyed, into each others' faces, acknowledging to each other they were willing to participate. Both turned back to look at me, and their happy, smiling, response was, "Sure, it will be our pleasure!"

"Remember, guys. This is an exercise to demonstrate the emotional impact of Pure Unconditional Love energy," I remarked. "It might be a good idea to go easy on the sexual aspects of this for now. I'll leave that up to you two."

Turning toward Robyn, smiling warmly, I expressed my gratitude and thanks, acknowledging her for the powerful, wonderfully loving Being that she is. We both allowed the feeling of Love to well up inside us as we hovered there, tears of joy in our eyes, looking into each others' hearts. Then I turned back, looking toward the 2ndGathgroup spokesman. As Robyn and I hovered there, watching, I could clearly see him smiling in anticipation as Julie and Rollo swooped toward their positions behind the two volunteers. That was my last contact with 2ndGathgroup. As I accelerated away, that last image faded into the blackness.

Checking, I discovered we were still in the free flow portion of the tape exercise. Robyn and I split up to continue exploring on our own. I decided to go back to my original intent, and began looking for other members of our group. Consciously bringing each person's name to mind, I focused on that person with the intent to find them. I went to each one to see if there was any way I could assist, without interfering with what they were doing. I found every one of them and realized none needed me to do anything. They were all busily exploring. Some had joined in little groups, others were on their own. It gave me the realization of just what a powerful, capable group of Beings I was with in this program. After I visited each one, Dar's voice on the tape let us all know it was time to return to the crystal at TMI-There. I focused on the image of the crystal and let it pull me in.

When I arrived, the rest of our Exploration 27 group was there already. We could hear cheering and applause surrounding us. The energy of Love was shooting around the room like fireworks. I couldn't see everyone who was making all the noise, but the feelings accompanying it were heartwarming. Bob, Ed, Rebecca, and Nancy were in plain view, smiling and waving toward our entire group and extending their gratitude and joy to all of us.

Then Dar's voice on the tape reminded us we were to continue our exploration with return trips to the Education, Planning and Health, and Regeneration centers. All traveling together, we arrived as a group at each of these locations. We entered each place to the sound of cheering and clapping from all the workers in the vicinity. All of the people working at each place we visited stopped what they were doing as we arrived. They stood wherever they were, looked at us with smiles and happiness, and cheered wildly. Everywhere we went they mimicked the sound and movement we had made as a group, when we first energized the crystal at TMI-There. We could see them all, standing where they'd been when we entered. In unison, each stepped forward with their right foot and pointed their hands and arms downward, just as we had in our circle around the crystal. Then, while stepping back, raising their hands upward, high up over their heads, they made our sound. "WOOO-AAAHH . . . WOOO-AAAHH" reverberated throughout Focus 27 everywhere we went. There is such great joy in that sound and such a profound feeling of gratitude emanated from everyone we met. They all had happy, smiling faces as they greeted us and mimicked our movement and sound. It felt like all of them were aware of what we had been doing during the entire program, and they wanted to demonstrate their approval, appreciation, and gratitude. In response to their heartfelt demonstrations of affection, I felt like we were all a cross between celebrities and astronauts returning from a successful mission.

At the Planning Center, one of the workers gave me the title used for this book, which became more of the title of the series, along with encouragement to finish writing the first one and get started on the second.

"You've got a series of books to write," the worker said. "Don't worry about the financial aspects of what you're doing. Trust the energy of Pure Unconditional Love to support you and provide for your needs," I was told. "Help is already laid into Focus 15 to further your efforts."

At the Health and Regeneration Center, I was treated to a session of energy work on my entire body. As I stood with one of the workers, strong pulsations of energy surged through my body, charging each chakra in succession. I left feeling a tremendous sense of heat running throughout my body.

Then Dar's voice told us it was time to return to TMI-There to complete the last task of our program. Once there, we joined hands, standing in our circle around the base of the crystal for the last time. Waves of Pure Unconditional Love flowed from the crystal and washed over all of us. I could see Rebecca, Bob, Ed, and

Nancy smiling, waving, and expressing their gratitude for what all of us had done. Back in my CHEC unit, I could feel happy tears streaming through my hair and down the face of my physical body. The level of Pure Unconditional Love ebbed for a moment, and I thought it was finished. Then it started again as a powerful wave of Love moved from all the other members of the group and washed over me. Words fail to describe the ecstasy I felt, as I watched each member of our Exploration 27 group extend their Love to me. It brings tears of joy and a lump to my throat as I write about it now. I can remember saying to myself, "I'm open to be receiving as much Love as there is."

Then it was on to the final task, to complete the program. Our instructions were to gather up as much of the Pure Unconditional Love energy at the TMI-There crystal as we could carry. We were to then bring it down to the Earth Core Crystal and anchor it there.

All of us stood around the base of the crystal, gathering in as much of the energy of Pure Unconditional Love as we could hold. I watched as others in our group jumped into the crystal and dropped downward, toward the center of the Earth. Robyn and I were the last to jump. We looked into each other's hearts and gathered armload upon armload of Pure Love energy. I could feel tears of joy again streaming down the face on my physical body. Then, smiling at each other, we jumped into the crystal and plummeted toward the center of Earth. When I landed I could still feel myself holding the energy of Pure Love in my arms. I could also feel the low frequency, telltale vibration of the Earth Core Crystal throughout my body. The now familiar tension had every muscle in my body bouncing and jerking as usual. Then I released Pure Unconditional Love into the Earth Core Crystal, intending to anchor it. I could feel the crystal absorb the energy, and when it did, its vibrational frequency increased! I

stopped and took special note of the vibration I was feeling in my body. It was definitely much higher now than it
had been during any of my previous trips! Judging by the
much smoother feel of it in my body, I'd say the frequency of the crystal was somewhere in the range of 20
cycles per second. It was no longer rough and tension
filled, instead it felt smoother and warmer. The muscles in
my body were no longer jerking and bouncing. It was
more like they were smoothly humming.

As I looked around, I could see all the other members of
our group celebrating. They were dancing, singing, and
skipping around, arms swaying in the air above their heads,
with smiles on their faces and smiles in their hearts. We
joined hands in a circle again and repeated our lotus blossom opening, WOOO-AAAHH sounding, energizing
movements, filled with joy and gratitude. Then the circle
broke up and people continued dancing and hugging for
quite some time. In fact, the celebrating went on for so
long I started looking around for something else to do.

Then, it occurred to me that if carrying the energy of
Pure Unconditional Love down here once was a good
idea, it would be a good idea to do it again. With that
thought, I used the one-breath technique to rocket myself
back up to TMI-There in Focus 27. On my way up I saw
Robyn zooming upward too and realized she had the
same idea. When we popped up through the floor together, the place looked and felt deserted. We'd caught
everyone there by surprise! We each gathered up as
much Love energy as we could carry and leaped, laughing like fiends all the way down to the Earth Core Crystal.
Robyn landed right beside me. We anchored our loads in
the crystal and then, smiling at each other, one-breath
rocketed ourselves back up to TMI-There.

This time when we popped up through the floor, Bob
was standing close by, with a befuddled look on his face.
Robyn and I turned toward each other, laughing hysteri-

cally at our ability to take Bob by surprise. For some reason it struck me as ultimately funny that he had no idea
we were coming back. Soooo . . . . the great one doesn't
know everything! Standing in front of Bob, smiling into
each other's hearts, Robyn and I gathered up armloads of
Love again. Then we stood, with our bodies facing the
opening in the floor we'd just emerged from. Turning just
our heads around, we both looked into Bob's befuddled
grin as we leaped into the air and fell happily toward the
Earth Core Crystal.

We were both laughing so uncontrollably when we
landed, it was hard to unload and anchor the energy.
Putting one over on Bob was just so hysterically funny at
the time. Giggling and laughing so hard our bodies were
swaying like drunks, we were on the verge of collapsing
into big happy heaps. It took at least half a minute to get
enough control of ourselves to one-breath rocket back up
again. This time Bob was waiting for us when we popped
up in TMI-There.

He smiled his "lifted eyebrow smile" at us, as if to say,
"Yup, you got me!" and we giggled our way through gathering another load.

After unloading and anchoring it, on the way up,
Robyn and I slowed down and tried to suppress our giggling out of respect for the old man. When we popped up
through the opening in the floor again, our bodies were
still jiggling in mirth. Bob, Rebecca, and several others
were standing there waiting for us. I could tell they had
hurriedly concocted something this time for each of us to
take back with us. Lucky for them, Robyn and I had been
delayed this last time while we laughed ourselves silly on
the way up from the Earth Core Crystal.

Bob looked at me and said, "This was . . . uh . . . quite
unexpected. You two caught us unprepared." Bob
thrust something into my hands that looked like a wide,
yellow-colored silk ribbon. It must have been at least a

foot wide and was very thin, with a soft, silky texture. "Here, take this with you and anchor it in the middle of the Earth Core Crystal," he said.

I got a firm grip on the end of the ribbon with both hands and turned, getting ready to jump. Looking over at Robyn I could see someone had handed her a ribbon like mine, but with different coloring. It could have been pink or green, I don't remember. I caught her eye and smiled just as we jumped. We rolled over on our backs and watched the ribbons trailing behind us like giant streamers. Before landing I realized these ribbons would serve some function for participants in later Exploration 27 programs. I don't know exactly what.

When I landed among the rest of our group, they were still dancing and singing and celebrating. Standing there, looking around, I didn't see anything nearby to tie the ribbon to. I shouted to my buddies closest to me, asking them to give me a hand tying this ribbon to something. Several came over and then a huge eyebolt-looking thing appeared out of nowhere next to where I was standing. We tied the end of my ribbon to it and I looked over to see how Robyn was doing. Several others were just finishing helping tie her ribbon to a similar eyebolt.

We went back up one more time to see if there was anything else Bob and company would like us to carry back down. Bob was standing there, waiting. He reached out, and putting his left hand on my shoulder, looked into my eyes with Love and said, "You two go on back down, enjoy yourselves, and have fun!"

So we did. I joined in again with everyone in celebration of our completion of Exploration 27. We danced and hugged and kissed and shook hands, laughing and singing all the while. Then Dar's voice on the tape called us back to C1. We slowly separated from each other for a last, private moment alone, and then, one by one, we slowly drifted back up to C1.

Later that evening, after dinner, while walking along the dirt roads around the institute, I pondered the concept that Love's true opposite is No Love. As I did, I realized we are probably confused in the same way about much of our emotional expression. The opposite of Hate is probably No Hate, Joy, No Joy, Sorrow, No Sorrow. Many of us, myself included, have misidentified the true, polar opposites of these feelings, these energies. Their power or intensity each runs separately on a sliding scale from zero to full on. I knew from my experience during the first Exploration 27 tape exercise a little more about the full-on end of the Pure Unconditional Love energy scale. The effect of my realization had me staggering along the dirt road. I understood that the path to Loving *does not* involve or require that I move along a continuum between Love and Hate. It's between Love and No Love. Hate is a totally separate energy. I realized removing Hate from my Being will not automatically move me closer to Love. The only thing that will move me toward more Love is to move away from a state of No Love. I can't stress to you enough how profoundly this has affected my thinking, feeling, and Being. It became clear to me that if I desire to stop hating and start loving, these are two separate issues. All I, or anyone, need do, is grab the knob labeled Love on my internal, emotional graphic equalizer and slide it up, away from zero. To turn down hate, slide the knob with that label back toward zero. I'm still dazzled by the feeling of being able to understand the true duality nature of feelings and emotional energies.

chapter 15

Speculation

Thursday evening, long after dark, I stepped outside to smoke and ponder some of the things that had happened during the program. Walking the deck at a lazy pace, I started thinking about the impact of what we'd done during our contact with 2ndGathgroup.

2ndGathgroup is a telepathic race of beings and I wish I better understood more of what it means to have the thoughts and feelings in the awareness of one be in the awareness of all others. When my partners and I stepped into the bodies of the volunteers and allowed the expression of Pure Unconditional Love energy to build between us, all members of the crew felt those feelings. The emotional impact was so foreign to them that they all clicked out.

What disturbed me so was 2ndGathgroup's telepathic nature and the implications for the rest of their race. If they were all connected to each other, I thought that meant members of the ship's crew were not the only ones who experienced the incapacitating click outs. Not just the volunteers, the spokesman and the crew experienced it, *all of them* did. Our experiments affected those at the

Gathering, those living on their home world or anywhere else, and those living in their nonphysical world. *All of them* simultaneously experienced the effects of our demonstrations—every last one of them. After our experiments, *all* of 2ndGathgroup's race was left with the memory and knowledge of Pure Unconditional Love. If that experience took root in the collective mind of their race, it changed them forever. What might their initial experience have been like?

At first they *all* experienced just short bits of missing time during the click-out periods. Most on their home world probably didn't notice the missing time unless they were doing something that brought it to their attention. Any who were watching clocks might have noticed the second hand appear to jump three seconds and then seven seconds during the first two experiments. During the third experiment it would have jumped twenty seconds and in the fourth, two full minutes or more. That's fine for someone sitting through a boring lecture in high school, watching the clock. But what about those in their version of a car driving in their version of rush hour, freeway traffic? It could have been like everybody in rush hour traffic falling asleep at the wheel for first three seconds, then seven, then twenty and then, finally, for at least two minutes. What about them? What could happen to them? Wondering about this concerned me greatly.

If it happened in Denver at the peak of rush hour, I can tell you what would happen. Thousands of cars, with unconscious, physically incapacitated drivers, would have kept moving until something got in their way. After the third experiment, those who weren't killed outright during the twenty seconds of chaos would have regained consciousness in a twisted mass of thousands upon thousands of wrecked cars and trucks. Just on I-25, our main north-south freeway, the dead or injured could have numbered in the tens of thousands. By the end of the

third experiment, enough wrecks would have piled together to stop all traffic on I-25 for days, while bulldozers
worked to clear the roadway. And that's just one fifteen-
to twenty-mile stretch of one freeway in one moderate
size U.S. city.

What would happen to 2ndGathgroup's version of pilots landing a commercial airliner at Denver Interna-
tional Airport during the third and fourth experiments?
Those 747s on final approach would descend toward the
ground with unconscious, incapacitated pilots, crews, and
passengers. When those people regained consciousness,
they would be dead. And what about other people? Any
in the midst of potentially dangerous activities—surgeons,
air traffic controllers, construction and factory workers,
nuclear power plant operators—could be seriously injured
or killed if they were suddenly, unexpectedly rendered
unconscious. Their unconsciousness could potentially
cause injury or death to millions of others.

And that's in Denver, just one medium-sized U.S. city.
But these click outs are happening simultaneously to every single member of 2ndGathgroup's race, no matter
where they are, no matter what they're doing. Can you
imagine the scope of such a catastrophe?

I know it sounds nuts, but considering these possibilities nearly drove me crazy. The experiments with 2nd-
Gathgroup were only intended to assist them in fulfilling
their mission to observe and record the Earth Changes.
None of us even considered the possible consequences of
our actions, beyond effects on the crew at the Gathering.
But it's conceivable that *all* members of their race experienced the emotional impact of Pure Unconditional Love
energy for the first time, and that may have jeopardized
the safety of *all* of them. Imagine you felt, as I do, some responsibility for what happened. It was hard to live with.

For quite a while there was no one to whom I could express my feelings about what happened. I kept visualizing

myself trying to explain that I was anxious and depressed because I might have caused the death of millions of aliens on a planet millions of light years from Earth. I kept seeing the person I was talking to picking up the phone to make reservations for me at the nearest psych ward. For the first time in my life I knew what it felt like to be seriously concerned about my sanity, to lose touch with consensus reality. When I was finally able to talk to someone who wouldn't judge me nuts after my first few sentences, I began to return to reality. (Dar, I love you, and thank you.) Over a few days the pins in my mental hinges slid back into place.

This brings me to my thoughts on the Earth Changes. Information from my first contact at the Gathering indicated that the Big Show, as Bob Monroe called it, is an alignment of the Earth Core Crystal with a very distant object. I understood this intergalactic alignment would make a connection that would bring the energy of this distant object into the Earth's nonphysical environment.

In response to my queries, 2ndGathgroup indicated that the energy this alignment brings in will be the energy of Love, Pure Unconditional Love energy. My visual interpretation of their information was a ring engraved with the word "Love," which slid along the Earth Core Crystal axis from the north pole to the center of the Earth. From this I speculate the Earth Changes are about an event similar to that experienced by 2ndGathgroup's race as a result of our experiments. What if the alignment were to infuse a tremendously powerful charge of Pure Unconditional Love energy into the Earth Core Crystal? What if every human being's awareness was flooded with an overwhelming level of such energy? What if that flood lasted for a long time?

If such a thing happened, some on Earth would at least have an advantage over 2ndGathgroup. There are some living on Earth who've experienced high levels of Pure

Unconditional Love. Many have experienced it at least to some level. Not everyone would be rendered unconscious as 2ndGathgroup was. But if Pure Unconditional Love energy were suddenly introduced at a very high level, we could expect all the rush hour freeway wrecks, airplane crashes, and other accidents. We could expect that globally, thousands or maybe millions could die within the first few minutes just from accidents alone. That scale of disaster could cause ripple effects resulting in death or injuries to many more.

There are some differences between this alignment possibility and what happened to 2ndGathgroup. Our experiments resulted in just a few, short-duration blasts of Pure Unconditional Love energy. The Big Show alignment on Earth would last far longer. It could last for hours or weeks or years. It could change Earth's environment at the energetic level forever. From astronomical alignments we could also speculate that the alignment would not occur as suddenly as the flip of a switch. Some energy transfer, at lower levels, could occur far in advance of perfect alignment.

Sunrise on Earth is an alignment of the eastern horizon with the Sun. The blackness of night doesn't instantly change to the brightness of day. As the sunrise alignment approaches, the Sun's energy, light, is gradually introduced. It starts as just a hint of light in the night sky and gradually builds toward a peak throughout the sunrise alignment. The Big Show alignment should be similar. Infusion of Pure Unconditional Love energy from the "source" should start gradually, like the dawn, and build to full force at perfect alignment. This could take a few hours or several years depending on how slowly we are coming into the alignment.

As with the sunrise alignment with our eastern horizon, we could also expect that once the Big Show alignment peaked, midday so to speak, it would begin to subside. The Love energy would gradually reduce over time, like our sun heading for the western horizon. Sometime after the Pure Unconditional Love energy from the source peaked, it would begin to gradually disappear. Like sundown, there would come a time when the infusion of energy would gradually taper off, and then stop.

So, what could this all mean? It could mean that the Earth Changes are about a window of opportunity. One in which the sun of Pure Unconditional Love energy will shine on all inhabitants of the Earth Life System, *all* inhabitants, physical and nonphysical, living and dead. If the energy involved is Pure Unconditional Love, it could be a time when *all* of us become acutely aware of experiencing and expressing Pure Unconditional Love. If this is a slow process, those of us who have experienced it before will begin to notice a gradual buildup of such experience and expression. Those who are unfamiliar with Pure Unconditional Love will have the opportunity to become aware of it and to begin to change our beliefs, our thinking, and our lives. If enough of us make such changes, we could be living in a Heaven on Earth long after alignment is over. The Earth Changes could forever change the entire Earth Life System. We could *all*, like 2ndGathgroup, carry the memory and knowledge of Pure Unconditional Love into our future forever.

If too few of us take this energy into our hearts, if too few of us learn to experience and express this energy, whatever it is, our lives after the alignment will at best return to their old ways. If this event is a culmination of some sort, something our Creator always knew would happen, and we pass up the opportunity, our futures may be more bleak. If throughout all of human history, our purpose has been to bring this energy into sentient Being consciousness, and we fail, what further purpose can our existence serve?

I hadn't reread Monroe's entire *The Gathering* chapter in *Far Journeys* until just before I began writing about my 2ndGathgroup experiences in the manuscript for this book. While still smoking my cigarette and walking the deck that evening after the last tape exercise, I hadn't realized most of what you've just read. (It came into my awareness just before I wrote this chapter.) From a short excerpt of Bob's chapter, handed out to participants during the program, I remembered the INSPEC's statement that the Big Show might alter not only our time-space but all adjoining energy systems as well. Even then it boggled my mind to think about the potential impact of introducing the ability to feel the energy of Pure Unconditional Love so abruptly to their entire race. I felt then we had definitely altered 2ndGathgroup's energy system, but not to the extent that I realized later while writing this. It still boggles my mind to think about the potential impacts and wonder about how it might have affected the evolutionary path of their race.

As I've thought and written about my experience, I've wondered what about it is most important. I've settled on the understanding that the most important thing is that we *all* become aware of experiencing and expressing Pure Unconditional Love to the greatest extent possible. It's the only preparation for the coming Earth Changes that makes any sense to me. As more of us learn to consciously experience and express Love, fewer of us will be at risk as the alignment begins to peak. Survival of human consciousness as the dominant Earth species will be less at risk. The most important thing any of us can do is to learn and teach the experience and expression of Pure Unconditional Love.

I seriously considered not including any of what I've written in this chapter in the final version of this book. Who am I, after all, to tell anyone anything about what might supposedly happen regarding the Earth Changes?

But Dar, the one who helped me come back to consensus reality, gave me a reason to include it.

"Bruce," she said, "when I think about all the things written about the Earth Changes, yours doesn't sound nearly as crazy as some of what I've read and heard. In fact, I kind of like yours better than most. I mean, really, all of us living on Earth in a state of Pure Unconditional Love? I rather like that one."

chapter 16

Come on Bob, Who Is This Guy?

Breakfast on Friday morning is the last opportunity for members of TMI programs to come together as a group. The program's over, the experiences are tucked away in notes and memories, and now it's time to say good-bye to fellow Explorers who've become friends in the past six days. It's Friday morning, a little after sunrise and three time/event lines are about to form a single crossover point.

After filling my plate with eggs and pancakes, I started looking around for a place to sit. As I did, I noticed a stranger walk into the room, and it was a déjà vu experience. There, walking across the room, was the man I'd seen standing next to me with Bob Monroe and Ed Wilson during the program! I'm sure my mouth must have dropped open as I stared at him. He looked exactly like I'd seen him nonphysically, about five foot ten, dark complexion, black hair, long sideburns, no mustache, and average weight. As I watched him walk over to fill his plate, I remembered saying, "Come on, Bob . . . Ed . . . Who is this guy?" the last time I'd seen him. Now I was seeing him and I was really curious! Then Ed Carter walked over to the stranger and the two of them started talking. Within a few minutes I was introduced to Frank DeMarco, one of the owners of Hampton Roads Publishing Company. I sat dumbfounded with him and Ed Carter for the first several minutes, as I remembered references to meeting someone a little after sunrise, Friday morning.

Frank and I talked a little about the program Ed and I had just finished and then he started in with the publisher's quiz. After an hour and a half of talking about what I'd been writing and why, Frank said that if I needed a book publishing contract to continue writing, we could sign one for my first book before I left Virginia. I was dumbfounded! Bob Monroe had been busy working from his side all along. Other authors I'd heard about told of sending manuscripts to several publishers and waiting months to find out if any of them were interested. Here I was, an engineer with a skeleton of a book, and a publisher was willing to put together a contract now! I didn't need a contract to keep writing–after this experience there was no way I could stop. I'd agreed to give Hampton Roads the first look at my finished manuscript when it was completed and then work out a contract. I left Virginia feeling well supported by the Universe.

When I returned to work I found that while I'd been gone several new projects had been funded. When I'd taken two weeks unpaid vacation to attend Exploration 27, the workload on my job had been pretty low. I was only working three days a week, which left two days and weekends to write. Now my supervisor informed me that the increased workload would require five or six days a week of my time. That started a long series of events that turned out to be the biggest exercise in trust of my entire life. The inner drive I felt to continue writing was something I couldn't put off. Within five days of returning to work, I gave my employer my two-weeks' notice. I had no idea how I'd financially support myself, but I had to write. Then things just started falling into place to make full-time writing possible.

chapter 17

Multidimensional Integration

That first Exploration 27 program opened my awareness and perception to aspects of myself and the nonphysical world that Lifeline's retrievals had only hinted at. I've always subscribed to the belief that we are all multidimensional beings, without any real understanding of what that meant. When an Education Center tour guide, seemingly miffed at my "playing dumb," told me he'd seen me there many times before, I thought at first he was joking. I've since come to understand he was pointing out something about the multidimensional aspect of who and what I am. I had absolutely no memory of ever being in the Education Center or Hall of Bright Ideas. Yet, this guy claimed I was a regular visitor. Could it be that some part of me exists in another dimension and has been making these regular visits without my Conscious Awareness?

Over the years in my work as an engineer and inventor I have developed a strong talent for solving difficult design problems. It was after a promotion from an engineering supervisor to a research and development project manager that I really began to notice this ability. I was assigned to a team attempting to develop a laboratory curiosity into a viable production process. There was no book to go by, no one knew how to do what had to be done. We hit lots of brick walls, and after smacking into quite a few, I found a technique that seemed always to lead to a solution.

Instead of trying to find a solution, I focused on trying to more clearly define the problem. I'd run experiments to learn more about why something didn't work. I'd immerse myself in the details of the problem, thinking about it day and night until I was sick of it. At that point I intentionally stopped thinking about it. I'd do anything possible to avoid thinking for one more second about the insurmountable conundrum we were facing. It usually took at least two or three weeks before the light bulb experience would bring the solution. I'd be sitting on the john, or staring out the window, not thinking of anything in particular, when suddenly the solution to the problem would pop into my mind's eye as a detailed, completed, working design that always worked! Over the three years of that project the time between being sick of defining the problem and the light bulb coming on shortened to a couple of days.

I concluded that the solution to every problem must already exist, somewhere out there in the ethers. All I needed to do to find it was to define the problem clearly enough and I would somehow be connected to where that solution was. I had no idea how it really worked and most other engineers laughed at my explanation of the process. But it always worked for me no matter how tough a problem I was handed.

When I left my research and development engineering job at Coors Brewing Company several years ago, my manager let me in on a secret. During my exit interview he asked if I'd noticed that others in the group often came to my cubicle to talk about what they were working on. I hadn't really noticed anything out of the ordinary.

It turned out that for more than two years, whenever someone in the group got stuck on their project, my manager would suggest they talk to me. The person would just walk into my cubicle, sit down, and proceed to talk about whatever aspect of their project had them stumped. As I relaxed and listened, pictures immediately popped into my mind. I'd sketch the images on my blackboard and offer them as a potential solution. If there was more to the problem, the person kept talking and I just kept seeing pictures and sketching. My boss's secret was that he knew fifteen minutes of such conversation would move my coworker past the project stumper. Back then I just took it as a nice compliment. Now I realize the Hall of Bright Ideas was probably involved.

Over that period of years I evidently had integrated my multidimensional access to information into my physical world awareness. It was seamless and I never suspected another "me" existing in another realm was finding the solutions for me. Yet, after my visits to the Hall of Bright Ideas, that's the explanation that seems to best fit the facts. It kind of makes me wonder just how much more than my physical body I am and what it would be like to be consciously aware of more of my multidimensional Being. And it makes me wonder where else in my life such integration has already taken place.

2ndGathgroup's information during this first Exploration 27 program also brought up questions about the role of Pure Unconditional Love in my Being. Why is it so important that we unconditionally love and accept ourselves and others? Why is there a Gathering of other intelligences from the Universe surrounding the Earth to observe the Earth Changes? Why is there some sort of intergalactic alignment occurring that will bring the energy of Pure Unconditional Love into the Earth Life System of human beings? Did Nancy Monroe's devastatingly powerful blast of Pure Unconditional Love during the first program tape exercise have anything to do with my incredibly clear, 3-D color and stereo sound perception from that point on in the program? My second Exploration 27 program presented the opportunity for lots of answers.

chapter 18
Another Exploration 27

Through an incredible set of circumstances, the Universe provided for my attendance at a second Exploration 27 program in February 1997, almost a year to the day after the first one. A lot had happened in that year. I'd completed the manuscripts for my first three books and was working on a fourth. I'd been doing a lot of partnered exploring with friends from the previous program. Those experiences provided all the material for the fourth manuscript. Ed Carter, a man I had grown to love like a father, died in early December 1996. I approached my second program without any expectations as to what might happen or what I should be doing or looking for. This allowed great freedom to observe my "program Self" in action without worrying that it would be a waste of time to do so.

I discovered much about myself throughout the program. Sitting at a table and snacking with other participants the first Saturday afternoon of the program, I noticed I was looking closely at every woman already in the room and those that entered. I remember thinking, "No, that one's too short, that one's too old, that one's not pretty enough. Wait a second . . . that young, dark haired beauty maybe . . . nope . . . she's taken . . . that young guy who just entered the room is obviously with her. Hmmm . . . maybe Erica, a tall, bright, attractive blond with the lively personality, maybe her? Hmmm . . . there's another prospect. Estelle, young, pretty, nice figure, very intense woman, dark haired, focused on something going on inside herself. She's a little short but I give points for good looking. Maybe her, or maybe her too."

When I caught myself in this internal conversation, I began wondering just what it was I was looking for. "I'm a happily married man. Is it sex I'm thinking about?" As I pondered the question, feeling deep inside for the answer, I found a piece of it. I realized I was looking at each woman to determine if she was one who might join me in mutually building up the level of some kind of energy. It was a desire to connect with an attractive female in a platonic way, although one that has a sexual feel to it. It wasn't that I was fantasizing about a potential sex partner, I was instead feeling a strong desire to allow a certain feeling to build between a woman and myself. I didn't understand why I would want to do such a thing, especially if sex wasn't involved, but I realized this was something I always did in every Monroe Institute program I attended.

Standing outside later that evening I met the tall blond and felt like the first few words out of my mouth insulted her, pushed her away. That felt very strange. I'd figured out this platonic, sexual energy thing and I pushed her away with everything I said. Very strange. I got away before doing any more damage and noticed two other women who'd just arrived; Sabrina and Ellen.

Sabrina, a tall, youthful, attractive woman, at first seemed ideal, but then something about her felt hard as nails. Kind of a steel and concrete, corporate Dragon Lady persona. I was certain it couldn't be Sabrina—too distant, too cold.

The trainers gathered everyone together Saturday night to give an overview of the program and have everyone introduce themselves. The first words out of the mouth of Estelle (the young, intense, dark-haired woman) were, "I'm a lesbian, at least I think I am. I mean I'm married to a woman, so I must be a lesbian." This presented an interesting possibility. As she and I had made small talk earlier in the day, I could feel her willingness to build that same energy I desired. Perhaps we could both allow whatever this was to build without getting tangled up in the sexual feel of it. Maybe we could explore this energy, this feeling, since neither of us would have any sexual expectations. I found the possibility tantalizing.

Lurking in my background thoughts was concern that since I entered this program with zero expectations, zero would happen. I'd always come to programs expecting something to happen. While it seldom turned out to be what I expected, something powerful and interesting did indeed always happen. It wasn't until several tape exercises into the program, while we were visiting Focus 21, that anything happened at all. When I arrived I heard a chorus of voices coming through the pink noise of the tape, hundreds of them, chanting "You Love We Love You Love We Love You . . ." over and over. I recognized them immediately as the greater part of myself I call my Disk. I'd first met my Disk years earlier during the Gateway Voyage program, and hearing them again now, I felt encouragement that despite my lack of expectations, things were happening.

Listening to their chant, I could feel its meaning change in the flow of the sound. Sometimes I heard "We Love You" and sometimes "You Love We" and sometimes "We Love . . . You Love." It almost seemed at times like they were saying "We are Love, You are Love." Listening to this flowing chant, I just relaxed into the soft, warm, fluffy feel of its energy. When the chorus faded into the pink noise and disappeared, I started wondering what I should be focusing on for the week. "What's the most important thing to be gained this week?" I asked myself, projecting the question outward in all directions.

"Knowledge, knowledge of Self," came back to me in a clear voiced, determined tone. I hadn't been expecting to actually hear a response, so it took me by surprise—not that the answer seemed at all profound, just more of the same old *know thy self* stuff. As I lay there soaking up the feelings of encouragement, three dark, hooded people walked in front of me from left to right. Trailing a few feet behind them was Erica, the tall blond, carrying a white coffee cup.

"Erica! Over here! It's Bruce," I mentally shouted. She turned and looked at me. I could see that bubbly, child-like smile of hers register surprise.

I asked, "Where are you going with that coffee cup in your hand?" I was hoping to call attention to something she might remember back in the physical world. But she just pointed at the three hooded figures still walking in front of her. "I'm following them," she said. "They're my guides." With that, she turned and hurried up her pace. She caught up with them just as they disappeared from view into the deep blackness on my far right.

Next Ms. Hard-As-Nails, Sabrina, came walking toward me out of the blackness. She seemed to want something from me but I couldn't understand what it was. She was very forward, almost intrusively so, and I found myself feeling like I wanted to back away from her advances. Got a taste of my own medicine, as I'm usually the one barging into other people's experience uninvited. Guess I'm not used to having someone intentionally visit me when it wasn't my idea. I felt quite puzzled by this as I shifted back toward C1 consciousness, wondering what Sabrina was after.

During the program tape in which we first revisited our own place in Focus 27, a smile moved across my face, accompanied by an alternate burning and itching in the center of my chest. I was met at 27 by the sound of cheering and clapping, with a few "you made it, you're here" shouts thrown in for good measure. The whole gang was waiting for me. Bob, Rebecca, Tralo, White Bear, Coach, and the Woman from Sensuous came into view, sitting in the chairs around my table. When their welcoming racket subsided, Rebecca got up out of her chair and we embraced in a big hug. She and I took a walk down by the lake, where we stood quietly, just taking in the view of the lake, the dolphins, and the mountains.

"Big doings this time, Bruce," Rebecca broke the silence. "Probably not what you're expecting, but then you've managed to come without much expectation this time. Nicely done!"

"Yeah, it's a change from my usual pattern. It's a little scary, but I'm doing all right," I replied.

"Speaking of patterns, I couldn't help noticing you've become aware of one of yours this time."

"Funny, I never recognized this platonic, sexual energy thing before. It's so blatant and so familiar."

"Maybe there's something more there for you to become aware of," she remarked mysteriously.

When we walked back to the table, White Bear caught me eyeing the Woman from Sensuous. "Scroom, treep, balooom," I felt him say, immediately translating itself into, "Such genuine beauty can be quite captivating!"

I broke my dropped-jaw gaze and joined his tonal conversation.

"Your leaping exercises have been coming along well," he toned "A little more consistent practice would be good. Be that as it may, I've got a new leaping form I'd like to show you."

I turned to walk toward the lake, but everything went dark for a moment and when it got light again, White Bear and I were standing atop towering rock spires.

Steamy mists swirled through the air. It very felt familiar. Then the memory rushed back to me.

"This looks a lot like the first place I saw the Cliff Diver," I toned to White Bear casually. During Gateway Voyage, my first TMI program, I'd seen someone execute a perfect swan dive from a place just like where we were now standing. I hadn't understood what that experience was about, but its memory stuck with me.

"One and the same. If you remember being here before, perhaps you remember the diving form we'll be doing, as well," he toned back. "That first time you just stood here watching. At least the second time you dove with the Cliff Diver part of the way, outside the diving body, but at least part of the way."

The rock spire felt like it rose for miles above the Earth and was surrounded by a thick impenetrable blackness thirty feet below, as it had been during my Gateway program.

"The key to this kind of leaping is like all the others," White Bear toned. "Maintain your attention in your diving body from start to finish."

With that, White Bear winked, turned facing the blackness below, and leaped high out into the air. He hung there for a moment and then executed a perfect swan dive. It looked like he'd come up off an Olympic diving board and pulled off a perfect ten-point dive. Seconds later I watched his feet disappear into the thick blackness below.

"Wonder what's down in that blackness?" I thought to myself, as I brought my arms down to my sides, preparing to dive. "Sure hate to run into a rock or something on the bottom!" My nervous wonderings were distracting. I managed to maintain my awareness in my diving body until just before I started dropping from the peak of the dive. Suddenly, I was watching my diving body, arms outstretched, falling toward the blackness. "Whoops! I'm supposed to stay in there! Geez, I better catch up quick before I disappear into that blackness." I shot down and leaped into my diving body just as my fingertips entered the blackness. I could feel it pass by my face at incredible speed for what seemed like way too long a time. "This is just fine! I'm in my body, diving down through blackness. Now what am I supposed to do?" After falling for what felt like many miles, the blackness gave way to light. I watched myself land feet first, gently on another rock spire next to White Bear.

"Let's try that again," White Bear toned. "And pay more attention to your landing." Without saying anything more, he turned his back to the blackness and backflipped up into the air again, high over another thick blackness, and then disappeared.

His comment jarred memory of the landing I'd just completed and it was confusing. Something very peculiar was happening. I would have sworn under oath in court I was in my diving body the whole time. But my memory also held the impression I was standing next to White Bear on the next rock spire, waiting for myself to arrive. "Hmmm . . . That's weird," I thought to myself as I pre-pared to dive again, "I could have sworn I stayed in my diving body. . . ? Oh well, I'll do better this time." I turned my back to the blackness and my diving body leaped be-fore I was ready but I managed to rejoin it at the peak of the dive. I stayed with it, plummeting downward another several miles or so, feeling the blackness rushing by. Then just before I broke out into the light again, I felt White Bear standing next to me. I felt the warm rock under my feet. We were both looking up, laughing. And at the same time I could still feel the blackness rushing past my face. When I landed this time, atop another towering rock spire, White Bear turned and winked just before he leaped backwards and dove again. This time at the peak of his dive he tucked his knees to his chest and spun head over heels several times as he fell toward the blackness. He straightened out his body just before entering the blackness and toned "pay more attention to your landing!" When I tried to mimic his movement I spun wildly out of my diving body and had to scramble to catch up to it in the thick blackness below. "How much further down can we keep diving," I wondered to myself, "before I run into solid ground?" I was half expecting to plow into the Earth at any moment.

This time, as I broke through the blackness into light, I could have sworn I saw someone standing next to White Bear on the rocks below. "Looks like White Bear is working with someone else too on this exercise. Wonder who it is?" I thought idly. Then next thing I knew, I was standing next to White Bear in the middle of a conversation.

"You're concerned about crashing into the Earth below," he toned. "Let's take care of that on this dive." With that he leaped and disappeared again.

Now I was really feeling my anxiety about crashing into solid ground, wondering how White Bear would "take care of it." I managed to stay in my diving body the whole way but was ready to leap out in an instant if my worst fear materialized in front of me. When I broke into the light again, that same guy was standing next to White Bear, both their bodies stuck halfway into the rock. The place looked familiar. Then I was standing next to White Bear, my body stuck halfway into the rock too. "Wonder where the other guy went?" I thought to myself, realizing I had no memory of landing and the other guy was gone.

"See?" White Bear toned. "Rock here isn't quite as solid as you're used to!"

Looking around, I realized we were back at same towering rock spires where we'd started.

"Wait a second!" I let out with surprise in my tone, "we're back where we started."

"So we are," he laughed.

"But we've been repeatedly diving downward for miles? How did we end up way back up here?"

"Diving downward? Really?" White Bear toned in all seriousness. "Way back up here?"

"I think I just got the point of this exercise," I toned back sheepishly. "Down is a physical world concept. Where we are right now there is no up or down. That's the lesson here, isn't it," I toned, feeling pride that I'd caught on. "It's to remove another physical limitation in my thinking, isn't it? I associate downward movement with both gravity and moving my awareness toward the physical world's C1 consciousness."

"Well, that's part of the lesson," he laughed, "but if you pay more attention to your landings in future dives, you might discover more."

With that, the surrounding thick blackness moved outward like black clouds receding away from the central point where we were standing. As they did, the familiar mountains of my place in Focus 27 came sharply into view. Several people were waiting there. Some I recognized; some I didn't. Moving over to a hanging chair around the table, I sat down across from Ed Carter.

This was the same man I'd met almost a year earlier during my first Exploration 27 program, the man who saw to it that I connected with a publishing company. In December 1996, Ed suddenly and unexpectedly died. We'd been in brief contact several times after he died. Now here he was in the Afterlife, sitting across the table from me, under the beach hut roof, at my place in Focus 27. It was good to see him again.

"Bruce," Ed said, in his familiar slow pattern of speech, "I've got something I'd like to show you at the Education Center. Your energy seems a little low, otherwise I'd do it now."

"Yeah, my perception seems a little foggy yet," I replied. "I seem to be drifting a bit, having a little difficulty maintaining my focus of attention. Lots of fragmented bits of images and things instead of solid, coherent perception."

"Between now and the Education Center exploration tape exercise, perhaps you could do something about that," Ed suggested.

"What would you suggest?"

"Perhaps you'll discover something that helps if you explore White Bear's latest leaping exercise. And maybe make a point of opening a bit more to the energy of Love."

"Thanks, Ed. I'll work on that one."

"And you'll meet me at the Education Center later?" Ed asked in a tone meant to elicit my commitment.

"I'll be there, low energy or not," I responded.

chapter 19
Sabrina, There

At the beginning of the next tape exercise I placed my intent on learning more from White Bear's latest leaping form. Shortly after shifting to Focus 27, I found myself standing, nonphysically, in a circle with the two program trainers, around another participant, Ralph, who had been having difficulty perceiving anything during the tape exercises. His complaints about being unable to see, hear, touch, or sense anything in any way brought back memories of my frustration and disappointment during my first Lifeline program.

Each of us began projecting a beam of energy, emerging from the center of our chests, directly into Ralph. Moments later other participants formed a circle outside of ours, beaming energy from themselves to Ralph. As more participants joined and another circle was formed around Ralph and us, some didn't have a direct shot at him and so they were beaming through other participants into Ralph. There must have been some critical-mass analogy to whatever we were doing, because at a certain point some kind of chain reaction occurred, like a nuclear pile. The addition of a single person beyond this critical mass increased the energy flow to Ralph not by a factor of one, but more like a factor of five or six.

Suddenly, my awareness shifted and Denise, a friend of mine from the previous Exploration 27 program, came into view. We hugged and gabbed for a moment and then the scene suddenly changed again. Erica was standing in front of me, talking like we had been carrying on a conversation before I got there. Then in a flash Tony, a friend from last year's Exploration 27 and a participant in this one, was standing in front of me. Then he was gone and I got a brief flash of Ralph. For a while I was seeing just brief, fragmented flashes of these people as they popped in and out of view.

Then, I found myself floating in space, looking in front of and slightly below my position. From there I could see Denise and me, surrounded by a ball of light, as we hugged again and talked to each other. Just to the right of Denise and me, in a separate ball of light, Erica and I were in a separate conversation. To the right of that ball I could see Tony and me gesturing with our hands, pointing at something and commenting to each other. On the far right Ralph was in the middle of concentric circles of people and I could see another of my selves standing close to him, beaming energy from the center of my chest directly into him.

From my new location, "floating in space," I was simultaneously aware of what my four alternate selves were doing, heard both sides of the conversations, and saw activities with four separate people. I also noticed that there appeared to be light-filled fibers extending from somewhere on the front of my "central location body" to each of the other locations. Nothing like this has ever happened to me before. I played with this new multiple locational awareness state for the rest of the tape exercise. After the tape exercise Sabrina and I chatted outside during a cigarette break.

"That's quite a pogo stick you've got. Wish I had one!" she said.

"Pogo stick?" I asked tentatively, "what pogo stick?"

"I saw you during the tape exercise," she said. "One second you were standing right in front of me and then you shot straight up in the air and disappeared! I'd be looking up, trying to figure out where you went, and then you'd land in front of me for an instant before you took off like a rocket, straight up and out of sight again. It was like you were on a pogo stick! You were bouncing so fast and so high I couldn't tell where you were going."

"I don't remember any pogo stick," I said, "but I was kind of bouncing around between different locations."

I briefly explained the fragmented flashes and odd simultaneous awareness of different locations I'd experienced and began to think that Sabrina's observations of a pogo stick made sense in an odd sort of way. "What if focusing my attention at one of my alternate Self locations blocks awareness of all the other alternate Self locations," I wondered. "A pogo stick is a good metaphor for bouncing from one place to another." Unable to draw any firm conclusions, I decided to experiment more with this multiple location stuff later, assuming I could figure out how to do that.

It was time for the tape exercise that would send all the participants to their first encounter with TMI-There to find the crystal, and then to visit the Reception Center. I found TMI-There easily and was met by Bob Monroe and Ed Carter. At Ed's suggestion he and I headed for the doors that led outside. On the way we stopped at a small table, where Ed called my attention to a bowl filled with medallions on beaded chains. The round, dark blue medallions were perhaps an inch in diameter, with the TMI OBE symbol in the center of a six-pointed star, both in raised relief and bright gold in color.

"Take one and wear it if you like," Bob said, "they're

giveaways people can wear like a necklace to identify themselves as TMI Explorers in their travels."

"Maybe later," I responded absentmindedly, and then we headed outside.

The countryside, with its glowing trees and mountains, looked just as it had on my previous visits here. Later I realized Ed had been trying to point out something new to me but I hadn't become aware of what it was.

Back inside the building I was surprised at the bluish cast of the crystal's light. I commented to Bob that it was different from the reds, oranges, and yellows I remembered from my previous Exploration 27 program.

"Of course," he replied, " didn't you notice all the blue light, spiritual types in the program this time?"

"You mean the crystal takes on the coloring of the participants?"

"Well, it is a group energy you're working with. So, yes, the crystal reflects that group energy in its color and some of its other characteristics."

Something behind me pulled at my attention and I turned to see Sabrina come clearly into view. She seemed to rise up through the ceiling and I followed her outside, through the roof. Spinning slowly around, I couldn't see her. Then, an incredibly beautiful Being with flowing, fluttering, shimmering silken wings flew slowly past me. Like a giant butterfly, it slowly moved through the air. I suddenly realized it was Sabrina. "What a beautiful, fancy set of flying gear," I thought to myself, as I moved up alongside her, flying along on her right. We made a long, leisurely sweeping turn to the right, which brought us over the roof of TMI-There. When we were directly over where the crystal was, inside the building below us, our flight together changed. Instead of a leisurely float through the air, we suddenly spiraled upwards in a tight, double helix. It was like we had encountered a beam coming out of the crystal's axis. Then we began rocketing upward in tight, intertwining, spiraling, flight. The acceleration was tremendous and carried us upward faster and faster until I lost awareness of our flying together.

When I regained awareness I was inside TMI-There, looking at Ellen and Ed Carter. Ellen had known Ed when he was physically alive and in an earlier conversation had said she hoped to contact him during the program. I decided to try to facilitate a connection between them. I could feel Sabrina standing nearby and sensed she was feeling a little "put out" in some way. I tried to get Ellen's attention to point out that Ed was standing right in front of her, but it was obvious she was completely unaware of his presence. A voice on the exercise tape prompted me to head for the Reception Center, and I decided I'd try to get Ellen and Ed together again later.

As I moved through the blackness, I saw a large swirl of tiny lights standing out against the backdrop of the blackness of empty space. It reminded me of what a galaxy looks like through a telescope. Moving toward it, I next found myself standing on the stone plaza at the entrance to the Reception Center. A vigorous looking young man wearing white shorts, shirt, socks, and tennis shoes was standing next to me. By the terry cloth sweat band around his head and racket in his hand, I judged him to be a tennis player.

"Excuse me," I addressed the young man, "I'm part of a group exploring the Reception Center. Mind if I follow along with an intake process?"

"Not at all, but I would prefer you remain invisible so you don't interfere with it," he replied. He motioned toward the oncoming crowd with his head, indicating a man who was approaching.

"No problem. I'm just here to observe and learn. I don't mean to make your job any more difficult."

The approaching man, who looked like he was in his sixties, was also dressed in tennis clothes. He looked fit for a man of that age, but I got the impression he'd had a heart attack and died while playing tennis. He was very confused as to where he was and why he was walking across an open field with other people. My tour guide called him by name, getting his attention and motioning him over like they were old buddies who played together all the time. After small talk about what a great day it was for a little tennis, the tour guide invited the newcomer to go looking for an open court and to play some tennis with him. The man agreed, but I could feel he was suspicious that something wasn't quite right about all this.

After walking through the Reception Center entrance, we came to area filled with tennis courts. The green surface of the courts had a fine, uniform texture, like a perfectly flat pool table, not a blemish even between courts. The nets were absolutely spotless with zero droop in the center, perfect nets. The whole tennis court scene was blatantly, obnoxiously perfect.

I followed along as the two men walked to an empty court and warmed up with a little casual volleying. The tour guide suggested it was time to begin playing and took first serve. In a disarming, young-jock way, he started bragging about his stupendous ace serve no one had ever returned. He kind of egged the newcomer on to the challenge of being the first ever to return his service shot. When the guy was pumped up to a hyperalert state in preparation for returning the serve, the tour guide was ready to introduce him to some aspects of his new environment.

"I call this my disappearing ace," he called out as he began the motion of his serve. The newcomer focused more intently, getting ready to return it. As the tour guide's racquet launched the ball, it didn't look a very formidable serve at all. In fact, it sailed at a rather leisurely pace toward the net. Then as it crossed the net, heading for the totally focused newcomer's forehand, it just disappeared into thin air. The newcomer's jaw dropped and he spun around quickly, looking behind himself to see if somehow the ball had gotten past him. Turning back toward the tour guide, he looked befuddled.

"See what I mean?" the tour guide called out. "Now pay close attention. Here comes another one."

He repeated the disappearing shot a couple of times until the newcomer was in a hyperalert state of confusion about how this was possible and wondering where the ball went when it disappeared into thin air. The tour guide moved toward the net, motioning the man over with his finger.

"Now I suppose, technically that's not an ace serve," he said chuckling, "hard to tell if it landed in or was a fault, but that's part of the difference, playing tennis here."

With that he launched off into a conversation I could see was headed to introducing the fact that tennis was a different game when played in nonphysical bodies. He was breaking the news to this guy that he was dead.

About that time the tape indicated it was time to return to TMI-There. I waved to the tour guide, knowing that even though I'd remained invisible throughout the experience, he was aware of my presence throughout the entire experience. Remaining invisible definitely made the process of observing easier than my experience during that first Exploration 27 program. I didn't need to find the Disappearing Room this time! Something else did seem a little odd, though. As the tour guide acknowledged my wave and departure, it looked like he was also continuing to talk to the newcomer, like he was somehow doing both things at once. It made me wonder if the tour guide was using an alternate Self awareness ability, something like I'd experienced in the earlier tape exercise.

Backing out of the Reception Center area on my way to TMI-There, I had the impression I was leaving the star-filled swirl of a galaxy, and once I was far enough away, I realized what I'd actually seen just before I arrived there earlier. The galaxy-like swirl of tiny lights wasn't a pattern of stars, they were people, people on their way to the Reception Center, having just left their physical lifetimes.

Nancy Monroe was waiting for me when I returned to TMI-There. As I stood now in front of her, I felt a flow of Pure Unconditional Love energy begin to move from her to my heart. It carried a message of healing into me, a healing for me, for Sabrina, and between Sabrina and me. It brought to mind my previous feelings that Sabrina and I were intruding into each other's space. I realized I have a history of intruding by jumping into someone else's space uninvited, and part of my reluctance to interact with Sabrina came from not wanting to repeat that pattern with her. When I'd fully realized the nature of my reluctance, I felt a surge of unconditional, loving acceptance from Nancy that dissolved and rinsed it away.

When Nancy moved away and disappeared, Sabrina came into view, standing in front of me. We hugged, each acknowledging the healing that had just taken place between us, and then stepped back from each other as the tape said it was time to return to C1 consciousness. We reached out toward each other, holding hands, and began to spin around the axis of our hands like we were on a playground merry-go-round. I could clearly see the open, loving smile on Sabrina's face. Delightful childlike feelings of play began to run through me as we spun and danced, first floating upward and then, slowly, continually, down toward C1.

When I found myself standing outside of my body, watching the two of us spinning and dancing, I felt White Bear tone a suggestion to remember my leaping lessons and move back into my dancing, twirling body. As I did, I experienced a strong sensation of spinning, seeing Sabrina's bright smile against the whirling blur of rushing blackness behind her. After a few jumps in and out of my spinning body, I stayed in it, spinning and dancing with Sabrina all the way back to C1 like we were a couple of playful kids. Childlike joy and glee flowed through me. At C1 we parted company and I remember remarking to her that I had no idea her steel and concrete exterior had such a delightful, softer side.

chapter 20

The Essence

At the beginning of the next tape exercise I arrived at my place in Focus 27 and found my usual group of friends sitting around the table, with Sabrina waiting there also. We had been talking during our cigarette break before the exercise and she'd expressed an interest in meeting White Bear. So I moved toward her, toning to White Bear to join us, and made the introduction.

Looking around for the Woman from Sensuous, I became confused about who she was; for a moment she and Sabrina felt like the same person. Then Sensuous/Sabrina stepped forward and suggested a walk. She took my hand just as Sensuous always did and we headed for the lake. It felt like walks we had taken before, but images of Sabrina and Sensuous kept fading in and out of each other as I gazed at the beautiful woman walking beside me. My confusion turned to alarm as I realized my openly drooling feelings toward Sensuous were still there when her image changed to Sabrina. What bothered me most was that Sensuous was a nonphysical woman. Somehow it was okay to express those kind of feelings with her since they couldn't spill over into my physical life. But Sabrina was a woman I knew in the physical world. This somehow made those same feelings both delicious and repulsive at the same time. I'm a happily married man and there was no room in my life for the trouble that can come from expressing such feelings to another woman who lives in the physical world. By the time we reached the water's edge, Sensuous was gone and only the image of Sabrina, tall and beautiful, stood next to me.

I felt extremely uncomfortable as we removed our clothes, getting ready to jump in for a swim. It felt inappropriate for the two of us, physically alive people, to be disrobing in front of each other, but that didn't stop me. We jumped in and splashed around like a couple of kids. Sabrina remarked that the water was delightfully warm and felt a little thicker than physical world water. I thought, "Of course it is! Why would anyone create a lake too cold to swim in? And being a little thicker than normal felt so much better as it caresses your body moving through it!"

With Sabrina on my right, we raced, swimming toward the center of the lake. When we stopped, she asked which rock Sensuous and I had made love on during the last program. Feeling embarrassed to admit it, wondering how she knew and where her question was heading, I pointed to the huge, flat-topped boulder at the water's edge on my right. Suddenly we were both sitting on top of that rock, my back to the lake, and Sabrina facing me.

Our naked bodies were glowing a brilliant mix of colored, swirling lights. I knew what was about to happen and felt conflict bouncing around inside me about it. We sat gazing into each other and I could feel the rise of sexual energy between us. As it built up, stronger and stronger, I felt more and more conflicted about joining with her. But the energy just kept building up between us until I began to feel my body sliding toward Sabrina as though pulled by a powerful magnet.

Part of me was trying to dig my heels into the surface of the rock to keep from sliding any further toward her; part of me was feeling an ever stronger desire to keep approaching her.

Continuing to slide toward Sabrina, I saw that her body was beginning to glow and radiate light, as was mine. When our bodies touched, I was still internally vacillating between feelings of resistance and no reservations. In our embrace, at times we felt like two physically bodied people making love. Other times our joining had no sexual flavor to it at all, just bursts of Pure Unconditional Love, exploding in brilliant flashes of light that illuminated the darkness for miles around. Still, I felt myself moving back and forth through my conflict of ethics about our nonphysical joining. I kept wrestling with feelings that vacillated between immersion in total, ecstatic bliss and pulling away in complete resistance to it. I could feel how my internal conflict blocked a total and complete, unconditionally loving joining with Sabrina and how it limited the flow of its power.

Then, as if somebody had flipped a switch, all of a sudden Sabrina and I were catapulted from the rock back to a standing position near my table with my entire group looking at us. It's true, chagrin can make a nonphysical body blush just as bright a red as a physical one. It felt like Sabrina and I had been caught making out on the sofa by our entire families when they unexpectedly stepped into the living room and switched on the lights. Everyone there just smiled, projecting a feeling like, it's okay, don't worry, kids will be kids. I can't say that really relieved much of my feelings of embarrassment!

Then Sabrina turned toward me and said, "Bruce, our joining doesn't necessarily have to be sexual."

I was puzzling over her comment when the tape suggested it was time to explore sensing the essence at TMI-There. I left my place to look for the CHEC unit I was physically lying in now. Landing in the room with the crystal, I moved through the kitchen and floated up the stairs to the second floor. When I was part way down the hall, something started pulling me backwards. It pulled me back down the stairs and left me standing in front of a table in a lounge area called the Fox's Den at the Institute of the physical world. So I decided to practice sensing the essence by moving into the table.

As I moved toward it, I became aware of Sabrina, standing on my right, and a powerful surge of sexual energy pulling us together. My internal conflict was back again, full force for just a few moments and then it disappeared in a puff of smoke. We turned toward each other with the feeling of sex-crazed lovers pulling us into each other. Wrapping our arms around each other, we embraced in the feeling of a full body kiss, the kind you feel as a lover's first kiss in that electric, ecstatic, sexually charged touch of lips that quickly spreads to your entire body. Turning her back to the table, I gently but firmly pushed her toward it until the backs of her legs were against it. In a fury of flying arms clothes flew through the air around the table. Sabrina slowly fell back onto the table, stretching out her body with an inviting smile that said, *now*! It seemed neither of us were paying any attention to the tape's suggestions to sense the essence of the table in our joyous thrashing around of top of it, but, perhaps it was that suggestion that started our bodies moving into each other's. We locked in mad thrashing bliss, and then sank together through the table toward the floor. Some minor fraction of my awareness took note of the feel of the wood and its texture as our bodies moved through it, but only because it gave boundary to the feeling of the single body we had become.

Still, my feelings of internal conflict of ethics pulled me in and out of this experience at times. Repeatedly, I found myself suddenly appalled at what we were doing and then

I wildly joined in again. Somewhere in this mix of bliss and damnation the voice on the tape suggested we move outside to continue our "sensing the essence" exercise outdoors. Sabrina and I separated into our own bodies, got up off the table and headed outside, where I lost track of her presence.

I was standing close to a very odd tree, looking closely at its bark. It had the appearance and smoothness of a poplar, but the color was too much toward a very dark green, almost brown. And though it felt smooth like a poplar, it looked more like the rough bark of an oak. What an odd combination! I couldn't see the tree's leaves, but I knew they somehow contributed to this crazy, mixed up version of a tree. Looking around for something to interact with, at the tape's suggestion, I settled on an odd-looking flower. So strange! Bright yellow shapes like a mixture of iris, lily, and orchid somehow looked like a daisy with very large petals. I was about to ask this flower's permission to alter its appearance when a bright yellow butterfly landed on its outstretched petals. Quickly switching my intent, I asked the butterfly for permission to alter it and then enlarged it to something half the size of a Cessna 150. As I climbed onto its back, I felt Sabrina climb up behind me.

The butterfly's huge wings seemed to move up and down in slow motion as we took off in a gentle climb to the right. High above the ground we took in the spectacular view of the countryside, passing over the buildings at TMI-There. After landing back near the yellow flower, we climbed off and the butterfly went back to its original size. As it sat on the flower, gently pumping its wings, another bright yellow butterfly came into view. I moved my awareness into the butterfly on the flower just as the other one began circling around it, immediately sensing it was Sabrina. Leaping into flight in the body of the butterfly I joined her in a kind of mating dance as we moved through the warm air and bright sunlight in spiraling flight with each other. When it was time to return to C1 consciousness, we began a lazy, spiraling flight downward. After a few moments the scene suddenly changed.

With the feel of ocean surrounding me I felt my body moving through the water in the smooth motions of a dolphin. I was swimming near the bottom, watching a small octopus moving along the ocean floor. I could clearly see the trail the little octopus was leaving in the sandy bottom as it moved along. After swimming closer to get a better look, I had the distinct impression of grabbing the little octopus with my mouth and swallowing it, feeling the satisfaction of a full stomach.

The scene suddenly changed again and I was one of two exotic tropical fish swimming in a slow spiral downwards toward C1. We were both holding each other in constant view as we swam in slow, admiring circles around each other. The iridescent blues, purples, and yellows of the other fish were brilliant and beautiful. As we continued this slow dancing swim downwards, I moved in and out of the fish's body. I alternated between being outside the fish's body watching two surrealistically beautiful fish swimming around each other and being inside one of their bodies. When inside the fish's body, my vision changed to a peculiarly unfamiliar state. It was like I could focus my attention to the view of either eye on either side of my head or focus on the view of both simultaneously. The simultaneous focus was very odd, like swimming through a world with a 360 degree view of my surroundings and receiving all the spatial information in that view, a very odd sensation. Sabrina and I continued our dance as these fish all the way back to C1 consciousness.

In the group briefing before the next tape I expressed my ethical conflict about my nonphysical experience with Sabrina to Franceen, one of the trainers. She responded by sharing her own experiences, which included a similar dilemma during her Guidelines program at TMI years earlier.

During that program she'd nonphysically met someone she described as looking like a Greek god. He showed up repeatedly in her tape exercises and she found herself more deeply aroused each time they met. She too was married and feeling the internal conflict of being attracted to this nonphysical man/god and did her best to resist acting on her feelings. At one point she'd asked the man for his name, to which he replied, Iasman. Thereafter, at every opportunity she asked other participants in the program if they were familiar with Greek mythology and if they'd ever heard of a Greek god called Iasman. Someone she spoke with asked her to write down the name, suggesting the spelling might help identify this mythological being. When she did, Franceen immediately understood what the name meant. It wasn't the name of a Greek god, it was I-as-man! The man she was nonphysically meeting was her masculine self. She explained that, through further meetings with Iasman, her desire to join with that part of herself as a whole, human being became clear. She came to understand it wasn't necessarily a sexual union, but rather a rejoining of the feminine and masculine within her being. She said that since that experience her life has never been the same.

I began to view my nonphysical experience with Sabrina in a new light. Before the next tape exercise began I gave some thought to my resistance to participate with Sabrina. "Could this be an experience similar to Franceen's? Was it an I-as-woman experience? What did that mean?" As the next tape exercise began, I found Sabrina standing in front of me. Holding hands, we danced and twirled our way around each other to the lake at my place in Focus 27. Then, like Olympic figure skaters, we gracefully glided and swirled on top of the lake's surface, sometimes laughing and rolling around like a couple of kids on the water.

Then our bodies transformed into dolphins, swimming side by side, just beneath the water's surface. While swimming very fast, we began taking turns leaping over each other, barely rising above the water. One of us would be just reentering the water as the other came out of it and passed directly over the other, barely touching, sliding over the other's body. I became curious about what we looked like from a distance. I moved out of my dolphin body and was fascinated by the complex crisscross, intertwining pattern, which had such precision timing it should have taken much practice to accomplish. Yet as we swam along, leaping over and gently caressing each other's dolphin bodies, it was pure, effortless joy. Then in one final leap together, we were back in our human bodies, sitting face to face, just as before, on top of the boulder at the water's edge.

Remembering this might not be the sexual union I felt so conflicted about, I tried to relax into whatever would follow. I felt the magnetic pull toward Sabrina (Iaswoman?) and our bodies began to glow in brighter and brighter yellow-white light. My feelings of resistance came up again as my body started sliding toward Sabrina. Then, strangely, I looked down and watched as my left arm fell off and landed on the surface of the boulder. As I watched, it slowly dissolved into white light. Then my right arm, my legs, my head, and my torso fell off, landed on the rock, and dissolved into white light also. Sabrina's body must have been doing the same because when I looked back at her after the last of my body disappeared, she was a brilliant, too-bright-to-look-at light—a long, slender, tapering glow of white light, radiating Pure Unconditional Love.

Then, suddenly, we moved together, intertwining our light bodies like two of those long, skinny balloons people use to make toys at county fairs. We were spiraling around each other like strands of DNA. Immersed in feelings of loving acceptance as One Being, we were enthralled with the dancing shades of pink, lavender, yellow, and blue swirling within us. All my internal resistance melted away in an indescribably powerful, heart-charging blast of Pure Unconditional Loving Acceptance as these two beings rejoined into One. Then . . .

CLICK: We are in the crystal at TMI-There and I can feel Sabrina standing next to me, on my right. We are both long, tapering ovals of light, and I can feel the colors of Sabrina's light swirling inside her. The feeling of our rejoining distracted me completely from the Focus 27 exploration of the Entry Director (ED) and Planning Center purpose of the tape exercise. I'd much rather have continued operating as the One Being we became earlier. Reluctantly, I headed for the ED at Dar's voiced instruction without much interest in delving very deeply into the contact. My attitude was, "If you have something to say to me, just shout it out, I'm not going to take the time to interview you, ED."

From what I remember the ED was talking about a pet theory of mine that the physical human brain is not where thoughts occur or memories are stored. As I only half listened he explained that the brain is more like a transducer, a broadcasting and receiving device that connects me to my I/There. That all memories of my physical world experiences are stored in the consciousness of my Disk or I/There, all my thoughts occur There. That I have physical reality access to them, via the filament of awareness, through the physical brain. That the common understanding of the brain as a storage device is incorrect. It's only a transducer that brings our memories, stored in I/There, into physical world reality. I'm sure the ED had more profound information for me, but I was still floating in the rapture of recombining as a whole being and wasn't paying much attention.

When we moved to explore the Planning Center, I still wasn't much interested in gathering information. Someone there was explaining that in my present lifetime my identity was a mixture of I/There personalities selected to perform in physical reality as a retriever. Whoever it was who was speaking made a point of explaining that my Disk or I/There was getting close to graduation and my retrieving role was important because all the "lost and stuck" members of I/There had to return to the Disk before graduation was possible.

Some of the parts of myself I had committed to retrieving were "hard targets," the guy said, very difficult to reach. Joshua, from my first Lifeline program, was pointed out as one of these, as well as the me who died after the house fire that killed my children and the me I saw buried at sea when I first created my place in Focus 27. It was explained that if I became more aware that I was a "Retriever type," carrying out my retrievals would lead to greater awareness of who and what I really am. This would assure my present lifetime identity wouldn't need to be retrieved after my physical death.

The Planning Center tour guide droned on, adding more information about the compression stage of reentry into the physical world. He suggested the "veil of forgetting" is one way to view this, but it's more accurate to say all memories always reside with the Disk, accessible by Probes via the filament of awareness.

I probably should have been paying more attention, but my attention was more focused on the blissful, loving connection with Sabrina/Woman from Sensuous/Iaswoman still hovering at my right side. I was still basking in the feeling of being Whole again. When it was time to return to C1 consciousness, Sabrina and I transformed into dolphins and began our slow, circling, swimming dance downward. Before we arrived we transformed into the two, brightly colored, exotic fish and finally into two dazzling lights. In all these forms we slowly, lovingly spiraled around and watched each other as two separate parts of a Whole.

During the break between tape exercises I noticed a slight aching in the center of my chest. Not strong enough to be a physical problem, more like spillover from the nonphysical world into physical experience. Some alternative medicine doctors call this kind of pain an energy blockage.

As I relaxed into the beginning of the next tape exercise, I asked, "What belief is blocking what energy and causing this pain in my chest?" The answer came drifting back to me in my thoughts. "Any belief that Love energy must be channeled through only physical world expression. There are many such beliefs that say Love can only be expressed in the physical world via a narrow band of expression. One of the more ecstatic of these is the one that says it can only come through physical, sexual union. Any of these beliefs serve to restrict the flow of Pure Unconditional Love (PUL) energy. Any belief that suggests PUL can't ethically be expressed within the physical world serves to block the flow. Any conflicting feelings like ethical or moral conflicts arising from your belief's interpretation of what Love is restricts the PUL that is actually flowing. Believing that what's flowing is sexual in nature is causing you to restrict PUL's flow. This is the cause of the ache in your chest." All this takes ten times longer to write than it did to experience.

Before I moved into Focus 10 Sabrina was once again standing in front of me. Holding hands and spinning, we danced and swirled our way to Focus 27. I felt a brief movement through darkness and then found myself alone, standing near the table at my place there. I saw the whole gang sitting in the hanging chairs around my table and noticed Sabrina standing off to my right, perhaps twenty feet away.

Something grabbed my attention and I turned back toward the table, looking at Rebecca where she was sitting on the opposite side of the table. After a few moments Rebecca got up out of her chair, walked around the table, and approached me. As she got closer she opened her arms, moved close, and hugged me. I felt something start to move from her to me and then I instinctively moved my body away from her, bringing my hands up to my chest as if ready to block a punch.

CLICK!

Something grabbed my attention and I turned back toward the table, looking at Rebecca where she was sitting on the opposite side of the table. I vaguely felt I'd just been in this scene, like a déjà vu experience. After a few moments she got up out of the chair, walked around the table, and approached me. As she got closer she opened her arms, moved close, and hugged me. I felt something start to move from her to me and then I instinctively moved my body away from her, bringing my hands up to my chest as if readying to block a punch.

CLICK!

Something grabbed my attention and I turned back toward the table, looking at Rebecca where she was sitting on the opposite side of the table. I remembered being in this same scene quite clearly, like living through my own instant replay. As Rebecca got closer, opened her arms, and hugged me, I felt something start to move from her to me and again instinctively moved my body away from her, bringing my hands up to my chest as if readying to block a punch.

CLICK!

You get the point. The scene CLICKED! back to the previous starting point several times and reran exactly the same sequence as before, like living through several instant replays over and over again. Then . . .

CLICK!

Something grabbed my attention and I turned back toward the table, looking at Rebecca where she was sitting on the opposite side of the table. As her hug approached, I began to wonder what it was that I felt moving from her to me and why I instinctively moved to block it. I started to focus my attention on the internal resistance I was feeling toward whatever she was extending. As I did I realized she was extending a flow of PUL to my heart. I realized my resistance was about physical world sexual attraction. It was like I had on sex-colored glasses. She was extending PUL to me but my glasses colored and changed its appearance, making me think this was a sexual overture. Since Rebecca was not sexually attractive to me, I was resisting the flow of PUL she was actually extending. I released my resistance and felt an incredible surge of PUL move through me from Rebecca's hug.

CLICK!

My attention is drawn to Sabrina, still standing off to my right. I have no memory of the previous experience with Rebecca. With a smile Sabrina begins walking toward me and extending her arms outward to hug as she approaches me. I feel something starting to move from her to me and then instinctively move my body away from her, bringing my hands up to my chest as if readying to block a punch.

CLICK!

My attention is drawn to Sabrina, still standing off to my right. With a smile she begins walking toward me and extending her arms outward to hug as she approaches me. I vaguely remembered I just being in this scene and am reliving an instant replay. I feel something starting to move from her to me and then I instinctively move my body away from her, bringing my hands up to my chest as if readying to block a punch.

CLICK!

This scene repeats at least three more times before it finally dawns on me to focus my attention on my resistance to Sabrina's hug. I still have no memory of the previous sequence with Rebecca at all. Then finally . . .

CLICK!

My attention is drawn to Sabrina, still standing off to my right. I fully remember all the previous scenes with her and focus my attention on whatever is moving from her to me in our hug. I look down at my hands, wondering what my resistance is about. I realize that since this X27 program began, I've been projecting an image onto Sabrina. It's the image of a tough-as-nails, corporate, Dragon Lady. I realize in all our previous tape exercise experiences she has been extending PUL energy to me as she is now. I realize I'm looking through my sex-colored glasses again and altering her extension of PUL energy into sexual energy. I realize my fears of intruding on her space and my ethical and moral dilemmas have been because I was misinterpreting PUL as sexual energy. I drop my hands and my resistance. A surge of PUL energy blasts through me and blissfully blows me away.

CLICK!

Pharon, my wife, appears on my right as if she's been standing out of view the whole time watching this entire episode. I have no memory of the previous sequences with Rebecca or Sabrina. Pharon moves toward me with a loving smile, wraps her arms around me, and we start to kiss. I feel something starting to move from her to me and then I instinctively move my body away from her, bringing my hands up to my chest as if readying to block a punch.

CLICK!

The scene repeats several more times with still no memory of the previous sequences with Rebecca and Sabrina until finally . . .

CLICK!

Pharon, my wife, appears on my right as if she's been standing out of view the whole time watching this entire episode. As she moves toward me I clearly remember I was just in this same scene before. I know I'm reliving an instant replay. When I feel my arms move up to block, I look down at my hands, wondering what my resistance is about. I realize my resistance feels like resentment. My sex-colored glasses have been altering the appearance of PUL coming from all other women, making it look like sexual energy. I've projected onto Pharon that because she is my mate I am not allowed to accept this sex-colored PUL from other women and I'm projecting my resentment onto her.

CLICK!

Rebecca gets up from her chair and moves around the table as Sabrina smiles and begins walking toward me. As they draw near, Pharon appears on my right like she's been watching this episode from the beginning. For the first time I clearly remember the previous sequences with all three of them. As all three of them reach me, I'm surrounded and hugged by three women extending their PUL to me. I feel no resistance. I extend the energy of Pure Unconditional Love back to each of them and we explode in a heavenly blast of warm, gentle feelings and showering sparkles of Love. In the bliss of that moment my physical body is crying in joy, grief, and gratitude. I feel great joy at allowing the energy of PUL to flow through me. I feel grief that I've allowed myself to color this Love into something it wasn't and thereby blocked its flow for so long. I feel gratitude for the unselfish, loving assistance of these three women who've helped me understand.

When the tape exercise was over I lay quietly sobbing so long there was no time to write any notes before going to the group debriefing. It really didn't matter. No notes are necessary, this is an experience I could never forget.

As I walked to the group debriefing I wondered how I would be able to integrate its lesson into my physical world existence.

chapter 21
Déjà Vu

Twirling again with Sabrina at the beginning of the next tape exercise, exploration of the Focus 27 Health and Rejuvenation Center, we arrived at my place in Focus 27. At the center I asked to be given my own personal healing demonstration, following the voice prompt on the tape. In the blackness a clear visual image formed that at first looked like a painting and then transformed itself into a puzzle.

It was a large, rectangular image that looked like a young child's jigsaw puzzle with oversized pieces. Each piece was a different color and texture—soft pastel colors, blues and purples, greens and reds, pinks and yellows. At their boundaries all the pieces were sewn together with colored yarn.

The healing demonstration image faded and I found myself back at my place, sitting across the table from Rebecca, Sabrina, and Pharon.

"So?" they all said in unison. And I understood it was time to review the previous tape's instant replay experience lesson.

I turned to Rebecca and began speaking.

"Rebecca, I allowed my sex-colored glasses to change my perception of your extension of Pure Unconditional Love (PUL) to me and resisted because I didn't find you sexually attractive."

She smiled and nodded.

Turning to Sabrina, I added, "I projected a hard-as-nails, steel, and concrete persona onto you. I couldn't conceive of such a person extending a sexual overture, but that was a misinterpretation of your extension of PUL. Out of my fear I was reading you wrong, and from fear of offending you I resisted that flow."

Sabrina nodded and smiled.

Then turning to Pharon, "I projected onto you that, because of our relationship, I was precluded from experiencing PUL from other women because my sex-colored glasses always changed it to look like sexual energy. As a result I felt resentment and resisted PUL energy from you because I wasn't allowed to receive it from others."

She nodded her head, indicating I correctly understood.

CLICK!

In the blackness the image of the puzzle again came sharply into view. While I was looking at it, a thought drifted through, "This is a metaphor for the fragmentation of a whole into separate, individual pieces." Then a hand appeared and its fingers grabbed the yarn between two pieces and pulled the stitches out between them. As the yarn was pulled out, the colors and textures of those two puzzle pieces merged and joined, forming one larger piece with the same color and texture. Thoughts floated into my mind. "Though the fragments appear to be separate, individual, and different, they were really parts of a Whole. As the boundaries between them were removed, an ever larger portion of that Whole was revealed." The visual pun didn't escape me, "As our boundaries are PUL'd, we discover we are all a greater whole."

Then that scene faded and I found myself in a darkened room with large overstuffed furniture, a fire in the fireplace, thick carpets and rugs on the floor, and intricate tapestries hanging on the walls. As I relaxed into the comfort and ambiance of the room, a very bright light suddenly flashed for several milliseconds, like a giant flashbulb it overilluminated the room with its stark, blinding glare. After several more randomly spaced flashes, I began to wonder what was going on. I asked this overpoweringly bright flash to explain its meaning. It kept flashing, washing out all the detail of the room with its brilliance all the way back to C1 consciousness without once giving me a clue. I left my CHEC unit not knowing the answer. To this day it's still a puzzle.

As I climbed into my CHEC unit Tuesday evening to retire, I noticed a strong aching pain in the center of my chest again. The more I relaxed to go to sleep the stronger it felt, until it became so uncomfortable I was unable to relax and go to sleep. I decided to open a dialogue with this ache to find out why it was there and what I could do to get rid of it.

"The ache in my chest is too strong to sleep, what can I do to get rid of it?" I asked.

"You might start by focusing your attention on it to determine what it is," some part of me answered.

I realized it was not physical. That's why it got stronger as I tried to relax into the nonphysical world of sleep. "It's some kind of blockage to the flow of energy through my heart center," I remarked.

"Perceptive of you," that part of me replied, "a major theme of yours for this program, don't you think?"

"Yes, I suppose so. What can I do to let the energy flow and get rid of this pain?" I asked again.

"Let it flow, obviously! Focus on it and let it take you to where the blockage is. Maybe the experience will be a useful exercise," that part of me commented dryly.

Focusing my attention on the ache in my chest brought an immediate awareness of Sabrina's presence nearby. She seemed to be projecting an extremely strong charge of sexual energy in my direction. Images started forming in my mind's eye that matched with the sexual flavor I sensed, and I felt the tiniest trickle of something beginning to move through my heart. Opening my awareness further to Sabrina's presence, I began to feel aroused and I suddenly shut down my awareness to the sexual energy I felt. The pain in my chest immediately intensified.

"You had it moving for a second there and then you stopped it. Why?" that part of me asked.

"It feels sexual and I'm still feeling conflicted about that kind of nonphysical encounter with someone I know physically who's not my mate," I replied. "Let me see if I can find a way around this one."

I opened my awareness again and tried to change the presence I felt as Sabrina into Pharon. I tried to allow my imagination to run with it, but it was no good. The harder I tried to alter the images into something acceptable to my ethics, the stronger the pain in my chest became. I gave up and pulled my focus of attention away from the pain.

"Well, that didn't work. It just made the pain more intense," I thought to myself. The other part of me was quick to critique my efforts.

"You didn't learn much from your experience with Rebecca, Sabrina, and Pharon today did you?"

"I sure thought I did at the time," I snapped back.

"How many times have you told other people that acceptance of a concept as a belief is completely different from learning by your own, direct experience?"

"But this is different! I have to do something my ethics say is wrong!"

"So tell me, how are your ethics different from your beliefs?"

I had me there!

"Okay, I'll try to go with it," I said reluctantly.

Focusing into the ache again, I felt Sabrina's sexually charged presence move into my awareness again. As she moved closer, my feelings of arousal became more intense. I let them build up quite a bit and then shut my awareness of them down again.

"Do I have to do this? Isn't there some other way to stop this blockage and let the energy flow?"

"Of course there are other ways. Lots of ways. But you're just going to have to do it in the way you are able to experience it."

"I'm not sure I can do this. What are my other options?"

"Well, you could just get used to the pain, I suppose. You probably won't sleep much tonight, but you could choose that way."

"But if I can't do this?"

"Then feel the pain of your blockage to the flow of Pure Unconditional Love energy. The choice is yours!"

I tried that for a short while, but it was becoming very uncomfortable.

"Okay, okay, okay! I'll do it!" I mentally yelled out.

"An attitude of relaxed abandon might be a good place to start," some part of me remarked.

I focused on the center of my chest and felt Sabrina's sexually charged presence approaching again. The air suddenly felt very warm, humid, and seductive, as the exotic ambiance of a steamy room began to take hold around me. As it came into view I could see that the floor-to-ceiling, glass walls of the room were dripping with warm condensation. Little rivulets of water broke loose here and there as they streamed toward the soft beige, polished terrazzo tile floor. The blackness of night behind the glass walls made them an impenetrable barrier, focusing all my awareness inside the room. It had the feel of an exotic jungle-theme atrium: palms, ferns, and vines growing everywhere, lazily draping themselves over mock fallen trees and covering much of the floor.

In the center of the room a sunken hot tub breathed clouds of warm, steamy vapor into the air. The beige tile of the room's floor seamlessly circled the round tub and disappeared into its gently bubbling water. An uncorked champagne bottle, nestled into a fancy silver bucket of ice, waited on the floor next to the softly bubbling water of the tub. Two crystal champagne glasses stood waiting to be filled, each resting on neatly folded white cloth napkins. Crystal ashtrays and freshly opened packs of cigarettes rested next to the glasses, waiting for "afterwards." I moved down from my floating overview, landing gently near the edge of the tub. I stood there, quietly drinking in the sensuality seeping from every pore in the scene, igniting my body with escalating feelings of sexual arousal.

Then I saw her, the Woman from Sensuous, in Sabrina's body, standing ten feet away, facing me. At the sight of her I am gripped in a feverish surge of raw, human desire. As she slowly moves toward me, I can see she's savoring every surge of energy the sight of the silken robe clinging loosely to her seductively swaying body shoots through me. I can feel something in my chest is beginning to bubble. Its effervescence is relieving my pain.

Sensuous/Sabrina stops, standing in front of me not a foot away, flooding me, engulfing me in flames of passion that pour into me through her smiling eyes. Standing perfectly still in front of me, her eyes are inviting, beckoning.

Reaching toward her, my hands slide through the opening in her luxurious, white silken robe at her waist and begin gently stroking the baby-soft skin of her sides. A fire of pure sensual passion bursts into flames in both our bodies. Whatever was effervescing in my chest now feels like a soft, continuous breath, flowing through my physical body.

My hands are like light fluffy feathers caressing, softly passing over her body. As they move upward, my arms are spreading her robe open wider and wider, exposing to the moist heat and passion in the air more of a body only meant to be seen by gods. Feathers slide seductively up-ward, stroking the sides of her breasts so lightly she might think the touch accidental, and an electric charge surges through both our bodies. When I reach her neck, my hands move outward over her shoulders and down her back just far enough so that her silken robe is released from her body and flutters silently to the floor in soft folds around her feet.

Now my hands are commingling with her hair, pulling her toward a deep, passionate kiss. We both turn and float, more than step, down into the hot tub's swirling cloud of vapor and sweet, warm, bubbling water. I feel first our faces, joining in a kiss, begin to pull us into each other's bodies. Our bodies totally merge into each other. White hot passion vaporizes the scene into a stunning, all con-suming blaze of the single white ball of light we've become. I realize there is nothing sexual in the bliss where we're floating, just unconditional, fully accepting Love that these two parts of the Whole now share in Being as One.

The scene fades and I'm alone in my CHEC unit again, basking in the flow of Pure Unconditional Love that is wafting through my body. Somewhere far away champagne is gently splashing into two crystal clear glasses. Somewhere gentle curls of smoke arise from matching crystal ashtrays at the edge of a hot tub amid smiles and laughter.

"Now that wasn't so hard, was it?" some part of me asked. "You did pretty well on the relaxed abandon part. Learn anything?"

"If I allow myself to see without my sex-colored glasses there's no ethical block to accepting Pure Unconditional Love for what it is, just the energy of Love."

"You might consider practicing that in your everyday life," some part of me advised. "Lots of opportunities to experience that energy, if you're open to it. Does wonders for one's perception."

All traces of the pain in the center of my chest were gone and had been replaced by a warm, gentle breeze flowing through my heart. I relaxed. Then I felt Sensuous/Sabrina floating toward me from my left. She floated down, gently stretching out her body beside me, resting her crossed hands on my shoulder, laying her head down on her hands. A warm, comfortable glow enveloped both of us and we drifted off to sleep.

chapter 22

A Visit with Ed Carter

I'd made a commitment to meet Ed Carter at the Education Center, though I didn't know exactly what we were going to do. Clearing my resistance to the flow of Love through my heart had boosted and cleared my perception. Without realizing it, I'd taken Ed's suggestion from our earlier meeting at my place in 27 to "make a point of opening a bit more to the energy of Love."

When I arrived at the Education Center in Focus 27, amid its familiar surroundings of high, book-filled shelves, Holodesks, and people milling around, Ed came into view almost immediately, standing just a few feet away.

"Well, glad to see you made it," Ed remarked. "Come on, I've got something to show you."

I followed Ed a short distance, feeling more than seeing the doorway into the Hall of Bright Ideas as we passed through it. I couldn't see the linear shelves of books morph into a hollow sphere. This time we just walked into the blackness of the room a little ways and then stopped moving. Right in front of me an image began to form in the blackness.

"It's a communication device," Ed said matter-of-factly. "It's to be used to allow communication between the physical and nonphysical worlds."

Unfortunately, patent application considerations prevent me from including a detailed description of the device here. Ed described each component of the device and its operating theory. After he finished, I repeated to him my understanding of all he'd told me to make sure I had it.

"Yep, that's how this thing works," Ed said, "you've got the principles. Now, when you first start working with this device, the voice might have a Morse code quality to it as we nonphysicals learn to speak through it. When you hear a Morse code kind of voice, you'll know you're on the right track."

"If we can get this thing to work, it looks like it has the potential to allow real-time conversation between our worlds," I commented.

"Development of that capability is the purpose of this proof-of-concept prototype," Ed remarked. "Once you've got it working you'll understand the operating principles more clearly and from there the device can be scaled down to something half the size of a bread box."

The image of the prototype faded into blackness and suddenly I was standing in someone's living room looking at what could have been a 1950s vintage radio. It was about the size of a large toaster, dark colored, and it had two round, white knobs on it. A young boy walked into the room and sat down in a chair next to the gizmo. He turned one of the knobs and I understood he'd just turned it on and brought the volume control to the place he usually set it. Then he put his hand on top of the device and turned the other knob like he was selecting a radio station. His grandfather's voice began talking to him. Grampa had been dead for several years and the boy liked to listen to him describe what it was like where he lived. It all felt normal and natural, no fear, just a talk with Grampa.

"What you're watching is a probable outcome of development of the prototype I've shown you," Ed commented. "Sony could manufacture these things by the millions if we get past the transition point."

"Transition point?" I asked.

"It's a timing problem. You see, the turn of the millennium is approaching and coincidentally so is the alignment of Earth with the energy of Pure Unconditional Love (PUL), which is the Earth Changes. Development and distribution of this device could be a critical piece of technology to help people in the physical world make the shift of awareness that's coming. It's technologically based, so a greater number of people might trust what comes from it. Look at it this way," Ed said, holding his finger three feet above a table that materialized beside him out of nowhere. "The distance from the table to my finger represents the number of physically alive people who are now on Earth, and only this many are presently open to PUL energy," he said, placing a finger on his other hand a fraction of an inch above the table. "Between my fingers is the vast majority of human beings who will have difficulty with the coming shift of awareness. The biggest percentage of those people will have difficulty making the shift because of their religious beliefs. It's very difficult to shift out of such a strong belief system, as you know."

"Yeah, my experience with Max's Hell and partnered exploring of other Hells and Hollow Heavens in Focus 25 taught me such folks can be very hard to reach," I commented.

He started moving the finger closest to the table slowly upwards. "As this part of the population increases we begin to approach a threshold, the transition point I spoke about earlier. Once the threshold number is achieved it will be easier for those between my fingers to make the shift. It's a lot like when television first came out, you remember?" Ed asked.

I did. "Somebody in the neighborhood bought one of those newfangled TVs and pretty soon others in the neighborhood began showing up on *I Love Lucy* night. People brought food and drinks and gathered around the tube to share a good time together. Pretty soon more people in the neighborhood bought TVs and it wasn't long before everyone had shifted to a life in which pictures and sounds came into their homes. It profoundly changed the way they lived their lives."

"You've got the idea," Ed smiled. "When developed to the point that a toaster-sized unit is possible, the same thing can happen with it that happened with television. Neighbors getting together to see the new toy, trying it out, experiencing communication between the physical and nonphysical worlds. If this happens in time, it can be an immensely important factor in the coming shift of human awareness. But there's a problem with timing I alluded to before."

"What's that?"

"Many religions, Christian in particular, believe the Messiah will return at or near the turn of the millennium. Many prophesy that before that happens Satan will make one last attempt to win all the souls for himself and that, in the ensuing battle, the Messiah will win. It's quite possible that when the device you're going to help develop begins to come into common use, it will be branded by many religions as that return of Satan. Things could get hairy. No telling what people will do if their fears are used against them and that's just what some religions will be doing, whipping up their fears in an effort to maintain control of the sheep in their flocks."

"That sounds a little scary," I thought out loud.

"If a high enough percentage of people are ready to make the shift when the device is ready for widespread distribution, there's a good chance it will work. If too few people have the new toy, it and they will be more easily vilified. If that happens, this technological communication device won't have a strong enough root to survive and it won't be of much use in the coming shift."

"So this could potentially be a critical piece of technology to assist the shift in human consciousness everyone else calls the Earth Changes."

"Yes, and the timing is a critical area."

"I'll give this information to every person I know who might be able to turn it into hardware," I said.

"Good, now let's turn to something else," Ed said. "How about we go find my old friend Ellen and I'll take another crack at getting through to her."

Moments later Ellen came into view. She felt very busy, intensely focused on whatever it was she was doing. I tried everything I could think of to break into her awareness to get her attention. I called her name, jumped up and down in front of her, all kinds of crazy things in an attempt to get her to look my direction.

"I'll stand behind you," Ed piped up. "We'll use the 'look through your eyes into hers' trick."

I felt Ed step behind me and begin looking through my eyes at Ellen. This trick has been used by many others during retrievals. You might remember from my second book that this is how Ribby finally got through to Chelik during his retrieval after the kiosk explosion that killed him. I could feel Ed intently focused on Ellen, standing not five feet away, intensely involved with whatever she was doing.

"Ellen!" I barked loudly, "Ellen look into my eyes!"

By loudly barking her name I got her attention for brief moments. She'd stare at me with a curious look on her face as if she had heard her name called but didn't really see me. Once she even looked into my eyes but there was no flash of recognition on her face. Then her face started to change. It looked like an accelerated aging process, in which her face looked progressively older and older and then disappeared.

"Ed, I don't think she was aware of either of us," I said after we had been at this for a minute or so.

"No, her focus is so tight we didn't get through to her," he remarked. "Thanks for helping for now and let's try again later on in the program."

With that, Ed wandered off into the blackness. Then, as I prepared to return to C1, Sabrina appeared in front of me. Reaching out, we took each other's hands and began spinning as we had before. We continued all the way to C1.

chapter 23

Multiple Location

Coincidentally, Franceen had a copy of a book whose author does research into electronic devices similar to the one Ed Carter showed me. In that book there were suggestions for improving the chances of hearing nonphysical voices in the white noise of a radio tuned between stations, the method the author suggested. The book also suggested developing the ability to feel compassion and love, as well as being helpful to others. Thinking it might somehow improve my perception during the program, I decided to focus on helping other participants. Over late night snacking and gabbing, Sabrina suggested that since we were meeting during every tape exercise, perhaps, we could do it together. She and I met nonphysically shortly after the next tape exercise began and we did our now-familiar spinning and dancing all the way to Focus 27.

By now I was having a pretty easy time of staying in my spinning, nonphysical body. I'd mentioned to Sabrina earlier that I'd been trying to help Ellen make contact with Ed Carter. So I wasn't surprised to see her come into view in Focus 27 almost immediately. I asked

Sabrina to stand behind me and try beaming Pure Unconditional Love energy through me into Ellen, as a way of opening Ellen's perception. After trying that for a few moments . . .

"I can feel your energy coming through me," I remarked to Sabrina, "there's definitely some kind of boost factor in doing this. She's getting more than just two times the energy of both of us."

"She knows me better than she knows you," Sabrina's voice behind me said, "let me get in front."

Sabrina whirled around in front of me and began beaming energy into Ellen. I began beaming through her, still wondering what this boost factor was.

"No, that doesn't seem to be getting through to her," Sabrina remarked, "let's try this." Sabrina moved to the opposite side of Ellen so she was between the two of us.

"There, now beam in," Sabrina suggested.

Something in Ellen's demeanor shifted. She wasn't so intensely focused on whatever she'd been doing before we arrived. A short time later Ed Carter appeared, standing in front of Ellen. She looked up, immediately recognizing him, and they began a conversation I couldn't hear. Sabrina and I continued beaming energy in for a while and then it was apparent that Ellen and Ed had made contact, so we moved off to the side.

"Think she'll remember her conversation with Ed?" I asked Sabrina.

"Well, even if she doesn't, at least they've finally made contact," she replied. "What's next?"

"Of the people in the program I'd like to help, Bill feels like the one who could most use a little boost. He nearly left the program early because he wasn't getting anything during the tape exercises. It reminded me of my first Lifeline program. What do you think?"

Moments later Ellen and Ed faded into the blackness and Bill appeared. He seemed to be gazing off into the surrounding darkness, unaware of our presence. We moved close to him and then stood facing each other with Bill between us. Sabrina and I reached out and held each other's hands, just as we been doing in our spinning before. We elongated our arms to make room for Bill and then began spinning. I focused on staying in my spinning body and looking over at Sabrina. We were smiling, laughing, and experiencing a joy like children must feel, spinning around and around. Suddenly, our bodies changed. Instead of feeling like I was a human body shape holding hands and spinning with Sabrina, we transformed into a hollow, spinning ball. I could feel my awareness everywhere within this hollow spinning ball and feel Sabrina's there at the same time. It was a very odd feeling, difficult to describe.

Watching Bill from my "hollow ball" perspective, I noticed a small ball of light beginning to form near what would be his heart. As the ball expanded, it seemed to be illuminating the space around him. When the ball of light was a little larger than his body, I could see him looking around, focusing his attention on something. I began to feel some concern about whether we were helping or interfering with Bill by what we were doing.

Then something else strange happened, something of a multiple-location experience. I found myself outside the spinning ball, watching Sabrina and me spinning around Bill. From this vantage point I could clearly see Bill engaged in some kind of interaction with his now-illuminated surroundings. I decided to leave that part of myself there, spinning around Bill while I went to do something Sabrina had suggested just before the tape exercise began.

I mentally pictured myself leaving my CHEC unit and moved toward the hallway entrance to the building, stopping between the two paintings I knew hung (physically) on the walls, one of Bob Monroe and the other of his wife, Nancy. The entire scene was in a uniform blackness, but I could feel the carved wooden dolphin I knew to be there along with the paintings. I got a sense of some kind of energetic shift between the paintings but couldn't get a fix on what it was. I moved outside the building and then back in, through that shift several times, but still couldn't get it.

While hovering in the hallway, trying to figure out what this energetic shift was, I bumped into Sabrina and we decided to check on Bill. When we got there, I could see myself in the spinning ball of light still surrounding Bill. We rejoined our hollow, spinning ball body, recharging and enlarging it. Then Sabrina and I left to check on Ellen and Ed Carter. We saw that they were still in conversation and stood watching them until it was time to return to C1. We went spinning and dancing from F27 all the way to C1.

During the break after the tape exercise, Sabrina told me that the energetic shift I'd found in the entrance hallway was her sister. They'd spoken on the phone the night before and agreed to try to meet each other there. She remembered moving outside the building and back in several times, suggesting she'd been following along with me while I was there.

Unbeknownst to me, Bill had remarked to one of the trainers after the tape exercise that he felt like he was spinning. During the debrief he reported that for the first time in the program he'd been aware of things around him and was happy to finally be perceiving in the nonphysical world again. I was relieved that what Sabrina and I did had helped. As the debrief ended I looked around the room, thinking about who to assist during the next exercise. I selected Vern, Bill, Dick, and Barbara.

When I next arrived at my place at Focus 27, White Bear was waiting.

"So?" White Bear toned. "You seem to be paying more attention to your landings."

"The leaping exercise from those towering rock spires wasn't just about releasing my physical world beliefs about C1 being down and Focus 27 up, was it?"

"You seem to be catching on," he toned back.

"When I felt myself still falling through the blackness and at the same time standing next to you on a rock spire below, I was in both places at once, wasn't I."

"That's your perception?" he toned back.

"The guy standing half in the rock next to you was me, wasn't it?"

"Well, he looked pretty familiar, don't you think?"

"You sneaky old Indian! Why didn't you just explain you were trying to teach me about this multiple-location business? I might have caught on a little quicker!"

"Preconceived notions," he buzzed.

"Preconceived notions?"

"You seem to have an extremely hard time getting past your ideas about how things are supposed to be. It blocks your perception something terrible. Without those notions you're much more open to learn directly from the experience. Besides, you seem to be doing quite well letting your direct experience teach you."

"Yeah, you're right. I just wish I could learn by listening to someone tell me how these things work. Wouldn't that be nice?"

"Perhaps, but then you would have little chance of discovering anything unknown to your teacher. After all, that's the reason for teaching anything in the first place."

White Bear's image faded into the blackness and Sabrina and I went to look for Vern. When we found him, I extended a filament of awareness from my solar plexus area to Vern. Moving through the filament to him, Sabrina and I spun a ball of light around him so his surroundings would be illuminated. I left an alternate Self spinning around him, while I also returned to my "central-Self" location. I repeated this process with Bill, Dick, and Barbara, then returned to my central-Self location and observed all four of them simultaneously. These balls of light were all in front of me and a little below my central-Self location. I could see them all clearly and was able to be aware of all my activities at once.

Once in a while I'd note that a ball of light had gotten smaller around one of them and would shift my awareness to the alternate Self that I'd left spinning around them. Joining that Self, I spun up the ball to be larger and brighter and then shifted back to my central-Self. Then I experimented with keeping my awareness at the central-Self location while I simultaneously joined my spinning alternate Self around one or more people to recharge it. I pretty much ignored the stated purpose of the tape exercise we were supposed to be doing and continued to play with observing various facets of my new, multiple-location toy for the entire exercise.

chapter 24

2ndGathgroup Again

I approached our first tape exercise excursion to Focus 34/35 with feelings of anticipation. Since my last contact with 2ndGathgroup a year earlier, I'd wondered what happened to them after our Pure Unconditional Love experiments. At times I'd worried that their clicking out during those experiments might have had disastrous results for 2ndGathgroup's home world population. I hoped I'd be able to find them again during this Exploration 27 program a year later.

During the prebriefing Franceen asked me to introduce the group to the Whooaah exercise I'd seen in the previous program. Holding hands in a circle, we Whooaah'd until I could feel the energy of the group come together in joyous celebration. Then we all left for our CHEC units for what was for me a return to a nonphysical reality Bob Monroe had called the Gathering in his second book, *Far Journeys.*

During the shift from C1 to Focus 27, one of the trainers, Joe, joined Sabrina and me in our spinning, dancing joy. When we reached the crystal at TMI-There, the other program participants gathered in a circle. Holding hands around it, we repeated our Whooaahing in this nonphysical world. In moments energy began building in the crystal; then we were showered in its explosion of colors and light.

After several cycles between the crystal at TMI-There and the Earth core, we made the leap to Focus 34/35. Arriving, I saw a large, white circular structure that from the outside resembled an ancient coliseum with huge windows between white stone columns. I remember seeing a similar-looking structure, a space station in the movie *2001: A Space Odyssey.* It looked like a huge, white bicycle wheel slowly spinning around its central axis. Inside this structure, white overstuffed furniture sat near the windows. Telescopes were also placed near the windows and, looking out, I could see planet Earth floating in the blackness of space below. The place had a man-made feel to it. After spending half a minute or so looking around inside this empty space station, I moved outside to explore.

I first saw eyes, like the wide-open, curious eyes of a gorilla. The high squeaky voice of something I'd encountered a year earlier came into my awareness, followed by his low-pitched voice companion. We exchanged greetings. I was a little surprised they remembered me. Then a huge snail shape drift by in the blackness above me, followed by something that looked spiderlike from underneath it. A long cylindrical object with a dish antenna on one end floated by, followed by lots of cone-shaped objects and something that looked like a flower. I didn't try to make contact with any of these, I was looking for someone else. Then I spotted the 2ndGathgroup spokesman and his ship again. I was overjoyed at seeing them and moved closer so we could open communication, hoping to get answers to some of my questions.

Something about 2ndGathgroup had changed. It was almost as if I was experiencing a friendly feeling of welcome from a group that last year hadn't a clue what feelings or emotions were. I began toning my greeting to him.

"Romba, pop, pop, squeeeeeeek!" I toned, saying something like, "Boy am I glad to see you guys again," and filling him in on my concerns about our interaction.

"Bruce, the toning is no longer necessary," the spokesman replied in perfect American English, "it's been a year, after all, since our last meeting. In that time we've learned to communicate in your language."

He said it so matter-of-factly, yet I could have sworn it had the feel of an Englishman's deadpan humor delivery.

"That's great!" I responded. "There's so much I want to talk to you about! Like what happened after our interaction last time. I've been so worried that our experiments might have had some kind of disastrous results."

"There will be plenty of time to talk about that in the next tape exercise," the spokesman said. "Take the time now to explore and do what you need to be doing. Come back in the next tape exercise and we'll be happy to share with you."

"Oh, okay. Yeah, there are a few people in my group I wanted to check on. Maybe lend a hand if they need it."

"We'll be waiting right here for you when you get back," the spokesman said.

As I turned to home in on one of my group members, I remember wondering, "Did he say 'happy to share with me?' Last time he wouldn't have put it that way. Something about 2ndGathgroup has changed."

After the tape exercise the level of energy running through my body was so strong my body felt hot to the touch. It felt much the same as the result a year earlier using Whooaah power to charge up for the Focus 34/35 exploration!

During the debriefing many group members commented on being in the coliseum place with windows and telescopes. As I listened to their descriptions, I began to feel lots of pieces coming together. It was my impression that this coliseum/space station is something that is being assembled as a meeting place, a place human Explorers can use as a "target" in Focus 34/35, very much as TMI-There is used to facilitate working in Focus 27. A meeting place between human Explorers and other intelligences of the Gathering perhaps.

Thursday morning finally arrived and I anxiously awaited the beginning of the next tape exercise, holding the spokesman's promise we would meet again during it. Sabrina wasn't with me this time as I shifted toward TMI-There. Moving through the various focus levels, I became aware of all the alternate Selves I'd spun off previously to assist others in the program. After expanding my awareness sufficiently to bring them all clearly into view, one by one I consciously pulled them all back into my central-Self location. There was a popping sound, like the cork coming out of a Champagne bottle, as each Self returned and reentered. I began wondering if it was all right to do this, feeling concern about withdrawing my support from others in the group. Yet, it felt like I had to do it to get all my awareness back in one central location. I was pondering this as I arrived at TMI-There. Bob Monroe and Ed Carter were waiting for me, both smiling.

"Don't be too concerned about pulling your alternate Selves back in," Bob said. "It was necessary as preparation for your contact with 2ndGathgroup. Having gathered up your Selves like that will give quite a boost to your awareness level."

"I still feel like I might have hindered someone else's progress in the group," I responded.

"It might help to think of it as helping while you could," Ed said. "Right now it's more important that you're at your best."

"By the way," Bob piped up, "you're right about the coliseum/space station. It's a construct in Focus 34/35 to be used by Explorers from both humankind and intelligences from the Gathering. It can be used in a future TMI program that will focus on Focus 34/35 exploration in more detail."

"I thought so, but from what they said the trainers didn't seem to want participants in this program focusing attention on it that way."

"All in good time," Bob replied. "All in good time."

"It took some fancy footwork to get you into this program," Ed said.

"I noticed! Lots of Celestine Prophecy coincidences," I replied.

"It was important that you and Sabrina met and got to know each other," Ed went on. "It's important to your future, her future, and the future of TMI. In addition to you completing the book you're writing, she's got one to finish too. There's also much work to be done on the communication device I showed you at the Education Center."

"I'll show it to anyone interested in such things," I assured Ed.

"There's more to it than that, but for now it's time to focus on your connection with 2ndGathgroup."

I left TMI-There and headed for Focus 34/35, finding the 2ndGathgroup and its spokesman almost immediately. I felt relief at getting in contact with them.

The previous year the spokesman had said they were members of an intergalactic federation sharing information regarding the Earth Changes with others in that group.

"We've become teachers, translators, or transmuters, if you will," he now said. "We have experienced great change since our last contact with you and we are passing along to others here Gathered what we learned as a result of that contact. We teach and explain what these Earth Changes are and what they mean. We've become disciples of Pure Unconditional Love here amongst the

Gathering. We are able to communicate this with a far greater scope of intelligences than humans can since we are more like some of the others Gathered here."

I asked what proportion of those Gathered were Earth school graduates. The previous year the spokesman had responded that their numbers were few but their power great. This time he said, "We are graduates of the Earth school! Our time in it was short and we learned the lessons very fast. Very soon after our experiments with you last year all members of our race graduated from the Earth school. We are a telepathic race and the lesson of Pure Unconditional Love passed to all of us very quickly.

I began to feel bathed in the gratitude of all members of the 2ndGathgroup toward me and toward all humans. I was overcome with emotion at their gratitude and got so choked up I had difficulty speaking out loud to record notes in my voice-activated tape recorder. The feeling of gratitude coming from them was overwhelming.

"Bruce," the spokesman said with quiet urgency, "we are a sensitive race. Your emotional radiation is far too strong for us. Could you please attenuate your radiation level? We are having great difficulty maintaining contact with you under its influence."

I stopped talking and tried to regain my composure. After ten or fifteen seconds I was still having a hard time smoothing out my emotions.

"Bruce," with more urgency in his voice this time, "please attenuate your radiation level! You're frying us!"

In another ten seconds or so I felt my emotional level dropping down a little, calming some.

"There, Bruce, that's better," the spokesman said. "We can maintain awareness of our contact with you at that level of your radiation." And as I calmed down a little more, "That's much better, we can now fully open up to you again, thank you."

"Something is very different about you. You guys don't feel the same as you did last year," I blurted out. "The cold, emotionless feeling is gone."

"Of course," the spokesman replied, "as a result of our previous contact with you and those other members of your group, we are now an emotionally sensitive race. Our telepathic ability spread that capability to every member of our race soon after the experiments. If it happened on Earth the way it did to us, you could expect the population of the Earth to increase by half the present total nine months later," he said with a chuckle.

I still didn't fully understand the implications of what the spokesman had said. I went on asking him the questions voiced on the tape.

"How do you identify yourselves and your current locale?" I asked.

"We are from a home world that orbits a distant star," the spokesman replied. "Its name is not important. Its location is not important. What is important is that our consciousness is enveloped in Pure Unconditional Love. That is the most important thing for any race anywhere."

"And what is your interest in being Gathered here?" I asked.

"Our interest is in spreading understanding of Pure Unconditional Love to other alien races," he stated. "As I said before, we are graduates of the Earth school. From our perspective the purpose of this school is to teach all who attend it to experience and express Pure Unconditional Love to an ever greater capacity.

"That's the purpose of the Earth school?" I questioned.

"As graduates that is our understanding, yes," the spokesman replied. "Alignment of the Earth's Core Crystal with a distant source of this energy was foreseen before your school opened its doors. It's no accident the energy of Pure Unconditional Love is pouring into your school now, as humankind reaches the pinnacle of its purpose.

We now live in this energy as you and other Earth school graduates may some day."

"How do you spread this understanding?" I asked.

"I cannot explain this to you in terms we would use to describe it to others like us, other telepathic races. To explain it in human terms, we send expeditions to other home worlds. In human terms we fill many of our ships with members of our race and send them to the distant home worlds of other alien races. Some of these are in the physical Universe you know, some are in other dimensions. We send many ships to the far reaches of the known Universe and beyond to carry out this mission of spreading awareness and understanding of Pure Unconditional Love throughout. We came here to the Gathering as Explorers. We came here looking to understand this thing that was happening to Earth, to this race called humans. We came without knowing that what is happening is a birth of something extending far broader than the farthest reaches of human consciousness. We now understand we are a part of this birth. It is happening to us and to others also. We now understand we are a part of the process of birthing awareness of Pure Unconditional Love into the farthest reaches of Consciousness."

A year ago when I asked 2ndGathgroup if they had a message for Earth's inhabitants, the spokesman had talked about huge numbers of humans shifting into the nonphysical world of the Afterlife. Now his message was completely different.

"It is of the utmost importance that Earth's inhabitants learn to experience and express Pure Unconditional Love energy to a higher and higher intensity. This is the mission, the duty, the purpose of all those living in the Earth system. The people of Earth are bringing this into awareness not just for themselves but for all beings to promote what it does in the relationship between its Selves. Our message is to keep up the good work, continue expanding your understanding of Pure Unconditional Love, and continue pouring it out into the Universe. We, as one of the Gathering's first recipients of this gift, will continue to spread this understanding to the far reaches and beyond."

The emotional impact of what the spokesman was saying began to sink in. I began having a little difficulty maintaining my composure as I felt the gratitude of many directed at all humankind for its mission.

"Bruce, we are now an emotionally sensitive race. We very much appreciate that you are emotionally affected, but the radiation of your emotional energies is too strong for us. You need to attenuate your radiation level again please."

When I had smoothed a bit, I continued asking tape-prompted questions. Last year the spokesman had shown me the approach of a previously unknown comet in response to my request for a sign his information was correct. This time his answer was twofold.

"Before you entered this program you had a conversation with Ellen about the books you are writing. She told you your subject matter was timely because the question of the Afterlife's existence seems to be 'written in the sky for all humans to see and wonder at.' Humans as a group want to know about their existence beyond the physical world in the Afterlife, as you call it. Human consciousness has a widespread intention to move past its limiting, physical existence to expand into a new home you would call nonphysical. That this desire on the part of human beings is so prevalent is evidence of the strengthening alignment of the Earth's Core Crystal with the distance source of Pure Unconditional Love."

"I don't see the connection."

"Bruce, experiencing and expressing Pure Unconditional Love to a greater and greater degree automatically opens human perception to realms beyond the physical world."

"So?"

"The Earth Changes alignment is increasing the capability in humans to experience and express Love. This automatically opens more humans to perception of the nonphysical world. This is bringing experiences of such perceptions to an ever increasing number of human beings. That's what is generating such widespread interest in knowledge about the Afterlife. So many more people are having these experiences that it is getting talked about and written about by a far wider portion of the human population then ever before in your history.

"We have given you other signs (referring to the comet last year and huge population shifts to the Afterlife) at other times. We did not understand then. We saw this as purely a physical world event. We did not understand Pure Love as anything but an energy, not much different from heat or light. Now we understand more about these Earth Changes and the process of birthing Pure Unconditional Love into the Consciousness they represent. The sign we would give is what your friend Ellen has said. It is written in the sky."

I felt a shift in the tone of feelings of the spokesman and the rest of 2ndGathgroup's crew. Then the spokesman continued.

"Bruce, as another sign that what we have told you is true . . ."

I saw the entire crew, everyone in their ship stand and turn, facing me.

"This sign is given not to you, Bruce the individual human, but to you, Bruce, as a representative of all humans."

With a gesture of his hand the spokesman pointed to the standing crew.

"These are the same crew members who went through the experience with you a year ago. We'd like to demonstrate a result of those experiments to show you what we've learned since then."

285

There was a short silent pause as I looked over the crew, wondering what would happen. Only those of you who have been near the detonation of high explosives will have a hint at what I felt next. When high explosives are detonated, something odd happens. A shock wave blasts through your body at about seven hundred miles an hour just an instant before the horrendously loud noise reaches your brain through your ears. In that instant you have almost enough time to realize the horrendous noise is coming before it hits you.

Just after the entire 2ndGathgroup crew stood and faced me, I felt that seven hundred mile per hour shock wave pass through me. In that instant I was confused, because instead of the horrific feelings of a bomb blast, I felt a whiff of Pure Unconditional Love pass through me with the shock wave. Then the full force of it hit me like the explosion of a bomb. I was totally and completely blown away. The force of their blast of Pure Unconditional Love blew me twenty light years away in between ticks of the clock. My shoes were left where I had been standing an instant before, but they were now smoking wisps of Pure Unconditional Love, rising, curling up from where canvas and rubber had been. The meaning of their demonstration was quite clear.

In the time since our meeting a year previously 2ndGathgroup had learned about the emotional impact of Pure Unconditional Love. Their dazzling, devastating display of its power left no question about their ability. I couldn't talk for a solid two minutes. Just an occasional "oh god!" squeaked out of my vocal chords as wave after wave washed through me. I was completely overcome. It felt like every member of their race, those in the ship, those on their home world and everywhere else were pushing gigawatts of Pure Unconditional Love energy through me. Gradually, they let the level come down. When I had calmed down, the spokesman continued.

"We return this gift of Pure Unconditional Love to all people of the Earth. We are with you in your mission. We will continue to beam this gift of Love to all people of Earth in gratitude for our receiving it and in the hope it will help you all on your path to a greater ability to experience and express it. As I said before, we are graduates of the Earth school. We understand that the purpose of that school is to teach all who enter to experience and express Pure Unconditional Love to a greater and greater degree. As graduates we, like human graduates, have the desire to spread this teaching as far and as wide as possible."

Dar's voice on the tape called us back to TMI-There and then back to C1 consciousness.

When I'd shifted my awareness fully back to my CHEC unit, I lay there, soaking in that joy. Yet I felt sadness. I realized it was the same bittersweet sadness and yearning to feel that strength of Pure Unconditional Love I had sensed in 2ndGathgroup the previous year after our experiments. A part of me remembered what it feels like to be joined in that way, to be joined to the other parts of myself in the energy of Pure Unconditional Love.

chapter 25

Last Contact

In the next tape exercise, the last of the program, I moved quickly to Focus 34/35 and reconnected with the 2ndGathgroup spokesman.

"Your radiation has attenuated nicely after our little demonstration," he said.

"Thanks to a little tree hugging during the break," I remarked. As promised, the spokesman began to talk about some of the immediate repercussions of our experiments the previous year.

"There are similarities and differences between ours and the human race. Our existence is not so neatly divided between physical and nonphysical. Members of our race are in constant, telepathic communication with all other members. This includes members who, in human terms, are no longer physically alive. We maintain contact in this situation. Not that we have a physical existence like humans, but in your terms this is how I would explain it."

He continued, "Shortly after the experiments last year we produced something you might call training films with which to acquaint our race with human ways of expressing this Love energy. You could think of this like a public service announcement on television. We in a sense broadcast to all our members the image, for example, of two human beings kissing. In our 'training films' these images were accompanied by the feeling of this energy. These were what you might call documentary films, showing members of our race how human beings live. So in our form of physical existence our race learned to use kissing as a means of expression also."

I became confused several times during the spokesman's explanation as he attempted to translate his race's experience into physical world, human terms. He took several cracks at it, doing his best to explain activities of his alien race in human terms I could understand. He was careful to point out that this was not how it actually was for them, but was the best he could do to explain their existence.

"After all," he said jokingly, "we are aliens! As beings alien to humans it is difficult to explain our existence to humans in precise terms. We are alien to your race, as you are to ours."

In human terms their learning to kiss, though the spokesman was careful to point out that's not exactly what they did, brought about other changes. Kissing is a means of expressing Love energy between individuals. A year ago any attempt at individual expression led to complete and utter chaos in their group that sounded like a thousand turkeys "squabble, squabble, squabbling" in a big tin can. Through their form of kissing they began to learn to express themselves as individuals. Their race now has incorporated some level of individuation. They are still a telepathic race with no way to hide any of their thoughts and feelings, but somehow their expression of Love by individuals doesn't interfere with the group mind activities.

In the middle of my conversation with the spokesman the voice on the exercise tape interrupted with the suggestion that I ask for a key phrase that describes what my contact at the Gathering has learned.

"We pass on all our learning not through our words, but through our acts of Pure Unconditional Love," the spokesman replied. Then he continued to tell me more about the effects of our experiments.

"As you attempt to perceive what happened to us as a direct result of our experiments last year," the spokesman said, "please do not become concerned or emotionally upset at what may have happened in your visualization of it in human terms. For us this was the birth of an energy within our entire race for which we are most grateful. We made a giant leap in consciousness over a very short span of time. We went from a race of emotionless beings to a race of beings living within the energy of Pure Unconditional Love. Unlike humans, our experience of this is not tainted by the polarities of the human school. Essentially, we went from ordinary beings to your version of Heaven on Earth in an instant, compared to the long struggle of humanity to harness this energy, to . . . to understand it . . . to share it . . . to live in a pure state of Unconditional Loving Acceptance. It has moved us to your version of Heaven on Earth. Please do not be concerned."

"Perhaps I misunderstood your meaning last year when you said huge portions of Earth's population would be dying and moving to the nonphysical world," I said.

"Perhaps," came the reply.

"The device Ed Carter showed me could move the awareness of physically living human beings to the focus levels of the nonphysical world without all the dying."

"Perhaps."

Then the spokesman began to talk about effects that occurred a little while after their initial disruption. Images of pollination of flowers by bright specks of light buzzing around the universe formed in my mind.

"After we had shifted to living in this Heaven on Earth

state of Being, we felt a strong desire to share what we'd learned with other telepathic races and civilizations that lacked, as we had, the ability of emotional understanding. To carry out this work we first assembled what you might call a documentary rote of our experience. It contained all the information, starting with our first observations of the Earth Changes, showing the experiments we carried out with you last year, the disruption it caused, and our present existence as a continuingly evolving result.

"Many we communicated with could not understand how such a calamity could be viewed with such positive importance. In our contacts we do our best to give assurances that what may be viewed as a calamity from the outside was well worth the price we paid. By our experience we are able to mitigate these calamitous events for those we teach, since our way of being is closer to theirs.

"We have in some cases taught a form of what humans might call meditation to other telepathic beings as a way of preparing them for the way in which they will receive this understanding. In human terms, you might say we are able to get every being on the entire planet to sit or lie down in a safe, comfortable place in which to experience this Love energy. A planetary holiday, perhaps, that is how a human could understand this. During this planetary holiday, two of our race move into the body space of volunteers from the receiving beings. They are like us. They are telepathic beings and experience of this Love energy moves into their consciousness as it did for us during your experiments with us. That is all I have to say on this point, Bruce, unless you have another question."

"Thank you for your explanation. It seems our little experiments did cause some type of disaster for your race. This has weighed heavily on my mind," I replied.

"As I have said," the spokesman responded sympathetically, "our telepathic nature means, in terms a human can understand, that our existence is not so neatly divided between physical and nonphysical realms. Our 'calamitous disruption' would be by your standards no more than a period of disorganized thinking. Do not concern yourself. We are grateful for the gift we received with your assistance."

"Thank you. I am curious about other aspects of the differences between your race and mine. For example, how does your race reproduce itself?"

"It is difficult to translate into human terms. There is a joining that results in a new being, but you might view this more as a factory. Perhaps something akin to cell division. A 'cell' within our being in effect divides, producing a new being. We do have a populated home world where we exist in ways similar to humans," the spokesman replied. "And I sense your next question. You are curious if those on our home world 'work for a living.' One must work to provide sustenance for the body. Yes, we have something akin to your understanding. But again, we are an alien race and there is quite some distance between our ability to explain our way of being and your understanding, when you have no point of reference."

A voice on the exercise tape cut in, saying it was time to return to TMI-There, time to say good-bye. I beamed a short blast of Pure Unconditional Love energy to the crew and then directed one at the spokesman. When I'd attenuated my other human radiations that usually accompany good-byes, I continued. "I am so grateful to you and your willingness to share your experience with me," I thought out to the entire 2ndGathgroup race. "I hope to be seeing you again."

"If not, at least know that sharing human consciousness's purpose of bringing Pure Unconditional Love energy to the far reaches of Consciousness is one we aliens share with you," the spokesman replied. As the scene faded, I could have sworn I felt from him the very human feeling of sadness we all feel at the parting of friends.

From TMI-There I went back to my place in Focus 27 after a short final tour of several of the centers in Focus 27. When I arrived, the whole gang was waiting there, including Sabrina, who was standing off to my right. The Woman from Sensuous stood up from her chair and walked to where Sabrina was standing. Then the two of them merged into each other and they stood there smiling.

"At the beginning of this program you asked about its purpose," they said. "Remember?"

"Yes, I remember hearing 'knowledge of Self' in response to my question," I replied. "And you two have certainly helped me understand something I became aware of at the very beginning of the program. It kind of fits together with something the spokesman said about the Earth Changes."

"What's that?" they asked, as if they didn't know.

"He said capability to experience and express Pure Unconditional Love automatically opens one's perception to the nonphysical world. I now understand that at the beginning of every TMI program I've attended that's what I've been trying to do. The platonic, yet sexually colored feeling I search for is really a search for a woman willing to share with me in building the energy of Pure Unconditional Love. Those feelings were my sex-colored-glasses' interpretation of Pure Unconditional Love energy. I was unknowingly trying to build up the flow of Pure Unconditional Love energy to boost my perception during the program. That's what I've been doing all along."

"Now that you know, perhaps you can use this technique more consciously in your everyday life. There are certainly lots of opportunities do so," they replied.

"And Soulmates, I see what they are now," I blurted.

"Really!"

"Everyone, as a Whole Being, is both masculine and feminine. In the physical world we live in a body that accentuates the traits of one side and reduces the traits of the other. We run around looking for the other half of ourselves, thinking it is living in a human body of the opposite sex. All this trying to find your Soulmate stuff is really searching for the missing half of our selves, in my case, my feminine side. That's what you were referring to, Sensuous, when you told me there was a surprise waiting for me when I remembered your identity. You are the feminine side of my Whole Being. You are me!"

"There are still a few surprises to come as you remember my identity," she replied.

"Sabrina, I was so confused early on by how I reacted to our relationships in the physical and nonphysical worlds. I'm grateful to you for physically embodying Sensuous and helping me struggle through the internal conflicts that were brought to my awareness. You made Sensuous *come alive* in the physical world. My sex-colored glasses painted Pure Unconditional Love into something my beliefs caused me to block. I'm so grateful."

"You're welcome and, I might add, you weren't the only one who benefited," she replied.

The tape exercise voice interrupted to call us back to C1 consciousness for the last time in the program.

"Before we go, how about one more trip to the lake," I thought out to Sabrina/Sensuous. "There's someone who lives there I'd like to introduce to Sabrina."

"You mean the dolphins?" she replied. "We know about the dolphins."

She/they approached and we walked arm in arm away from the table, bathed in the feeling of Bob, Rebecca, Tralo, and White Bear, who were standing and cheering. At the water's edge Sabrina and I stood looking into each other, smiling.

"We're both going in with our clothes on?" came to mind, like a thought we both shared at that moment. Our smiles broadened, our bodies jiggling every so slightly as we giggled away physical world feelings of embarrass-ment. Then our bodies fell away, like the peelings falling off pieces of fruit, leaving us floating side by side as two long, slender, brilliant orbs of white light. Still by the shore we, as two lights, moved into the same space as each other, into One Light, One Being.

Now, I could say that when we dove into the lake and swam toward the middle, we had all the body sensations of being a dolphin. I could say I felt the full length of our spine rhythmically undulating through the water. I could describe it as swimming to the middle of the lake and be-ing greeted and nuzzled by the ring of dolphins who live in there. Saying it that way all would be true.

But I could also say that a Whole Being, the rejoined parts of a Greater One, moved through eternity in the joy of being Pure Unconditional Love. In our travels through eternity I could say we are greeted by the encircling Love of other such Beings, and that would be true too. Perhaps I'll just say that we are Dolphins of Light, swimming end-lessly through the power of Pure Unconditional Love.

Epilogue

Is human consciousness opening more and more to the focus levels beyond physical world reality? I see it happening everywhere, like yesterday over coffee with a woman I barely know.

Trish had had an experience she didn't understand, and she wanted my opinion. She'd been getting ready to leave home in the morning on her way to the chiropractor. As she gathered up her purse and car keys, she was thinking about talking to the receptionist at the chiropractor's office. As she put her key in the ignition, she was suddenly overwhelmed by concern for her dog. While it was a totally irrational feeling, it was so strong she went back into her house to check on her pet. She checked the dog's license tags and collar to make sure they wouldn't fall off and checked the backyard fence and made sure the gate was closed. Absolutely nothing was out of order and she dismissed it all. When she arrived at the chiropractor's office, the receptionist she'd been thinking about was beside herself with worry. It seems her dog had gotten out of the yard through a damaged area of her fence. Trish's question to me was, "What happened? I was worried about my dog and then it turned out it was the reception-ist's dog that had gotten loose and was missing."

This sort of thing is so typical of experiences occurring as awareness opens beyond our physical body. I feel they will be happening more and more as the Earth Changes alignment moves closer and closer to its peak.

My answer to Trish was, "While you were thinking about talking to the receptionist, you were intending contact with her and she came into your awareness. You became aware of her strong concern about her missing dog, but you didn't realize they were her thoughts, not yours."

Trish sat back in her chair and took in my statement.

"If you'd said that to me a month ago, I'd have said you were full of hooey. But this sort of thing has been happening more and more to me lately and your explanation makes sense. Now my only question is, how do I know when I'm thinking my thoughts or somebody else's?"

In her question, the issue of M-band noise and our evolutionary adaptation of closing down our awareness to avoid it stood out like a thumb just smacked with a hammer. There wasn't time to go into all of that. Trish had to leave for work in a few minutes. So my answer for her on that one will have to wait until our next cup of coffee.

My answer will have to do with intent and how important it is that we become aware of placing it. When she placed her intent on talking to the receptionist, it brought the receptionist into Trish's awareness. If she'd understood any of this was possible and remembered placing that intent, it could have been a clue to where irrational concern for her dog came from. What it turned out to be instead was a direct experience lesson with the potential to teach her more about what awareness is.

I hope reading about Trish's experience triggered a memory of something similar that has happened to you. I hope that if it did, you are able to accept the part of yourself capable of such awareness as deserving of your loving acceptance. So often we discard such experiences as flukes or mere coincidences, when they really point to the greater awareness that we possess. It's my feeling that as the Earth Changes progress, these experiences will become increasingly common for all of us. It is my greatest hope that we will all learn from such experiences more about who and what we really are.

Moving on from there, I'd like to tell you a little about what came after Exploration 27 for me. As I neared completion of my second book, *Voyage Beyond Doubt*, something was bothering me. My third book, the one you're reading now, was beginning to take form in my mind as one that would go beyond the retrieval experiences of Lifeline. My only problem was that the small volume of notes I had didn't seem enough for a book. This was running through my mind one day as I sat at my word processor, when Bob Monroe popped in with his usual suggestion.

"Don't worry about it, Bruce," I could feel Bob say. "Lack of material won't be a problem."

"But what can I do about it?" I asked, feeling helpless.

"You can stop worrying about it, that's what you can do about it," Bob thought back to me. "And you can finish the second book."

So, while writing and editing, I put my worry on a back burner and kept busy finishing what I was working on. Then a week later, in early August, came an e-mail out of the blue from Denise. I hadn't spoken with her since the last breakfast our group shared on that Friday morning in February. In her e-mail Denise asked if I'd be interested in exploring Focus 27 with her. That was the beginning of a three-month, twice-a-week adventure of partnered exploring, which continues off and on to this day. In partnered exploring, as a brief reminder, two or more people meet and work together nonphysically. Upon returning to physical consciousness, each person records in a journal everything that happened during the experience. These journal notes are later shared with partners in the group for cross verification of the information.

Denise was new to the concept of partnered exploring and was quite surprised at some of the things that happened. We always worked out a set of questions on a topic of mutual interest before beginning one of our partnered exploring sessions. Denise's first surprise was that Bob Monroe met us at the beginning of every exploration. This always resulted in conversation and other unplanned interaction with Bob, which we both recorded in our separate notes. This led to Denise's second surprise. Upon reading my notes Denise discovered that her experiences of these interactions with Bob were the same as mine. That had the effect of verifying her experience. Additionally, there were always unplanned interactions between her and me, such as conversations, side trips to unexpected locations, and meeting other people. Denise's notes matched mine in these areas too. She found exploring together is a marvelous, verifiable way to build confidence in the reality of one's experience.

Some readers will remember that early in my training I'd been introduced to partnered exploring by my friend and teacher, Rebecca. Accounts of many of our activities together are in my first two books, *Voyages into the Unknown* and *Voyage Beyond Doubt.* These experiences greatly accelerated my acceptance of the Afterlife as a valid reality, for which I'm grateful to Rebecca. Working with Denise and with others who joined our group gave me the opportunity to give back a little of Rebecca's gift to me.

And Bob was right. I didn't need to worry about having enough material for my third book. For a time, after Denise and I started our "forays," as she called our partnered exploring, I thought the information we were gathering would be needed to fill out the third book. As it turned out, material from Exploration 27 was more than enough to complete the manuscript. Besides, there never would have been room to include what our forays yielded. By the time we slowed down our activity, I already had more pages of just notes than would fit in a book. That material will be published as my fourth book, tentatively entitled *Voyage to Curiosity's Father.*

One of the amazing aspects of the foray material is Bob Monroe's direct participation and continuing assistance in active exploration of the Afterlife and beyond. Bob always met us, ready to guide us to sources of information who could answer our preplanned questions. Like Sacajawea for Lewis and Clark, Bob became our native guide who knows the territory and the people who inhabit the Afterlife. After our first few explorations Denise and I got over the novelty of Bob's meeting with us and began to rely on his guidance. It became a simple matter of working out a set of questions via e-mail and then meeting at the TMI-There crystal on Tuesday and Thursday nights to gather the information. Often we ended up with information from more than our preplanned questions.

Since taking up Afterlife residence, Bob has continued to explore. Sometimes, after gathering information for our selected topic, he would suggest exploration of something entirely different. During many of our forays, he led us to places and information he'd explored during his out-of-body experiences, while he was living in the physical world. In many ways I felt that from his new perspective he'd understood more about things he wrote about in his last book, *Ultimate Journey.** He seemed to want to pass along what he'd found out since his death.

For example, he led us to something he called "the Aperture" in *Ultimate Journey** and showed us more about what it is and how it fits into the evolution of human consciousness. With his assistance we revisited Max's Hell in Focus 25 and learned more about what holds people in such places and how they get out. We explored the Hollow Heavens of Focus 25, learning what they are and why it's so difficult for people to leave them and go to a better place. Our forays led us to discover other centers in Focus 27 and to learn about their function and operation. Bob led us to people who work in these centers and they explained what they do and why. As we continued exploring, a pattern emerged in the activities of all these people that showed us how Earth school training continues in the nonphysical world. We learned what it means to graduate from the Earth school and what graduates do.

During Exploration 27 my tour guide at the Coordinating Intelligences spoke of an area of the Grid they fed with information but never received anything back from. He spoke of rumors claiming that a portion of the Grid was connected to something called the Planning Intelligence. Bob led us to several connections with this Planning Intelligence. From those contacts we began to understand how and why the physical/nonphysical Universe was created. We learned the primary purpose behind the lives we all live in the physical and nonphysical sides of the Earth Life System. What we gathered during our forays will be included in my next book. Until then, please accept my invitation to express and experience all the Pure Unconditional Loving Acceptance you can handle, and more.

Appendix A
The Science of the Earth Core Crystal

The following information is taken from a copyrighted, April 4, 1995 article in the *New York Times* by William Broad. Its title read: "The Core of the Earth May Be a Gigantic Crystal Made of Iron."

The article explains that early in Earth's formation its most prominent element, iron, formed the molten core of the planet. And that in time this iron core formed and, "some experts say it may be a solid crystalline structure of gigantic proportions." Using data gathered by monitoring earthquakes, present-day mapping by scientists of earth's interior suggests this crystal is aligned along the rotational axis of our planet.

The article cites research at several universities supporting the possibility that temperatures and pressures at the earth's core can form the type of iron crystal geologists and other earth scientists' theories point to.

The article also mentions some of the magnetic effects of such an iron crystal, including a reference to what I see as possible evidence of an ancient magnetic pole located off the western coast of Australia.

Readers interested in learning more about this theory are encouraged to read the article by William Broad, which may be available at the website of *The New York Times*.

Appendix B
The Birth of Exploration 27

All of the material contained in this book was gathered and experienced during my participation in a Monroe Institute program called Exploration 27. During this program, one of the trainers, Franceen, told the story about how X27, as participants call it, came into being. I was fascinated to be given the opportunity to see behind the scenes into the birth of this powerful, extraordinary program. Thank you, Franceen, for graciously accepting my invitation to repeat that story below.

By Franceen King

Exploration 27 (X27) was first conducted at The Monroe Institute (TMI) in June 1995, only three months after Robert Monroe's rather sudden death. Bob had agreed to develop this program in December 1994 and originally planned to design the program and tapes himself. At the time of his passing, however, no program design or tapes existed, despite the fact that the program had been announced and participants were already registered for the June and August sessions. Because I had been instrumental in encouraging Bob to develop this program, the design responsibilities fell to me.

The entire process of bringing this program into manifestation was quite fascinating, filled with sychronicities, and genuinely inspired at each stage. My involvement began in September 1994 in a very personal way—through my own meditations at home. Although I spend much time in altered states, I did not normally "sit in meditation," and for a variety of reasons had decided to start doing this in a disciplined way on a daily basis. One evening as I meditated, I was simply noticing the shifts in consciousness that occurred naturally as I sat. I noticed that I passed through the states that Bob Monroe's system would call Focus 12, 15, 21, and so forth. I noticed the familiar energy of Focus 27, then gradually noticed that I had shifted out of that energy into a different state that was familiar, yet definitely *not* Focus 27. I wondered to myself what this state might be in Bob's system. I was aware of many intelligences operating in a slightly different manner and realized that this was the place that Bob described in *Far Journeys* as the Gathering. I also got the clear impression, perhaps a "rote," that this could be designated as Focus 34/35, so noted because there were two slightly different, yet qualitatively distinct, energies that composed this state, which was in itself a kind of boundary area. I thought this was interesting and made a mental note.

In October 1994 I trained a Lifelines program at TMI. On the first evening that Bob came to talk with the participants, he asked if there were any questions. The first question came from the back of the room: "In which focus state is the Gathering taking place?" I thought this was an unusual question—especially for a Lifelines group. In the mid 1980s, following the publication of *Far Journeys*, Bob would often get questions about the Gathering. But during the 1990s such questions had been rare. Bob's normal response to most questions over the years was to be somewhat evasive and then to encourage participants to "go find out" for themselves. This evening was even more unusual in that Bob immediately responded with a direct answer: "The Gathering is taking place in Focus 34 and 35." Again, I thought to myself, "Gee, that's interesting," and made a mental note of this exchange.

Later that week, Bob and another trainer and I were chatting casually in the employee "lounge" area. Bob was always very interested to hear how the participants were responding to the "rescue and retrieval" activities of the Lifelines programs. We were talking about some of the fascinating experiences associated with Focus 27. After almost four full years of conducting Lifelines, we had become quite comfortable with the rescue work and had developed more curiosity about the nature and activities of Focus 27 itself. Bob was particularly fascinated with the ease with which humans could create and manifest in that energy—and with the stability of human creations. At some point I said something to the effect that I thought it was time for us to develop a program that would take participants to the Gathering. Bob did not make any kind of response to this suggestion, although I assume he heard it. This was simply a casual suggestion, or expression of my opinion, so I did not take offense to his lack of response.

I live in the Tampa, Florida, area where, among other things, I am a licensed psychotherapist as well as an ordained minister. The local church with which I was affiliated had been conducting a "psychic development" class over the fall. On a particular night, a couple of weeks after this Lifelines program, the class instructors needed volunteers to come to the class so students could practice doing psychic readings. I decided to participate. While I was there, a student approached me with a "message." As she tried to convey the information, it seemed to get jumbled, so eventually the head minister approached and offered to communicate it clearly. The essence of the message was this: she said I had recently made a suggestion to Bob Monroe for a new program or course at TMI, and he did not respond. She said it was important for me to approach him about this again. She suggested that I draw some pictures to make my point and suggested some specific images. She emphasized that it was important for *me* to convey this information to him, and that I should tell him that "This is important. Do this now."

I was in a bit of a quandary. Having been a trainer at TMI for about eight years at that point, I knew Bob fairly well. And I knew that he definitely did not like being told what to do. I had always been careful to think and communicate that these were Bob's programs, despite having trained them for so long. I also had a little bit of a feeling like, "Why me? You want me to tell Bob 'This is important. Do it now?' Why don't you tell him yourself?"

After reflecting on the best approach to take, I finally decided to write a very casual memo (careful to not appear like a proposal), detailing the events that had occurred, describing some visual images, mentioning several specific content areas and types of processes that had been emphasized in my reflections, and suggesting that he take this within and see what guidance he might receive. At the end I wrote: "With this memo I will consider that I have fulfilled any obligation I might have to communicate this information."

During my next training assignment in early December 1994, I gave the memo to Bob when I saw him briefly at the beginning of the week. Days went by with no response. As the week drew to a close, I wondered whether or not to ask him about the memo. Finally, I decided that the most responsible action would be to at least ask him if he had read it. Much to my surprise, he had, and had decided to create such a program. In fact, he was rather excited. He told me that I could announce to the group that night that we would be developing a program that would take participants to the Gathering in Focus 34/35—and I did.

A couple of weeks later I was talking on the telephone with Dr. Darlene Miller, Director of Programs at TMI. I inquired as to whether or not Bob had mentioned this program to her. She had not heard anything, so I filled her in and sent her a copy of my memo. In early January 1995 she called me to say that Bob finally told her about it and asked her to set aside two weeks in 1995 to conduct the program. She asked me if I would be available to train them. I put the weeks on my calendar. A program announcement was sent to Lifelines graduates. It was to be called Exploration 27. Within one week the first session was full. By the end of the following week the second session was almost full.

I was at TMI in January 1995 and discussed the program with Bob very briefly, and he assured me that he was going to do the tapes, and so forth. In March I was again at TMI. Bob was not feeling well, and by the time I left on Friday morning I realized that Bob would be leaving. When I arrived home in Florida, there was a message on my answering machine from Dar. I called back, and heard her say, "Well Franceen, Bob checked out this morning (and in the same sentence) and are you going to be able to design this program for us?" Of course I said, "yes," not really having given it much thought for several months. Bob's passing was, in my opinion, quite sudden and very conscious. It had been an amazing week, and that story would take many pages to relate.

I was scheduled to train a program in April, so I arranged to arrive a day early to meet with Dar and Mark Certo, the TMI sound engineer. About a week before that meeting, I sat down to make notes about this program. First I laid out our assumptions about Focus 27, based on both participant reports and my own experience with this energy. (While I had trained the first Lifelines Program in 1991, my own experience with rescue and retrieval began while I was a ministerial student in a Spiritualist church in the late 1970s.) I then laid out the purposes for the program based on conversations with Bob and others as well as my own intuitive guidance. One point that I emphasized in my original memo to Bob—and that was repeatedly emphasized by my own guidance—was the necessity to move into the Earth Core and connect strongly with the Earth energies before moving into the F34/35 energy. This idea, and the kinds of energetic movements that grew out of this, were very new to TMI programs. But they were strongly supported by both intuitive guidance and synchronistic happenings. For example, during this time I was wondering how best to symbolize and execute this movement to the Earth core, when I happened to see a *New York Times* article about the Earth core on-line. The article told how many scientists were beginning to think that the Earth core was a large, six-sided crystal made of iron. So I decided to use the crystal symbology to represent the Earth core. Part of my guidance was about the need for participants to be willing to operate more as group consciousness before moving into F34/35. The crystal symbology also provided a mechanism to build the group energy/consciousness. Before the first training session I also came across a segment from one of Jose Arguelles's books (written in 1989) that included a section on "Earth diving." This validated both the importance of this activity and the Earth core as a large crystal made of iron.

It was also clear to me from the beginning, and verified in discussions with Bob, that this program was very much related to a rote that Bob had often sent to Gateway groups as part of their closing. This rote can be represented by a blue triangle with a red circle in the center. This is consequently the logo used for X27. There are far too many specific content details about this program for me to go into in this brief history. The intuitive reader might want to tune into this rote and see what they get.

After laying out the assumptions and purposes of the program, the specific tape exercises and other procedures flowed quickly and naturally into form. When I presented these ideas to Dar and Mark in April, they understood immediately, and by the end of the day we were all quite high from the synergistic energy. Dar agreed to write and record the tape scripts. Mark understood the kinds of sounds and movements needed on the tapes. Everything proceeded with remarkable ease. This in itself was highly unusual. Typically, the development of new programs included a fair amount of struggle, revision, and sometimes overt conflict.

The workshop includes exploration into a variety of functions and processes that seem to occur in Focus 27. We used very broad labels to help participants focus on these functions: that is, the Healing and Regeneration Center, the Planning Center, the Educational Center, and so forth. Dar had conducted approximately thirty Lifelines programs by this time. While writing the tape scripts, she reported that she had clearer, more stable, and more prolonged experiences of Focus 27 than she had previously had in training the Lifelines programs.

We conducted the first program and were very pleased with the outcome. By the end of 1998 the program will have been conducted eleven times. Not a single tape or exercise has been changed from the original. Both TMI and participants have received a wealth of information from these explorations, as well as personal healings, and a profound new level of spiritual integration. Since only Lifelines graduates are eligible to participate, the pool of applicants is relatively small. We have had approximately thirty participants repeat the course at least twice. The learnings are virtually unlimited.

Participants are asked to fill out written reports after most tape exercises, which are then copied for data gathering by TMI. As a result, TMI has acquired a large volume of experiential and informational data, some of which may be published in the future.

Appendix C
Glossary

I've included this glossary for those who haven't read my previous books yet. A fuller understanding of these terms will be gained by reading the first two books in the series.

Celestine Prophecy Coincidences Refers to what James Redfield called the First Insight in his book, *The Celestine Prophecy.* Redfield suggested that one of the first indications of spiritual growth was the increased recognition and understanding of coincidence in our lives. I highly recommend Redfield's book.

Chakra One of the seven energy centers of the spiritual body, according to Eastern metaphysical philosophy.

CHEC Unit Controlled Holistic Environmental Chamber. A Pullman berth-like space at TMI that participants use as sleeping quarters and as a place to listen to Hemi-Sync tapes during six-day programs such as Gateway Voyage. Each CHEC unit has a mattress, a pillow, and blankets and provides a level of isolation from outside sound and light. Each is equipped with stereo headphones connected to the control room, lighting, and its own fresh air supply.

The Disk Refers to a vision described in my first book, *Voyages into the Unknown.* Robert Monroe described something he called his "I/There" in his books, and my experience of the Disk matches his description. I see the Disk as my Greater or Higher Self, or a larger version of me.

Exploration 27 program A TMI program for graduates of the Lifeline program. In Exploration 27 participants explore the infrastructure of Focus 27 and learn more about the various "places" There. Introduction to the Planning Center, Education Center, and Health and Rejuvenation Center are included as well as more detailed exploration of the Reception Center. Participants also explore Focus 34/35, an area Bob Monroe referred to as the Gathering in his second book, *Far Journeys.* Here participants have the opportunity to communicate with intelligences from other areas of our Universe.

Flying Fuzzy Zone An area in nonphysical reality I discovered during my first Lifeline program. It is described in detail in my first book, *Voyages into the Unknown.* It appears to be an area populated by nonphysical humans in a form that looks like small, swirling curls of light.

Focus Levels Each focus level is a specific *state* or *level* of consciousness or awareness. Each has specific *properties* or *activities* that program participants learn to access and use through Hemi-Sync sound patterns.

Focus C1 The level of ordinary, physical world consciousness. The level of physical world reality in which we *normally* live.

Focus 10 (Mind Awake/Body Asleep): The state of consciousness in which the physical body is asleep, but the mind is awake and alert. In this state one can develop conceptual tools for use in: reducing anxiety and tension healing, remote viewing, and other information-gathering methods. In Focus 10, much like an awake dream state, one learns to think in images rather then words.

Focus 12 (Expanded Awareness): This is a state where Conscious Awareness is expanded beyond the limits of the physical body. Focus 12 has many different facets, including: exploring nonphysical realities, decision making, problem solving, and enhanced creative expression.

Focus 15 (No Time): The state of "No Time" is a level of consciousness that opens avenues of the mind that offer vast opportunities for Self exploration beyond the constraints of time and space.

Focus 21 (Other Energy Systems): This level offers the opportunity to explore other realities and energy systems beyond what we call time-space-physical-matter.

Focus 22 The state of human consciousness where humans still in physical existence have only partial consciousness. In this state would be those suffering from delirium, from chemical dependency or alcoholism, or from dementia. It would also include patients who were anesthetized or comatose. Experiences here might be remembered as dreams or hallucinations. My personal experience of this arena is that many here appear deranged, lost, or confused. This can make them very difficult to reach and communicate with.

Focus 23 A level inhabited by those who have recently left physical existence, but who either have not been able to recognize and accept this or are unable to free themselves from ties to the Earth Life System. It includes those from all periods of time. Those who live here are almost always isolated and alone. Often the circumstances of their death have left them confused about where they are. Many times they don't realize they've died. Many maintain some form of contact with the physical world and thereby limit their ability to perceive those who come from the Afterlife to assist them.

Focus 24, 25, and 26 This covers the Belief System Territories, occupied by nonphysical humans from all periods and areas who have accepted and subscribed to various premises and concepts. These would include religious and philosophical beliefs that postulate some form of post-physical existence.

Focus 27 Here is the site of what we may call the Reception Center or the Park, which is the hub of it. This is an artificial synthesis created by human minds, a way station designed to ease the trauma and shock of the transition out of physical reality. It takes on the form of various Earth environments in order to be acceptable to the enormously wide variety of newcomers.

Focus 34/35 A level of consciousness beyond human consciousness, also known as the Gathering. Here intelligences from other areas of the Universe are gathered to observe the Earth Changes. Here contact, communication, and interaction with these intelligences is possible.

Free Flow Focus Tape A Hemi-Sync tape with minimal verbal instruction and maximum free time in the focus level.

Gateway Voyage program The first of the series of six-day residence programs TMI offers and a prerequisite for all other

TMI programs. Gateway Voyage introduces participants to Focus 10, 12, 15, and 21 in a structured program of learning. It teaches participants how to access each focus level and various conceptual tools for their use.

Helpers Nonphysical human beings who have lived in the Afterlife long enough to know the ropes. Helpers often volunteer to assist physically alive people explore the nonphysical realities. They also provide volunteer assistance to other nonphysical humans, usually upon entry into the Afterlife, but at any time the assistance is requested or would be helpful.

Hemi-Sync The following explanation is taken from a Monroe Institute pamphlet with their permission:

The Monroe Institute is internationally known for its work in the effects of sound wave forms on human behavior. In its early research, the institute discovered that nonverbal audio patterns had dramatic effects on stages of consciousness.

Certain sound patterns create a Frequency Following Response (FFR) in the electrical activity of the brain. These blended and sequenced sound patterns can gently lead the brain into various states, such as deep relaxation or sleep. A generic patent in this field was issued to Robert Monroe in 1975. Drawing on this discovery and the work of others, Mr. Monroe employed a system of "binaural beats" by feeding a separate signal into each ear. By sending separate sound pulses to each ear with stereo headphones, the two hemispheres of the brain act in unison to "hear" a third signal, the difference between the two sound pulses. This third signal is not an actual sound, but an electrical signal that can only be created by both brain hemispheres acting and working together simultaneously

The unique coherent brain state that results is known as hemispheric synchronization, or "Hemi- Sync®." The audio stimulus that creates this state is not overpowering. It is noninvasive and can easily be disregarded either objectively or subjectively.

While hemispheric synchronization occurs naturally in day-to-day life, it typically exists only for random, brief periods of time. The Hemi-Sync audio technologies developed by The Monroe Institute assist individuals in achieving and sustaining this highly productive, coherent brain state.

Hemi-Sync My Explanation. If you're a technical type, maybe my own explanation of hemispheric synchronization will be easier to follow:

> Using stereo headphones to acoustically isolate each ear, two different frequency audio tones are supplied, one to the left ear and the other to the right. For example, a 400 cycle per second tone might be supplied to one ear and a 402 cycle per second tone to the other. If you watched a real-time brain wave frequency pattern analysis of the result, you would see the brain wave frequency spectrum of both hemispheres begin to synchronize to 2 cycle per second. The brain wave pattern of both hemispheres synchronizes to the difference between the two input frequencies $(402 - 400 = 2)$. If this brain wave frequency pattern was the same as, say REM sleep, which it's not, then the person listening would begin moving into REM sleep. Another pair of audio tones could be simultaneously introduced that would match an alert, wide-awake brain wave state. Then the state the individual would move into would be Mind Awake/Body Asleep, or Focus 10 in Monroe Institute jargon.

> The most important point seems to be that both hemispheres of the brain come to a balanced, cooperative, information-sharing state that is facilitated by their synthesizing the third tone. In this balanced state both hemispheres of the brain, with their well-documented differences in perception and analysis abilities, cooperate constructively. In that balance comes Knowing.

INSPEC An acronym for Intelligent Species that Robert Monroe used to describe certain nonphysical beings he encountered during his out of body experiences. During his early explorations he saw the INSPECs as a species more advanced than humans. He later came to understand an INSPEC as "future self."

Lifeline program A six-day residence program at TMI that introduces participants to Focus 22, 23, 24, 25, 26, and 27. This is the area of the Afterlife. Participants learn to contact and communicate with those who inhabit these levels, including Helpers and other nonphysical humans. Lifeline uses the vehicle of retrieval to teach participants how to access and explore these focus levels.

My Place in Focus 27 In one of the tape exercises in the Lifeline program, participants create a place of their own in Focus 27. Each of these places could be considered to be a thought form projected into the nonphysical world that becomes a reality. My place is high in brightly lit, rocky mountains. My choice to add a lake to this place no doubt stems from my upbringing in Minnesota, the land of ten thousand lakes. At any point I am free to alter my place in Focus 27. It serves as a meeting place for me now and will perhaps some day be the place I "retire" to.

The Park An area of Focus 27 also known as the Reception Center. (See Reception Center.)

The Reception Center An area of Focus 27 in which the newly departed are assisted in their adjustment to leaving the physical world and entering the Afterlife.

Resonant Tuning A technique taught in the Monroe Institute's Gateway Voyage program. The physical voice is used in way that sort of 'tunes' one's awareness to the 'vibration levels' of nonphysical realities. It bears resemblance to vocal toning techniques taught by various esoteric philosophies.

Retrieval The act of locating, contacting, and communicating with a nonphysical human stuck in an area of consciousness from Focus 23 through Focus 26 and moving that person to Focus 27. Retrievals are the vehicle of training used in the Lifeline program to learn to explore the Afterlife.

Stuck (as in a focus level) A nonphysical person who is completely without contact with other nonphysical humans in the Afterlife is said to be stuck. This usually results from beliefs held by that individual at or before death. The circumstances of such a person's death may also lead to being stuck.*

Endnote

*   Robert A. Monroe, *Ultimate Journey* (New York:
       Doubleday, 1994), chapter 18, pages 247–9

Hampton Roads Publishing Company

. . . for the evolving human spirit

Hampton Roads Publishing Company
publishes books on a variety of subjects including
metaphysics, health, complementary medicine,
visionary fiction, and other related topics.

For a copy of our latest catalog,
call toll-free, 800-766-8009,
or send your name and address to:

Hampton Roads Publishing Company, Inc.
134 Burgess Lane
Charlottesville, VA 22902
e-mail: hrpc@hrpub.com
www.hrpub.com